THE CHARTERED INSTITUTE OF MARKETING

Professional Certificate in Marketing

STUDY TEXT

Assessing the Marketing Environment

Valid for assessments up to September 2013

The Chartered
Institute of Marketing

BPP
LEARNING MEDIA

First edition July 2012

ISBN 9781 4453 9142 7
e-ISBN 9781 4453 7615 8

British Library Cataloguing-in-Publication Data
A catalogue record for this book
is available from the British Library

Published by

BPP Learning Media Ltd
Aldine House, Aldine Place
142-144 Uxbridge Road
London W12 8AA

www.bpp.com/learningmedia

Printed in the United Kingdom by Polestar Wheatons

Hennock Road
Marsh Barton Industrial Estate
Exeter, Devon
EX2 8RP

Your learning materials, published by BPP Learning
Media Ltd, are printed on paper obtained from
traceable sustainable sources.

Lead Author: Deirdre Makepeace

The Chartered
Institute of Marketing

Contents

1 Studying for The Chartered Institute of Marketing (CIM) qualifications

There are a few key points to remember as you study for your CIM qualification:

(a) You are studying for a **professional** qualification. This means that you are required to use professional language and adopt a business approach in your work.

(b) You are expected to show that you have 'read widely'. Make sure that you read the quality press (and don't skip the business pages), read *Marketing*, *The Marketer*, *Research* and *Marketing Week* avidly.

(c) Become aware of the marketing initiatives you come across on a daily basis: for example, when you go shopping look around and think about why the store layout is as it is; consider the messages, channel choice and timings of ads when you are watching TV. It is surprising how much you will learn just by taking an interest in the marketing world around you.

(d) Get to know the way CIM write their exam papers and assignments. They use a specific approach (the Magic Formula) which is to ensure a consistent approach when designing assessment materials. Make sure you are fully aware of this as it will help you interpret what the examiner is looking for (a full description of the Magic Formula appears later).

(e) Learn how to use Harvard referencing. This is explained in detail in our CIM Professional Certificate Assessment Workbook.

(f) Ensure that you read very carefully all assessment details sent to you from CIM. There are strict deadlines to meet, as well as paperwork to complete for any assignment or project you do. You also need to make sure you have your CIM membership card with you at the exam. Failing to meet any assessment entry deadlines or completing written work on time will mean that you will have to wait for the next round of assessment dates and will need to pay the relevant assessment fees again.

2 The Professional Certificate Syllabus

The Professional Certificate in Marketing is aimed at anyone who is employed in a supporting marketing role such as Marketing Co-ordinator or Executive. You may also be a manager with a senior role within a small or medium sized company where marketing only forms part of a wider work remit. Or you may be looking to move into your first marketing role or to specialise.

The aim of the qualification is to provide a strong foundation of marketing knowledge. You will develop the breadth of knowledge of marketing theory but also appreciate issues faced within the organisation as CIM qualifications concentrate on applied marketing within real work-places.

The complete Professional Certificate qualification contains four units:

- Unit 1 Marketing Essentials
- Unit 2 Assessing the Marketing Environment
- Unit 3 Marketing Information and Research
- Unit 4 Stakeholder Marketing

CIM stipulates that each module should take 40 guided learning hours to complete. Guided learning hours refer to time in class, using distance learning materials and completing any work set by your tutor. Guided learning hours do not include the time it will take you to complete the necessary reading for your studies.

The syllabus as provided by CIM can be found below with reference to the coverage within this Study Text.

Unit characteristics – Assessing the Marketing Environment

The aim of this unit is to provide an understanding of the nature and scope of the internal and external marketing environment with broad consideration of the impact of international and global marketing.

The unit seeks to provide an overview of the significance of the marketing environment within the confines of the PESTEL model, but with consideration of issues including environmental and economic sustainability.

The unit addresses the key characteristics of the marketing environment and assesses the impact of market forces that are uncontrollable and how an organisation responds to them. At the same time, some consideration should be given in terms of how the factors within the micro and internal environment can be manipulated to the benefit of the organisation and its customers.

On completion, students should be able to demonstrate a detailed understanding of the internal, micro and macro environment. This should include consideration of the key controllable and uncontrollable drivers of change, and the challenges posed to market oriented organisations in today's volatile and dynamic business and marketing environment.

Overarching learning outcomes

By the end of this unit students should be able to:

- Explain the nature and scope of the internal marketing environment, including the resource perspective

- Distinguish between the types of organisation within the public, private and voluntary sectors and understand the different influences and challenges they face and how their objectives differ as a result

- Identify and explain the different characteristics of the micro environment and recognise the sources of information required to gain a good understanding of it together with its drivers and challenges

- Assess the importance of and potential impact on a market oriented organisation of key trends in political, economic, social, technological and legal/ethical/regulatory environment

- Consider the implications for organisations pursuing both economic and environmental sustainability as part of its agenda for CSR

 The Chartered Institute of Marketing

SECTION 1 – The nature of the organisation (weighting 15%)

		Covered in chapter(s)
1.1	Evaluate the different characteristics of the internal marketing environment, and consider the challenges facing the organisation in developing the customer value proposition including: ■ Resource capability ■ Competency ■ Internal politics ■ Objectives ■ Key internal drivers	1
1.2	Explain the classification of public, private and voluntary sector organisations in terms of: ■ Legal forms ■ Organisational characteristics, influences and challenges ■ Divorce of ownership and control	1
1.3	Explain how organisational objectives differ across a range of different sectors and consider the influences upon setting these objectives and the challenges they represent: ■ Identifying stakeholder needs ■ Satisfying stakeholder needs ■ The increasing need to address corporate social responsibility issues	1, 2

1.4	Assess the comparative strengths and weaknesses of small/medium and large/global organisations in the context of the marketing environment:
	
	■ Business/local focus versus global focus (ie, standardisation versus adaptation)
	■ Organisational constraints:
	  – Objectives
	  – Resources
	  – Risks
	  – PESTEL
	  – Shareholders
	  – Stakeholders
	■ Niche versus mass marketing
		1

SECTION 2 – The micro environment (weighting 30%)

		Covered in chapter(s)
2.1	Evaluate the stakeholders that constitute the micro environment within which organisations operate and their importance to the marketing process: ■ Company ■ Customers ■ Competitors ■ Suppliers ■ Distributors	2
2.2	Evaluate the micro environmental factors that have a bearing on an organisation's ability to meet customer expectations and generate customer satisfaction: ■ The importance of continuous marketing research ■ Product/service portfolio analysis ■ The link between service quality and customer satisfaction ■ Extended marketing mix	4
2.3	Explain the nature of the interactions between the organisation and its various stakeholders including shareholders, employees, customers, local communities, suppliers, channel members and competitors: ■ Understanding and managing stakeholder power and interest ■ Developing relationships with partners, pressure groups, consumer groups, etc ■ Competition for customers ■ Consumer protection legislation	4
2.4	Evaluate the different types and sources of information required to gain an in-depth understanding of the micro environment: ■ Company reports ■ Department for Business Innovation & Skills (BIS) ■ Office for National Statistics ■ Research organisations eg, Dun & Bradstreet, MINTEL, etc ■ Industry journals	4
2.5	Examine the nature, scope and impact of competition policies on the organisation and its marketing environment: ■ Legislation, regulatory bodies and watchdogs ■ Monopolies and mergers ■ EU competition policy ■ Bilateral international competition relationships (Europe, Japan and the USA) ■ Fair trade policies (local versus international) ■ Patents ■ Trademarks	3
2.6	Explain the process for undertaking a detailed competitor analysis and how the analysis influences the marketing decision-making process: ■ Competitor identification ■ Competitor strengths and weaknesses ■ Competitor strategies ■ Competitor response patterns (tactics) ■ Key success factors (KSF) ■ Company capability profiling	4

The Chartered Institute of Marketing

SECTION 3 – The macro environment (weighting 40%)

		Covered in chapter(s)
3.1	Explain the importance of the macro environment to the marketing process: ■ PESTEL market performance indicators ■ Identification and implications of market turbulence, complexity and dynamism ■ Effects of changing markets within the world arena	5
3.2	Identify key sources of information useful in analysing the macro environment. ■ Government statistics ■ Economic indicators ■ Business confidence indicators ■ Internet ■ Trade publications, etc	5, 6
3.3	Explain the social, demographic and cultural environments and, in general terms, their influence on and implications for marketing including: ■ Social cultural behaviour and change ■ Demographic/population trends, etc ■ The need for social responsibility and marketing ethics ■ The growth of consumerism	6

3.4	Explain the economic environments within an international context and, in general terms, their influence on and implications for marketing, including consideration of:
	■ Interest rates
	■ Exchange rates
	■ GDP
	■ GNP
	■ Effects of demand and supply
	■ Economic growth and unemployment
	■ The effect of changing economies eg,
	  – The single European Market (EU)
	  – Market driven economies in Eastern Europe
	■ European Monetary Union
	■ Business cycle
		7

3.5	Explain the political and legislative environments and, in general terms, their influence on and implications for marketing: ■ Political activities resulting in legislative changes ■ Green legislation ■ Customer protection legislation ■ Employment legislation, etc	8
3.6	Explain the natural environment and, in general terms, its influence on and implications for marketing including: ■ Policies relating to emissions and waste, etc ■ Governmental and pressure group influence on environmental priorities ■ Pollution and waste management ■ Moral and ethical responsibility ■ Green marketing – 5Rs (ROI, Reach, Responsibility, Reputation, Revenue) ■ Social responsibility and sustainability	5
3.7	Assess the potential significance of environmental challenges to marketing in the future: ■ Globalisation ■ Global warming/emissions/carbon footprints ■ Environmental decline ■ Shortage of natural resources ■ Reducing waste ■ Increasing re-cycling ■ Alternative energy sources (wind power, solar power, electric/gas cars, etc) ■ Alternative transportation	5

		Covered in chapter(s)
3.8	Explain the evolution of the technical and information environments and consider its actual and potential impacts on organisations, employment, marketing and communications: ■ The technical diffusion process ■ Technology and the workforce ■ Technology and the impact of social change ■ The convergence of technology ie, telecommunications linked with media communications ■ Digital superhighways ■ Credit transfer ■ The internet and other technology based communication tools	9
3.9	Evaluate the impact of economic and environmental sustainability on an organisation's CSR agenda including the impact it has on the organisation, its vision, mission and objectives: ■ Environmental information systems ■ Impact analysis ■ Codes of conduct ■ Social/conscience marketing/human rights ■ Ethics ■ Environmental sustainability ■ Shareholder activism (green shareholders)	10
3.10	Evaluate different methods for undertaking analysis of environmental trends: ■ Environmental audits ■ Quantitative and qualitative forecasting techniques ■ Trend impact analysis ■ Scenario building ■ Delphi method	11
3.11	Review the emergence of social marketing as an increasing trend in establishing social values associated with CSR: ■ Growth of social and cause related marketing ■ Traceability/transparency ■ Fair trade/local product policy ■ Government initiatives eg, packaging, labeling, recycling, etc	10

SECTION 4 – Undertaking a marketing audit (weighting 15%)

		Covered in chapter(s)
4.1	Explain the process of undertaking the internal and external market environment audit: ■ Environmental scanning ■ Collecting internal and external marketing information ■ PESTEL analysis ■ A competitor comparison of key competitors ■ Assessing opportunities and threats ■ Reviewing environmental and resource constraints	11
4.2	Describe the meaning and role of various analytical tools in the marketing auditing process: ■ PESTEL ■ 5 Ms ■ Ansoff's Growth Strategy Matrix ■ SWOT	11

The Chartered Institute of Marketing

3 Assessment

The unit covered by this Study Text (Unit 2 Assessing the Marketing Environment) is assessed in a three-hour formal examination. You will be sent a case study prior to the exam from which you are expected to complete PESTEL and SWOT analyses. In order to help you revise and prepare for the exam we have also written a Professional Certificate in Marketing Assessment Workbook which is available either through your usual book retailer or our website www.bpp.com/learningmedia.

4 The Magic Formula

The Magic Formula is a tool used by CIM to help both examiners write exam and assignment questions, and you, to more easily interpret what you are being asked to write about. It is useful for helping you to check that you are using an appropriate balance between theory and practice for your particular level of qualification.

Contrary to the title, there is nothing mystical about the Magic Formula and simply by knowing it (or even mentioning it in an assessment) will not automatically secure a pass. What it does do, however, is to help you to check that you are presenting your answers in an appropriate format, including enough marketing theory and applying it to a real marketing context or issue.

The Magic Formula for the Professional Certificate in Marketing is shown below:

Figure A   The Magic Formula for the Professional Certificate in Marketing

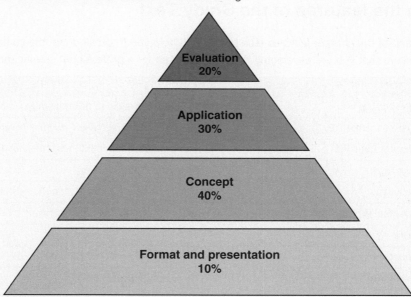

You can see from the pyramid that for the Professional Certificate marks are awarded in the following proportions:

- **Presentation and format – 10%**

    You are expected to present your work professionally which means that assignments and projects should **always** be typed. Even in an exam situation attention should be paid to making your work look as visually appealing as possible. CIM will also stipulate the format that you should present your work in. The assessment formats you will be given will be varied and can include things like reports to write, slides to prepare, emails, memos, formal letters, press releases, discussion documents, briefing papers, agendas and newsletters.

- **Concept – 40%**

  Concept refers to your ability to state, recall and describe marketing theory. The definition of marketing is a core CIM syllabus topic. If we take this as an example, you would be expected to recognise, recall and write this definition to a word perfect standard to gain the full marks for concept. Understanding marketing concepts is the main area where marks will be given within your assessment at the Professional Certificate level.

- **Application – 30%**

  Application based marks are given for your ability to apply marketing theories to real life marketing situations. For example, a question may ask you to discuss the definition of marketing and how it is applied within your own organisation. Here you are not only using the definition but are applying it in order to consider the market orientation of the company.

- **Evaluation – 20%**

  Evaluation is the ability to asses the value or worth of something, sometimes through careful consideration of related advantages and disadvantages, or weighing up of alternatives. Results from your evaluation should enable you to discuss the importance of an issue using evidence to support your opinions.

  For example, if you were asked to evaluate whether or not your organisation adopts a marketing approach you should provide reasons and specific examples of why you think they might take this approach, as well as considering why they may not take this approach, before coming to a final conclusion.

5 A guide to the features of the Study Text

Each of the chapter features (see below) will help you to break down the content into manageable chunks and ensure that you are developing the skills required for a professional qualification.

Chapter feature	Relevance and how you should use it
Introduction	Shows why topics need to be studied and is a route guide through the chapter
Syllabus reference	Outlines the syllabus learning outcomes covered in the chapter
Chapter topic list	Study the list, each numbered topic denotes a numbered section in the chapter
Key Term	Highlights the core vocabulary you need to learn
Activity	An application-based activity for you to complete
The Real World	A short case study to illustrate marketing practice
Exam tip/Assessment tip	Key advice based on the assessment
Chapter roundups	Use this to review what you have learnt
Quick quiz	Use this to check your learning
Further reading	Further reading will give you a wider perspective on the subjects you're covering

6 Additional resources

To help you pass the entire Professional Certificate in Marketing we have created a complete study package. The **Professional Certificate Assessment Workbook** covers all four units for the Professional Certificate level. Practice questions and answers, tips on tackling assignments and work-based projects are included to help you succeed in your assessments.

Our A6 set of spiral bound **Passcards** are handy revision cards and are ideal to reinforce key topics for the Marketing Essentials and Assessing the Marketing Environment exams.

The Chartered
Institute of Marketing

7 Your personal study plan

Preparing a Study Plan (and sticking to it) is one of the key elements to learning success.

CIM have stipulated that there should be a minimum of 40 guided learning hours spent on each unit. Guided learning hours will include time spent in lessons, working on fully prepared distance learning materials, formal workshops and work set by your tutor. We also know that to be successful, students should spend **at least** an additional 60 hours conducting self study. This means that for the entire qualification with four units you should spend 160 hours working in a tutor guided manner and at least an additional 240 hours completing recommended reading, working on assignments, and revising for exams. This Study Text will help you to organise this 60 hour portion of self study time.

Now think about the exact amount of time you have (don't forget you will still need some leisure time!) and complete the following tables to help you keep to a schedule.

	Date	Duration in weeks
Course start		
Course finish		Total weeks of course:
Examination date	Revision to commence	Total weeks to complete revision:

Content chapter coverage plan

Chapter	To be completed by	Revised?
1 The organisation within the business environment		
2 The micro environment and stakeholders		
3 Market structures and competition regulation		
4 Analysis of the competitive environment		
5 An introduction to the macro environment		
6 The demographic, social and cultural environment		
7 The economic and international environment		
8 The political and legislative environment		
9 The technical/information environments		
10 Corporate social responsibility		
11 Coping with the challenges of the environment		

CHAPTER 1

The organisation within the business environment

Introduction

The economies across the world are made up of a wide range of differing types, sizes and cultures of organisation. Each one will be driven by a range of factors; the sectors in which they operate, the culture of the organisation and the environment(s) in which it operates, and the legal form of the organisation. The finances, risk levels, ownership, governance and control will influence decision-making across the organisation including key decisions on marketing aims, objectives and delivery.

Topic list

1.1	Evaluate the different characteristics of the internal marketing environment, and consider the challenges facing the organisation in developing the customer value proposition including: ■ Resource capability ■ Competency ■ Internal politics ■ Objectives ■ Key internal drivers
1.2	Explain the classification of public, private and voluntary sector organisations in terms of: ■ Legal forms ■ Organisational characteristics, influences and challenges ■ Divorce of ownership and control
1.3	Explain how organisational objectives differ across a range of different sectors and consider the influences upon setting these objectives and the challenges they represent: ■ Identifying stakeholder needs ■ Satisfying stakeholder needs ■ The increasing need to address corporate social responsibility issues
1.4	Assess the comparative strengths and weaknesses of small/medium and large/global organisations in the context of the marketing environment: ■ Business/local focus versus global focus (ie, standardisation versus adaptation) ■ Organisational constraints: – Objectives – Resources – Risks – PESTEL – Shareholders – Stakeholders ■ Niche versus mass marketing

1 The importance of the marketing environment

The Chartered Institute of Marketing gives the following definition of marketing: 'the management process which identifies, anticipates and supplies customer requirements efficiently and profitably.'

Key dimensions encompassed by this definition are:

■ The importance of the marketing environment, including competitors
■ Identification and anticipation of customer requirements
■ Internal review of the organisation and how it manages the process of satisfying those requirements
■ External review of the marketing environment, in particular opportunities and threats

In analysing the marketing environment there are three layers to consider:

■ The internal organisation: how it works, its legal status, culture, resources and capabilities.

■ The micro environment, or competitive environment: the influences of a range of stakeholders and how these interact with or influence the activities of the organisation.

■ The macro environment: the uncontrollable factors existing in the global, national and local economies that influence market conditions for the organisation.

Figure 1.1   The marketing environment – the organisation

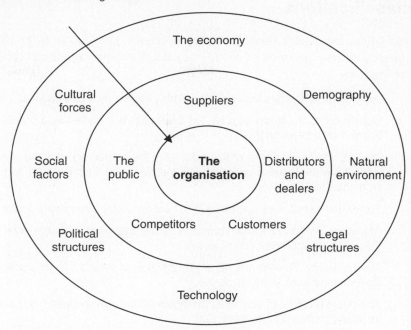

In this chapter we start our investigation with the nature of the organisation and the factors that affect the ways in which the organisation functions successfully in achieving its objectives. We also investigate the comparative strengths and weaknesses of a range of different organisations from SMEs (small and medium size enterprises) to global organisations.

2 Defining organisations

Organisations bring together people with common interests in a systematic effort to produce goods and services that they could not readily have produced as individuals. They enable the specialisation and division of labour. This saves time and raises productivity. They are social as they provide mutual support and opportunity for development.

Some common characteristics of organisations are:

- A framework of written or tacit rules (eg articles of association)

- A decision-making hierarchy (eg Board of Directors)

- A record of proceedings (eg minutes of meetings)

- A means of co-ordinating efforts and resources to determine what and how to produce, in what quantities, using what channels of distribution (eg CEO)

▶ **Exam tip**

Acquire the habit of checking your understanding of key terms as they appear in this study text. You can also refer to the CIM marketing glossary: www.cim.co.uk/resources/glossary. Start compiling your own list of terminology. For example be sure that you can explain the terms used so far including hierarchy, SMEs and resources. You can add to this as you go through the case study. The exam will ask you to define terms and explain them in the context of the case.

3 Business classifications

Organisations can be very diverse; operating in difference environments, for different purposes and with completely different perspectives on how they satisfy customer needs profitably. They may be classified in the following ways:

- Ownership: Is the business private, public, owned by a co-operative?

- Legal form: Is the business a limited company? Is it owned by a sole proprietor? Is there a partnership (more than one owner)?

- Control: Who is in charge of decisions? Are there directors? Are the shareholders the main decision takers? Are the trustees or the council members the main decision makers (this tends to be the case with charities)?

- Sector: Is the business operating in the public sector, the private sector or even in the voluntary sector?

- Objectives: What is the main objective of the organisation? Is the organisation in business for profit? Is the public welfare the main objective?

- Accountability: To whom is the organisation accountable? To its shareholders, to the ministers, to its customers or even to its employees?

- Activity: What type of activity is the organisation involved with? Is it agriculture, manufacturing, services, utilities, construction, tourism, etc?

- Size: How big is the organisation? Is it an SME? Is it a large corporation? Does it operate only nationally or globally?

ACTIVITY 1.1

Describe three organisations in terms of their:

(a)   Sector
(b)   Activity
(c)   Size

3.1 The public sector

Public sector organisations operate internationally, nationally and at regional and sub-regional levels to deliver services for their communities. Means of revenue include:

- Taxes imposed on wages and salaries (income tax), sales (VAT), sales of properties, properties (council tax) and profits of businesses. Television licences raise finance for channels run by the state.

- Governments also borrow money from either international sources (thereby implying foreign debt) or national sources.

Resources are allocated to the departments of the government or state.

- These departments historically plan their expenditure according to government objectives rather than market forces.

- Objectives may be socially desirable and involve the embracing civil rights. For instance, in the United Kingdom there are support allowances, housing benefits and old age pensions. These all have monetary value.

The state can also take responsibility of areas where provision by the private sector is not seen as adequate or even appropriate.

The Chartered
Institute of Marketing

- Public goods and services such as defence, law, order and emergency services comprise one major category.

- Merit goods, that is, health, education and other social services, are another.

- A number of other industries might come into the domain of the state for various reasons including strategic considerations, health and safety, natural monopolies and national security.

- In the United Kingdom although the private health sector is growing, the National Health Service (NHS) is state owned and largely run by the state. But, increasingly private consultants and sundry services are called upon to assist in operational activities previously led by the state.

THE REAL WORLD

Governments in West Europe tend to spend on average about 40% of their gross domestic product (GDP) on the provision of social welfare. However, Scandinavian countries have a history of more generous social benefit provision. Accordingly, Scandinavian countries spend closer to 50% of their GDP. In contrast, more free enterprise economies in East Asia for instance tend to opt for lower taxes and private provision. Driven by recessionary impacts, many governments have faced falling tax incomes and rising social expenditures. The UK's 2011 public spending dilemma forced the government to take drastic measures. Paul Johnson (2012), Director of the Institute for Fiscal Studies, described the measures in *Prospect* Magazine:

'These will come in part from [reductions in] social security and tax credits, but mostly from unprecedented reductions in spending on public services. Faced with a gloomy economic prognosis, the chancellor pencilled in two more years of spending squeeze for 2015-16 and 2016-17 in his 2011 autumn statement, in order to return us to a balanced budget by 2016-17.'

(Prospect, 2012)

Many governments introduce market disciplines into their public sector.

- Management and compulsory competitive tendering for central and local government services have been increasingly deployed in recent years. This has led to a degree of marketing orientation in a wide cross-section of public services, such as social care provision, cleaning and housing.

- Government, government agencies and businesses have realised that they need to relate their offerings to existing and even potential client needs for the necessary contract, budget or funding to be forthcoming.

- Private finance initiatives are being used to fund capital costs such as building schools and hospitals and public private partnerships can exist to manage service delivery.

3.1.1 Local authorities

- Services include fire and police, road maintenance, consumer protection, recreation, environmental health, education and may even include airports.

- They are managed by elected councillors through full-time professional officers.

- As in the rest of the public sector, they have been subject to radical structural and operational changes over the past decade. Central government control has increased, but authorities have been encouraged to forge mutually beneficial links with local business communities. This includes the formation of 35 private sector led, Local Enterprise Partnerships (LEPs) across England.

- Over the years, the role of local authorities has changed tremendously.

- Exposure to market forces through compulsory competitive tendering has transformed the council officer's role into that of a facilitator rather than a direct provider of local services.

  - Nowadays competitive tendering for refuse collection involves the submission of a tender meeting or exceeding stated service specifications, but assurance on standards and competitive pricing must also be provided.

3.1.2 Quangos and PPPs

Powers have also been devolved, through a large number of executive agencies, also known as quangos (from the term QUasi-Autonomous Non-Governmental Organisations), to supervise a wide variety of activities. The official term used by government is non-departmental public bodies (NDPBs).

- Quangos are publicly appointed bodies with considerable powers over the disposal of resources and important regulatory activities. Their non-elected nature and lack of direct accountability raised concerns in relation to their responsiveness, efficiency and the amount of work that appeared to be duplicated or conflicting. The government responded with what has been dubbed 'bonfire of the quangos', a programme of cuts that that saw the abolition of over 200 quangos.

- The BBC and the Bank of England could be classified as quangos as both are publicly owned and funded bodies with considerable independence and limited political accountability.

- Public private partnerships (PPPs) seek to combine the strengths of private sector management with the social concerns and community benefits of the public sector.

ACTIVITY 1.2

Match the terms with the correct definition: (1) Contracting out, (2) Privatisation, (3) Merit goods, (4) Public goods, (5) Quango.

(a)   Can also be provided by the private sector but concern for equity and doubt regarding sufficient goods and services lead to public provision.

(b)   A good or service which cannot be priced accurately and therefore cannot be efficiently supplied by the private sector. Consumption by one person does not reduce supply for others (eg TV signals/street lighting). No consumer can be excluded even if they refuse to pay (eg public health) and no one may abstain from consumption (eg defence). All people may consume equally. However they have no incentive to pay for what must be provided in any case.

(c)   A quasi-autonomous non-government organisation, which is neither an elected nor a private business organisation. However this type of organisation has executive or administrative authority to implement or advance government policy. The marketer is likely to encounter a large number of such bodies (eg regulators, standards authorities).

(d)   This is practised by governments and by businesses. Instead of doing so themselves, governments or businesses employ an outside agent to perform some specific task, project or part of a project.

(e)   The transfer of ownership of 51% or more shares from a nationalised organisation or state to private hands or ownership.

3.1.3 The efficiency of the public sector

There are of course many strengths and weaknesses of public sector organisations. Some are shown in Figure 1.2.

The Chartered Institute of Marketing

Figure 1.2   Advantages and disadvantages of public sector organisations

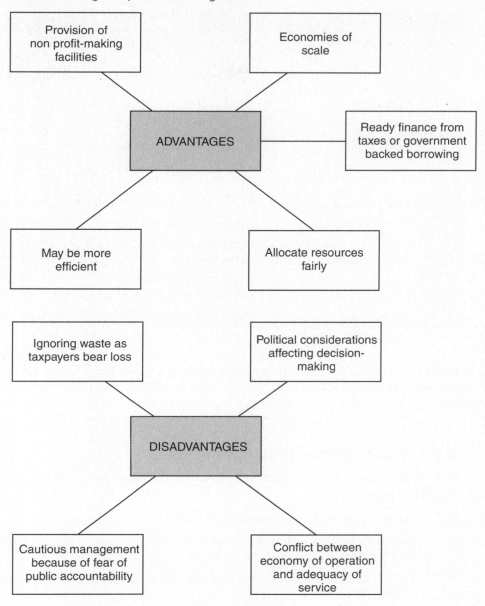

3.2 The private sector

This sector normally accounts for the majority of domestic output, investment goods and exports.

- Resources are privately owned and businesses compete to satisfy consumers.

- The majority of companies operating in that sector are profit motivated.

- Decisions are made about what and how to create products/services by identifying and anticipating market demands in line with available resources and capabilities.

- Although they are not part of the public sector, non-profit-making organisations, that is, trade unions and employer associations, would normally be classified as voluntary organisations.

Table 1.1   Strengths and weaknesses of the public sector versus the private sector

	Public sector	Private sector
Strengths (there are of course many more)	Provide essential but non-profit-making services	Private ownership can lead to enhanced initiative
	Avoid wasteful duplication of expensive resources	Strong motivation to use resources well
	Funds are easily raised through taxation	Funds are efficiently and effectively used and monitored
	Can overcome failings in the market	Companies tend to respond quickly to market signals
	Employees are motivated by public service	Employees are paid by results
Weaknesses (again, there are many more)	Tendency towards political interference	May mean ruthless exploitation
	Monopolies do not serve public	Competition may end in monopoly (mergers and acquisitions)
	Over-accountability may limit entrepreneurship	Competitive over-investment may ultimately be wasteful
	Unions tend to be powerful and taxpayers may have less power	Ignore costs that damage society
	Public expectations of 'free' services	Everything has a price!

> ▸ **Exam tip**
>
> You need to plan your work in line with the timescale associated with the course requirements. Intermediate targets or milestones will help you work towards completing this module. Your plan must be realistic, achievable within the time frame but also controllable through regular reviews of your progress against the targets you have set.

3.3 The voluntary or 'third' sector

The voluntary economy includes services, which are undertaken by individuals and/or organisations, with a not-for-profit motive.

- There is a non-commercial mission and ethos
- This sector includes various unions, clubs and associations that act to promote the common interests of their members.
- Many of these organisations have a special status. As such, services are performed out of friendship or simply acts of charity.

  The Salvation Army or the Samaritans focus on offering support to those in need within the general society. Others focus on specific segments. Oxfam focuses on alleviating poverty worldwide; Age UK focuses on helping to meet the needs of old age pensioners. The organisation Médecins Sans Frontières instead seeks to protect and assist communities and individuals affected by calamity, regardless of race, politics or gender.

Although these organisations satisfy important needs and generate considerable social welfare, they are however not counted in the statistics about national output. Thus the output of these organisations is not included in the GDP of the country. It must be noted that many of the organisations within the voluntary economy such as the Red Cross and CARE operate internationally while many only operate nationally. Features of organisations in the voluntary sector include:

- They are registered and controlled but generally attract tax concessions.
- Registration is dependent on principles, which are very different to those to which companies in the private or public sector have to adhere to.

The Chartered Institute of Marketing

- The type of employment is also sometimes different (paid or voluntary). More often than not, as is the case with the volunteers working in charity shops in the United Kingdom, no money is paid.

- Although making money is often not the primary objective of many of these organisations, their performance has generally become increasingly more professional and marketing informed.

- The competition for funding has arguably contributed to these organisations needing to become more professional and marketing aware.

    In the United Kingdom and the United States, their trading activities have been reflected in the increasing presence of 'charity shops' or 'thrifts' within retail environments. As such, in contemporary terms they constitute an added element of choice for consumers and are even regarded as competition to established retailers.

- Ironically, much of their funding comes from successful private sector entrepreneurs and private companies.

- Between 1994 and 2011 the Bill and Melinda Gates Foundation donated over $26 billion to support causes such as global health and education. In recent times, there appears to be growing pressure on the world's 'mega-rich' to contribute to charities for the benefit of those in poverty around the world.

Although the contributions and achievements of organisations operating within the voluntary economy are not measured in terms of a country's GDP, the effectiveness of their efforts and operations may however be measured in terms of the gross value of the contributions they raise, the degree of suffering they are able to alleviate and perhaps even their success in raising the public profile of the cause which they represent. Indeed, their skills in marketing communications are key determinants of their success with regard to the raising of their profile and the precise communication of their mission.

3.4 Informal and hidden economies

The household economy includes the unpaid domestic services of homemakers, mothers and house-husbands.

- Services include childcare, cooking and cleaning for instance.

- Do-it-yourself activities include gardening, improvements made on existing properties, regular maintenance and even repair.

- Subsistence agriculture primordially conducted to provide food for personal use is significant in many developing and developed economies.

The hidden or shadow economy involves transactions and activities that are 'undeclared' for tax purposes.

- Moonlighting workers perform services for cash in hand.

- Other elements of this sector include pilferage and outright illegal activities such as drug dealing, smuggling and stolen goods.

3.5 Classification of businesses

Governments normally develop a comprehensive framework that places businesses into classes, groups and activities as part of its annual measurement of national output. These are classified according to the sector within which the business operates:

1   The primary sector includes agriculture, fisheries and forestry.

2   The secondary sector includes manufacturing, energy and construction.

3   The tertiary sector involves business services.

4   The quaternary sector involves personal rather than business services, that is, health, education, leisure and other personal services.

4 The legal form of trading organisations

▶ **Key term**

Organisational cultures may vary but the **legal form of organisation** gives an immediate indication of priorities that lie within. A sole trader may expect to sell up or wind up on retirement. A plc will be heavily answerable to its shareholders, and particularly large institutional shareholders. A co-operative will have a shared culture with its owners – be they staff or customers.

Several types of organisations and businesses operate within the private sector. There are two broad categories of privately owned commercial organisation, incorporated and non-incorporated. The key issue is the degree to which a business is a separate legal entity from its owners – ie its legal form. In business a legal entity may be a person or a collection of people. An incorporated organisation is recognised in law as a legal entity in its own right and therefore will have the following rights:

- To make contracts
- To carry out business transactions
- To own property
- To employ people
- To sue and be sued for breach of contract

Non-incorporated organisations, on the other hand are not separate from the individual 'human' business owners. The diagram below highlights the differences.

Figure 1.3   Incorporated and non-incorporated organisations

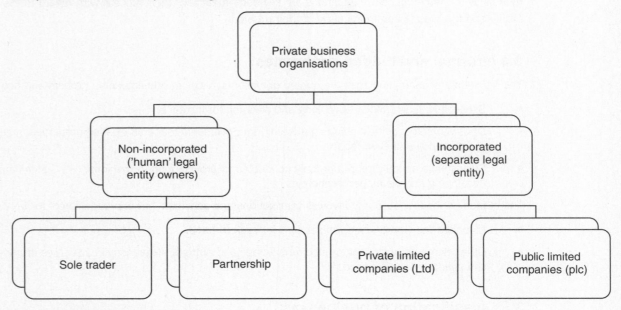

Non-incorporated organisations are:

- Sole traders
- Partnerships
- Registered companies
- Co-operatives
- Franchised businesses

4.1 Sole trader

An estimated 80% of small enterprises are said to be operated by sole traders but the total output is not as significant in terms of contribution percentage to the economy.

The Chartered
Institute of Marketing

Distinctive characteristics of sole trading:

- It is arguably the oldest type and also the most straightforward form of trading. It is also the simplest form of self-employment.

- It involves business usually being carried out in its own name. It implies that a business is not incorporated with any other type of business or people.

- The type of business is usually owned by a single person.

- Business is usually controlled by that same person, who assumes all the rights and is ultimately responsible for all the duties associated with the business.

- There is a sole owner of the business, who is legally responsible for the business.

- Information does not have to be disclosed to any other party. But information about operations and profits must be disclosed to tax authorities.

- There is no limit on the number of people which the sole trader can employ. There can be up to 100 employees.

- Sole trading is popular within farming, personal services, building and retail.

- Sole trading may originate in the hidden economy.

ACTIVITY 1.3

A range of merits and drawbacks associated with sole traders has been identified below. Stop and evaluate each merit and drawback in depth. Think about the environment within which the sole traders may operate. Think about trends. Think about the demands of business. Think about why an aspect is being hailed as a merit and why another aspect is being criticised as a drawback.

Table 1.2   Merits and drawbacks of sole traders

Merits of sole traders	Drawbacks of sole traders
Minimum formalities but also minimal privacy	Unlimited liability for any debts. There is no demarcation between the owner and the business
Complete control. No consultation is necessary if not wished for by the owner	Raising capital can be difficult and may only be possible from personal sources and from putting profits back into the business
Favourable tax treatment	May be perceived to be specialised and risky to financial and other services. It could be difficult to get insurance
The sole trader can be highly motivated and single-minded	The owner may in fact have a too narrow outlook for the ultimate benefit of the business
The least costly type of business to create	The status of the business depends on staying healthy. Thus, there may be a lack of continuity
The simple organisation implies that the owner can remain close to his or her customers and to the employees	The owner as well as the employees may have to work long hours and thus inadvertently lead to exploitation
Can be a very flexible type of structure. When needed, detail can be attended to promptly	Competition from large corporations and other small traders cannot be overruled and ignored
Can be a niche business within the market	Lack of management skills
Has exemption from certain legislation	No one to share burden

- Sole traders tend to operate in sectors where entry barriers are low and where capital requirements are limited.

- They tend to be financially weak compared to well-resourced companies.

- Many are self-employed in name only and work exclusively under contract to others.

4.2 Partnerships

This type of business involves two or more owners or associates. Partnerships are more attractive to the professions where capital requirements are limited.

Main characteristics of partnerships are:

- This is an unincorporated type of enterprise.

- There are two or more partners. However, they all should have a common view to how to achieve profit and conduct business.

- There is usually a limit to the number of partners, which can be included in a partnership. There could be a legally specified maximum number of 20 partners. This limit however does not apply to some professions.

- Legal formalities are few and the privacy of the partners tends to be high.

- The partners usually form an agreement or are bound by legislation. Codes of conduct may strongly limit the risk of financial malpractice.

- The partnership itself has no legal personality. It is in fact the partners who have unlimited liability and are jointly liable for what happens within their business.

- Partners share management decisions as well as any profit or loss that is made.

Table 1.3 Merits and drawbacks of partnerships

Merits of partnerships	Drawbacks of partnerships
Partners are able to raise more capital than a sole trader	Partners have unlimited liability unless the partnership becomes 'limited'. Even then, at least one partner must be fully liable for the business decisions
Partners can pool together their expertise and personal funds	There is a lack of legal identity associated with the business. It may dissolve in case of death or even disagreement
Partners have more possibilities of specialisation	Any potential disagreement may lead to heightened expenses and even unrest within the business
There is no company tax on the business	A partnership can be referred to a frozen investment

ACTIVITY 1.4

Re-examine table 1.3 and evaluate each merit and drawback. What do you think?

4.3 Registered company

The main characteristics of registered companies are:

- As opposed to partnerships, registered companies are incorporated. As such, they have a separate legal entity. Consequently, a registered company can enter into contracts.

- They are formed under specific legislations (eg the 2006 Companies Act).

- A registered company can confer various rights and duties.

The Chartered
Institute of Marketing

- Members of a registered company contribute capital and own shares.

- This type of organisation is dominant nowadays.

- Liability is limited to the amount of finance invested or guaranteed.

Recent UK governments have been simplifying registration processes, requirements and costs to encourage the development and growth of SMEs.

A registered company has a wider range of reporting and taxation requirements including submission of the following documents to the Registrar of Companies:

- **Memorandum of association**

   This regulates the external affairs of the company and protects its investors and suppliers. This document includes the registered name of the company, its objectives, its scope of business and its liability structures.

- **Articles of association**

   This regulates the internal administration of the company. It includes the issuing and transfer of shares, shareholder rights, directors' powers and accounting procedures.

- **Statutory declaration of compliance**

   This must be related to the relevant Act.

- **Independently audited annual accounts and directors' report**

   - Companies with less than 50 employees only need to provide a summary of their independently audited annual accounts and directors' report.

   - 'Unlimited liability' companies are exempt from filing accounting data.

> ▶ **Key term**
>
> **Divorce of ownership and control** is a term used to describe the weakening of connection between those who make decisions within organisations and those who provide the funding. Sole traders exhibit the ultimate unity of ownership and control. As organisations grow and ownership diversifies, the links may weaken and control rests with the structures established in the memorandum and articles of association. For example, the UK government has owned the majority of the Royal Bank of Scotland since 2008 but they declared themselves powerless in their attempts to regulate the controversial bonus culture.

Table 1.4   Comparison of public and private companies

Public company (plc)	Private company (Ltd)
Two or more members	Minimum of one member
£50,000 and a minimum of two directors including a qualified company secretary	Most will have a minimum of one director and a company secretary. Typical family business.
Shares are offered to the public.	Cannot offer shares to the public but can do so to friends and other family members.
A business certificate must be issued before any trading or borrowing can take place.	Trading can only take place when an incorporation certificate is received.
Similar legislation is followed globally. However a different terminology may be used (eg in the United States 'inc.' is used to refer to a plc; in Malaysia the term 'Sdn Bhd' is used to refer to a plc.	The raising of additional bank funds is easier. However, personal guarantees may be needed to do so.

4.3.1 Public companies

Plcs have traditionally been popular and hence constitute a significant percentage of the volume of business of companies operating within any market environment. The key difference conferred by their 'public' status is the ability to raise capital by selling shares on the stock market.

Table 1.5   Merits and drawbacks of plcs

Merits of plcs	Drawbacks of plcs
The plc represents a separate legal entity.	The company is bound by special and double taxation.
The owners have limited liability.	The structure of the company is complex, and hence it is costly to form such companies.
The plc benefits from greater financial capability.	The company is bound by disclosure requirements.
It is easy to transfer the ownership of such companies.	Special government regulations apply to plcs. They must also hold an AGM and comply with Stock Exchange regulations.
The company can fund innovation as well as new product development.	Plcs can be inflexible in terms of size.
Customers tend to trust plcs.	Plcs can become impersonal.

Business is not only conducted by public or private companies. Many companies in fact hold shares in other enterprises which they may have formed or acquired. However, if any one company exceeds more than 50% of the voting rights within another company, that company is then referred to as a **holding company**. Such holdings may sometimes form a pyramid, with the **ultimate holding company** having overall control. Such structures are common in Japan.

THE REAL WORLD

2012 sees the flotation of Facebook, a company that started only eight years ago and now has over 800 million users worldwide. The flotation is expected to raise £5 billion and will mark a significant milestone in the company's phenomenal growth. In an open letter to potential investors, co-founder and chief executive, Mark Zuckerberg emphasised the opportunities that flotation could bring:

'Facebook was not originally created to be a company. It was built to accomplish a social mission – to make the world more open and connected...We think it's important that everyone who invests in Facebook understands what this mission means to us, how we make decisions and why we do the things we do... Thanks for taking the time to read this letter. We believe that we have an opportunity to have an important impact on the world and build a lasting company in the process. I look forward to building something great together.'

(Zuckerberg, 2012)

The Chartered
Institute of Marketing

Review the *Financial Times* for details about a company, which is seeking plc status and offering shares for sale to the public. Read the offer carefully. Evaluate the possible advantages of this course of action for that company. What are the potential drawbacks?

Seek someone who owns shares. Ask them about the dynamics of an AGM and whether they attend these. Try to assess the person's response. Draw conclusions about who you think exercises the real control in this situation.

4.4 Co-operative

Co-operatives represent a significant but declining force in most sectors. Co-operation has contracted in the face of competition from the better-managed and more focused multiples, and has been forced to merge and specialise in other niches. Worker co-operatives among farmers and craft workers were generally established in times of recession or rapid structural decline in the industries concerned.

The main characteristics of co-operatives are as follows:

- Co-operatives were pioneered in the mid-nineteenth century.

- Traditionally, and nowadays, they are most prevalent in agriculture and retailing.

- They are governed by relevant legislation.

- Although workers usually retain the ownership and control of co-operatives, in recent times numbers as well as mergers of co-operatives have been dwindling.

- Co-operatives benefit from limited liability.

- Each member of a co-operative is allocated a vote.

- Co-operatives favour self-help rather than profit maximisation.

- Co-operatives usually operate through a management committee.

- Co-operatives favour the equitable distribution of dividends if and when a surplus is achieved.

Attempt to identify a co-operative. Try to find out how your selected co-operative operates differently to a private company of your choice.

4.5 Franchising

With the wide range of benefits, which it offers, franchising has gained much popularity during the past few decades.

Main characteristics of franchises:

- The franchisor sells the right to market a product under its name to a franchisee.

- Although the various outlets within a specific franchise are in fact financially separate entities, they are all interdependent businesses.

- Franchising has been benefiting from rapid growth especially within the retail sector. Well known franchises include McDonald's and the Body Shop.

- Franchising offers a ready-made opportunity for any entrepreneur who has the capital required for purchasing the franchise. By providing the franchisee with structured offerings to help them run their

business, risks to the franchisee are minimised. Given that the rhetoric goes that only 90% of start-ups actually survive beyond three years, franchising provides new entrants many risk reductions.

In order for a franchise to be agreed upon, the two parties, namely the franchisor and the franchisee, need to meet a range of terms and conditions.

Table 1.6   Franchising terms and conditions

A franchisor must agree to:	A franchisee must agree to:
Provide the business format and initial training	Pay an initial sum and pay a percentage of the profit to the franchisor
Supply product and quality control	Buy supplies of product from franchisor
Provide promotional support (eg advertising)	Maintain the standards stipulated by the franchisor

THE REAL WORLD

McDonald's and Subway are two of the world's best know franchises. A much smaller company using franchising to achieve growth is Riverford Organic Vegetables. With a base in the South West of England, their produce comes from their own farm and from a co-operative of producers. The distribution and marketing is fulfilled by a network of franchisees that sign up to service specific geographic areas, delivering vegetables to over 50,000 households across England every week.

4.6 Global versus SME

The size of organisations will have some influence over their preferred structure and legal status but scale also confers a range of strengths and weaknesses. Globalisation is a significant trend, with consumers and businesses often choosing international organisations and their ubiquitous brands. However, some may see advantages in buying from smaller organisations that may be able to satisfy their needs more effectively for a range of reasons. Some brands may be carefully positioned as small and geographically specific but in fact be part of large multinationals. For example Buitoni pastas and sauces, Bakers pet foods, Häagen Dazs ice cream and S Pellegrino soda water are all owned by Nestlé. Citalia, Hayes & Jarvis, VTB Reizen and Jetair are all owned by TUI Travel plc.

▶ **Key terms**

Small and medium size enterprises (SMEs)

The European Commission (2012) defines these as:

- Small – under 50 employees and 10m euro turnover
- Medium – under 250 employees and 50m euro turnover

They also define **micro businesses** which will have under 10 employees and 2m euro turnover, resulting in the less well known acronym of MSMEs.

Table 1.7　　Strengths of global organisations versus SMEs

The strengths of global organisations	The strengths of SMEs
Economies of scale may be exploited (eg discounts for volume) with regard to both supply and purchase. Thus bargaining power can be used with suppliers or even government to secure subsidies for instance	Attracts people unwilling to work in the confines of large organisations
The similarities between markets can be exploited. Risks may be spread across markets and similarities exploited	Tends to cater to local consumers
The homogeneity of product, image and advertising messages can be maximised. Thus, skills and other resources can be fully utilised. Best practice, ideas and even technological development can be exploited across the organisation	May cater to local tastes and purchasing habits
Global brand leadership can lead to sustainable marketing advantages	Attention to detail and to customers
Ability to centralise strategy and confront worldwide competition	The organisation can be more flexible and adaptable. Thus it may adapt or respond more quickly and easily when change is required
Because of its size and presence, such organisations can be more attractive to suppliers and other key resources	Can remain close to the business partners and its various stakeholders

4.7 Public corporations

Main characteristics of public corporations:

- These are publicly owned, controlled and accountable via specific ministers to the Parliament.

- These are separate legal entities created by Statute or Royal Charter (eg Royal Mint).

- They are controlled by boards of management, which are appointed formally and by ministers.

- Although they are designed to be commercially independent, they are however subject to ministerial control and may be part-financed from the revenue raised by the government or by central government funding.

- Their aim is to secure long-term strategic objectives as well as to control the economy.

- A shortcoming associated with these organisations is that the lack of competition and conflicting objectives may unfortunately lead to inefficiency.

- As they are governmental, they are susceptible to pressure group activity such as trade unions in particular.

UK examples include the Patent Office, Ordnance Survey, the Meteorological Office and the Civil Aviation Authority.

THE REAL WORLD

Met Office

The UK's national weather service is a world leader in providing weather and climate services, employing approximately 1,600 staff in 60 locations around the world. Originally set up in 1854 it has taken many forms during its long history but in 2011 it became a Trading Fund of the Department for Business Innovation and Skills. The Met Office Owner's Council (under the departmental Secretary for State) approves the strategy, sets long term goals and reviews performance. The Met Office Board's primary responsibilities are to develop the strategy and build beneficial external relationships.

Always the forefront of technology, the Met office installed its first computer in 1959 and now has a supercomputer creating 3,000 tailored forecasts and briefings daily for clients around the world. Despite being a thoroughly modern and commercially focused organisation it remains in public control due to the critical nature of its role.

(Met Office, 2012)

4.7.1 Nationalisation and privatisation

Politics and business trends have shaped leanings towards either nationalisation or privatisation. In the UK, British Telecom, British Airways, British Rail, British Aerospace and the regional water companies were once all owned and controlled by the public sector and are now privatised. The Royal Mail, has, to date, proved too challenging (or expensive) to privatise but the 2010 coalition Government kept privatisation on the agenda with mutual ownership (based on the model used by retail giant John Lewis) the favoured form. The justification for the move to privatisation for any public corporation could include the factors identified below.

Table 1.8   Justification for privatisation of nationalised industries

Political factors	Economic factors
The reduced role of the state	The achievement of efficiency improvements
The deregulation of the economy and some industries	The increase of competition and choice
The intention to enable worker share ownership	The pressure on management to become marketing orientated
The encouragement of shareholding democracy among customers	The improvement of industrial relations
To cut the running costs of public services	The exploitation of new opportunities
To cut borrowing (PSBR) and taxes	To improve supply and productivity levels

▶ **Exam tip**

Build a portfolio of case studies of organisations from your own experience, from past exam case studies and from other references in this Study Text. Identify their size, sector and legal form and evaluate how they are impacted by the marketing environment as you work through this unit.

4.8 Other legal forms

As economies continue to develop and to meet changing societal needs, the organisational forms made available to them continue to evolve.

- Companies Limited by Guarantee are often clubs, associations or other not-for-profit organisations. This status gives the people running the organisation the protection of limited liability but there is no share capital and the control lies with members rather than shareholders. Any profits or value on winding up is usually distributed to support the causes defined in the company's articles.

- Community Interest Companies (CIC) have a similar not-for-profit ethos. An asset lock means that assets and profits must be directed to the beneficiaries defined in a Community Interest Statement.

The Chartered Institute of Marketing

5 The vision and mission of organisations

Most economies are made up of a variety of organisations. Each organisation aims to achieve its objectives within a challenging environment. Consequently, the marketer needs to have a comprehensive understanding of, not only what these organisations are trying to achieve, but just as importantly what is driving the behaviour of these organisations both internally and externally.

5.1 Vision

Every organisation, whether operating with a sole trader or as a multinational company, requires vision. Effective vision is closely linked to the marketing environment since it requires the ability to discern future conditions in the industry or market concerned. It is a critical requirement at the strategic level and is normally the responsibility of the board of directors. Vision may be said to involve understanding the future, anticipating how markets, tastes and technologies may evolve as well as the mobilisation of resources to translate the vision into reality. This is the key to business success and competitive advantage and explains why the marketing environment is so central to the marketer's role and importance.

5.2 From vision to mission

Converting a vision into a mission statement produces a strong sense of overall purpose and direction and it seeks to clearly establish what the business does and what it should be doing. It encompasses the scope of its core activities and aims to distinguish that organisation from other organisations of its type by clearly defining its uniqueness. Finally, it may provide a set of corporate values intended to unify the various stakeholders in the organisation and generate a strong sense of common endeavour.

A business mission statement essentially expands on an identified vision. Accordingly, a mission statement would normally refer to a number of the following key elements:

- What is the organisation's philosophy, values, priorities and aspirations?
- What are the organisation's key strengths, competencies and competitive edge?
- What business is the organisation in? Why is the organisation in this type of business?
- Within which markets does the organisation compete?
- Who are the organisation's main customers?
- What are the main products and services, which the organisation offers?
- What core technology does the organisation use?
- What are the organisation's responsibilities towards society?
- What is the organisation's position regarding key stakeholders?

It is important to make a clear distinction between a vision, a mission and a promotional statement. The mission of UPS includes the words 'business solutions that contribute to your global supply chain success'. 'We love logistics' is the promotional slogan the company is using in the run up to London 2012. (UPS, 2012).

A mission statement should respect some fundamental criteria such as:

- It should be brief, achievable and clear.

- It should have a clear statement of purpose as it is meant to enable specific, relevant and realistic objectives.

- A mission statement defines a common purpose. Consequently, it could mobilise the loyalty and commitment of staff/management.

- It provides a clear statement for stakeholders about the values and future direction of the business and should motivate their commitment. Accordingly, it needs to excite and inspire, encouraging participation through a shared vision.

- It acts as a control or benchmark for comparison by senior managers in evaluating the success of the business in realising its purpose.

- It can motivate employees where stated organisational values coincide with theirs.

- The mission statement is part of the corporate culture and this is the glue that unifies contributions.

- Unless a mission statement changes organisational behaviour, it has little value, yet its absence is like being a traveller without a destination, with no way of determining progress.

- A mission statement should differentiate the organisation from others and establish its individuality, if not its uniqueness. It defines what the organisation wishes to be and provides a unifying concept that both enlarges its view of itself and brings it into focus. In brief, it states the intentions of the organisation.

- The mission statement must not, however, unduly restrict astute evolution of the organisation in response to changes in the marketing environment.

THE REAL WORLD

British Airways publish their goals and strategic objectives in their Annual Report as below:

- **Global** – What we offer will appeal to customers across the globe. Wherever we operate, individuals and business travellers alike will want to fly with us whenever they can.

- **Premium** – We will make sure all our customers enjoy a unique premium service whenever and wherever they come into contact with us. Our customers will recognise that the service we offer is worth paying that little bit more for.

- **Airline** – We will remain focused on aviation – moving people and cargo is our core business. We will develop new products and services to complement this.

Our five **strategic goals**:

1   Be the airline of choice for longhaul premium customers
2   Deliver an outstanding service for customers at every touch point
3   Grow our presence in key global cities
4   Build on our leading position in London
5   Meet our customers' needs and improve margins through new revenue stream

(British Airways, 2012)

5.3 Corporate Social Responsibility

The place of CSR as a tool for achieving competitive advantage is discussed in Chapter 4 and the wider macro environmental factors are discussed in Chapter 10. However, a true ethos of responsibility is one that sits at the heart of the organisation. The concept of the 'triple bottom line' suggests that organisations will aim to be responsible for:

- Achieving **economic** security for shareholders, directors and employees

- Striving for positive **social** impacts for employees, suppliers, communities and customers. Is it 'responsible' to sell foods with high sugar and fat content?

- Protecting the natural **environment** through management of land, transport, emissions etc

▶ **Key term**

Corporate social responsibility is the term used to describe a wide range of obligations that an organisation may have towards its stakeholders including the society in which it operates. Jobber (2010) clarifies that CSR it not a new concept – think of Cadbury's 19th century 'model village' at Bourneville, giving workers housing, healthcare and schools.

The legal status may tell us that the organisation is established on a not-for-profit basis. The leadership of the organisation and the priorities followed may be rooted in strong personal values. These values in turn may be influenced by the history of the business and the religious, ethical or cultural values of the founders or owners.

 The Chartered Institute of Marketing

6 Objective setting in organisations

Organisational objectives vary over time and are dependent on the type of organisation and the markets in which it operates. Setting objectives is part of the overall decision-making and planning process within the organisation and it is good to be familiar with the vocabulary of corporate and marketing plans.

- **Goals**: what you are trying to achieve; the intention behind any action.

- **Aims**: goals that cannot be expressed in quantifiable terms eg customer satisfaction or loyalty.

- **Objectives**: a goal which can be quantified.

- **Strategy**: the method chosen to achieve goals or objectives eg we will grow by increasing market share in existing markets.

- **Tactics**: how resources are deployed in an agreed strategy eg new call centre, campaign to target new customers, or a new distribution channel.

6.1 Objectives

- Objectives are the ends to be achieved in order to fulfil the business mission of an organisation.

- They are specific and concrete measures by which an organisation defines standards to be accomplished in key result areas such as profitability and customer service.

- They can be classified into distinct categories, namely strategic, tactical and operational. Each type is linked into a planning process, which seeks to identify and to implement effective strategies and tactics to achieve them:

  Strategic objectives are broad long-term goals set by senior management.

  - To achieve and maintain a position of leadership (be number 1 or 2 in a market)
  - To automate business-to-business transactions with supply chain partners

  Tactical objectives are set by middle managers and relate to functional areas like marketing. They tend to be more measurable.

  - To develop an informational website for the company
  - To reduce operating costs by 5% per annum
  - To achieve preferred supplier status with designated customers

  Operational objectives are usually set by first-line management. These tend to be more short term.

  - Daily production targets
  - To reduce customer complaints by 5% per month

6.2 General organisational objectives

Different types of organisation can have contrasting primary and secondary orientations.

Organisation	Primary orientation	Secondary orientation
Private business	Profit	Growth and increase in market share
Co-operative	Members' returns	Democratic processes of business
Public corporation	Public service and profit making	Efficiency
Social services	Public service	Equity
Interest group	Members' self-interest	Raise organisation's profile
Charitable	Alleviating suffering of the less fortunate	Raise contributions to help operations and mission

Primary and secondary orientations are decided by organisations. But, actual objectives can be diverse, complex and subject to considerable influence from market environments.

6.3 Profit and profit maximisation

Profit maximisation implies that businesses seek to make not only a profit but also the maximum possible profit through time. This is the most-quoted business objective. It provides a **measurement system** for assessing business performance.

In order to maximise its potential for profit, a business may choose to adopt the following course of actions:

- Supplying goods that consumers most wish to buy. Through careful research of customer needs, an understanding and anticipation of their changing preferences can be acquired.

- Combining resource inputs to produce planned output at minimum possible cost. Businesses will not satisfy consumer wants, irrespective of cost, just to make sales.

- Responding quickly to changes in supply and demand conditions. If consumer tastes change or input prices alter then it will be in the interest of the firm to adjust the marketing mix or production methods accordingly.

The pursuit of maximum profit therefore answers two of the basic economic problems arising from scarcity:

1   What to produce and in what quantities and
2   How to produce them efficiently

It also provides a dynamic growth incentive for the business system to:

- Innovate new and improved products that enhance value for money for consumers and revenue for the firm

- Invest in research and development of more efficient methods of production to reduce costs

Maximising profit would appear to promise an ideal allocation of resources by rewarding those businesses that produce and market the right goods, in the right quantities, using the most efficient methods and ploughing back resources into producing economic growth through new products and better methods.

When competition is very strong:

- Firms must market what consumers demand otherwise their competitors will.
- Firms must be efficient otherwise they will be undercut by lower-cost rivals.
- They must provide excellent service because the power lies with the consumer in such situations.

6.4 Market share

Many businesses seek to maximise sales **subject to a profit constraint**. There may indeed be a positive correlation between profit and market share, but beyond a certain point, extra share may only be 'bought' at the expense of profit.

The Chartered Institute of Marketing

- Prices and margins will be trimmed or extra promotional expense incurred.

- So long as sufficient profit is made to keep shareholders content, management may see an advantage in the stability and security of a dominant position.

6.5 Business growth

Growth and profits may be positively related but they are not unconditionally linked. The rapid growth in out-of-town grocery superstores appears to be a case in point. Growth may require takeovers and acquisitions, and these may prove unsuccessful, especially if they represent diversification into unfamiliar areas. Such strategies put pressure on the management of resources.

Growth may, however, be attractive for a number of reasons. For instance:

- It may help resolve conflicts between stakeholders
- It may provide opportunities for promotion and job satisfaction
- It tends to increase market power and thus management status
- It can raise morale in general
- It can reduce risk through having a wider product or customer base

Table 1.10   Judging success

Key result areas
Refer to academics to support your points; ie P.F. Drucker argued that there are at least eight key result areas in which a business organisation should be judged:
▪ Market standing: Desired share in present or new markets
▪ Innovation: In products/services and the skills/processes required to deliver them
▪ Human resources: The supply, skill, development, attitude and performance of staff
▪ Financial resources: Sources of capital and effective utilisation
▪ Management performance
▪ Productivity: Efficient use of resources relative to outcomes
▪ Social responsibility: Maintenance of ethical behaviour
▪ Profitability: The indicators of financial wellbeing

6.6 Making management objectives matter

If management is not under severe competitive pressure, it may decide to **satisfice** and may then only produce satisfactory performance and profits. Where there is a **separation of ownership from management** there is no automatic incentive for professional managers to maximise profits for shareholders. The organisation may operate with what is termed **organisational slack**; failing to minimise costs and spending inefficiently on pet projects or perks. Organisational slack may lead to more security and status for management in good times but such organisations will be poorly placed to thrive in more challenging times.

A lack of competition, the absence of a profit incentive and powerful stakeholder groups led to an accumulation of **slack** in health, education, local authorities, state-controlled industries and government bureaucracy. This resulted in efforts by the government to improve productivity across a range of public services through various means such as:

- Deregulating markets or introducing internal markets

- Making services client driven (through the introduction of service charters in addition to set service standards)

- Insisting on compulsory competitive tendering

- Attracting better-calibre managers while curbing the power of the trade unions

- Appointing powerful regulators to set price/performance standards

As the objectives have become more customer-orientated in the public sector, the nature of these organisations has also been transformed. Subsequently, the skills of the marketer have also come to the fore in the quest for more focused customer benefits.

7 The setting of organisational goals

Key influences may be summarised as internal and external.

Internal influences include:

- Memorandum of association

    - The **memorandum of association** or its equivalent sets limits in the objects clause to the powers of a company.

    - Pursuit of purposes outside these limits will be deemed *ultra vires* and therefore legally void.

    - In practice, this clause will be broadly defined to allow the directors to diversify outside their traditional business.

- Personal values, competencies and objectives of senior management

    - The personal values and objectives of senior management will exert significant influence on an organisation, in particular when represented to the board, for example by the marketing director.

    - Satisfying customer needs may be dependent on a shift of skills and expertise and this may be something that the organisation is unwilling or unable to develop.

- The expectations of the internal decision-makers and their degree of aversion to risk

    - This will strongly impact the risk avoidance or risk taking dimensions of tactics and even strategies.

- The limits set by resource availability

    - Internal financial and human resource may be seen as a limiting factor or as a driving factors eg optimising staff utilisation.

    - A minimum return on capital may be required in order to attract the necessary internal and external funds to finance other objectives.

- Key individual and institutional shareholders

    - Their expectations will greatly influence receptivity of ideas and change in particular. Internal politics may have a powerful influence over attitudes, change and overall direction.

- The force of inertia and past successes may prevent serious internal review of objectives

    - For example, Microsoft, a 30-year-old company, still relies on a ten-year-old suite of desktop applications for 80% of its sales, while newer products like the Xbox made significant early losses. The much younger Google attracts the software talent and releases a much faster stream of products directly onto the internet.

External influences include:

- Successful businesses recognise the importance of matching the capabilities of the organisation to its environment. Internal strengths and weaknesses must be set against external threats and opportunities.

- There are a variety of connected and external stakeholders whose interests and attitudes must be considered before objectives are set. Their contribution will often be crucial to the effective implementation of the objectives.

- Conflict between the interests of shareholders and various stakeholders may require a compromise to retain their contribution to the achievement of set objectives.

The Chartered
Institute of Marketing

- The competitive environment may constrain what are achievable objectives in terms of time.

- A change in government will alter previously set objectives, while changes in legislation will define what is, and is not, achievable for private businesses.

- External interests may be represented, for example worker or consumer directors.

8 The change of organisational goals

There are compelling reasons to regularly consider changes to goals. Most organisations operate in a dynamic and constantly changing environment. As these environmental forces threaten to throw the business off course, management must respond proactively by setting a new direction and a renewed focus to unify the organisation's efforts. Changes may include:

- Changes in consumer wants must be anticipated and responded to with matching goals.

- Changes in production possibilities transform resource availability and technological options.

- Opportunities and threats from the various environments represent new realities and require new responses.

- Objectives are intended to be achieved and so require renewal as this occurs.

- If control processes show that objectives are not being realised, then a change to more realistic goals will provide more effective motivation for management and staff.

- A change in the chief executive or perhaps a merger or acquisition will tend to change the strategic goals.

- Larger organisations may adopt corporate planning to formalise the above process.

- Every organisation must periodically review its objectives if it is to survive and succeed.

- Corporate planning is akin to a continuing process during which the long-term objectives of an organisation may be formulated and achieved by means of short-term as well as long-term strategic actions.

- Strategic objectives are the outcome of the above internal and external influences and considerations.

- They tend to revolve around a five- to ten-year time frame.

- Ongoing rigorous reviews and corrections are implied.

- Corporate strategy tries to determine what an organisation should optimally do.

9 The organisation as an open system

Organisational objectives must be regularly reviewed and set with reference to internal and external considerations. Understanding this interplay between internal context and the wider environment has led to the organisation being viewed as an open system. This approach focuses on the interrelated activities that enable inputs to be converted into outputs and provides a very useful framework for gaining insight into the relationships that prevail between the organisation and its marketing environment.

There are many different systems we could identify: ourselves, the marketing department, our organisation, the corporate system, the marketing environment, the wider society, the global economy, the ecosystem, our galaxy and the solar system. Each has a boundary that represents its interface with the others.

The interface between the organisation and its environment is represented in and possesses the following common characteristics:

- Productive inputs and energy are received/obtained from the marketing environment.
- The organisation adds value by converting these inputs into desired outputs.
- The organisation discharges its outputs into its environment – both positive and negative.
- The organisation applies control by monitoring the feedback on achievement of objectives.

Open systems are interdependent with their marketing environment and must adapt to change if they are to survive and develop.

Open systems are vital where the environment is unstable or uncertain. Closed systems do not respond to change and only function well in stable conditions.

Open systems will also scan the external environment for opportunities and threats. When the organisation adapts to this external environment it will impact on its **effectiveness**, whereas when it adapts its internal structure and organisation, it will impact on its **efficiency**.

10 The characteristics of organisational strengths and weaknesses

10.1 The internal characteristics of the organisation

Our final aspect of considering the organisation is to look at the individual elements within the organisation that make it what it is:

- Functions eg marketing, finance, production, HR
- Structures – lines of responsibility and reporting
- Management – setting goals, monitoring performance, organising resources and leading teams
- Systems and procedures
- Staff

- Culture – shared history, attitudes and opinions
- Competencies and skills
- Strategy, objective, mission and goals

Marketing not only operates over the external boundary with the wider environment but must also establish and maintain effective relationships across the internal boundaries with key departments such as finance, research and development, and production. How this works in practice will be shaped by all of the other elements, for example the culture and competencies.

10.2 5 Ms of business management

The 5 Ms is a model of the internal elements of the business environment. These elements may represent the strengths and weakness of an organisation and the model is commonly used to prompt analysis of priorities, actions, and challenges that may hold the key to success. As this unit progresses you will see that this model is helpful for identifying the elements within the organisation that need to be managed in order to satisfy customer requirements profitably. As a generic and well-used model there are a number of different definitions and terms that may appear. Other Ms referred to include Manpower (for men) and Management, however the version shown below is the approach used in this unit.

Figure 1.4   5 Ms – analysing the internal environment

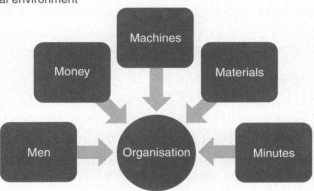

10.3 Orientation

In Marketing Essentials the concept of the general orientation of the organisation is covered in detail. In this unit its relevance is as once of the many elements that characterise the internal marketing environment. There are four main fundamental types of business focus related to the environment:

1   Production orientation
2   Product orientation
3   Selling orientation
4   Marketing orientation

Each one has implications for organisational effectiveness and the degree to which it is outward looking. Some businesses may evolve from an inward-looking focus on production efficiency and product quality or even selling quality to a comprehensive operational emphasis on anticipating and satisfying changing consumer requirements through greater sales awareness.

10.3.1 Production orientation

- Companies adopting a production orientation not only focus their efforts on improving the production process, but also the efficiency of distribution channels and processes.

- Such companies may by all means also aim to focus their operations on the reduction of operational costs or even economies of scale.

- Technical or finance specialists will tend to dominate the hierarchy while the sales function will be minor with no representation on the board.

- Primacy is given to products rather than to their customers.

10.3.2 Product orientation

- Focus is on quality and performance.

- Companies believe that customers choose products for their quality rather than their price.

- The aim is to produce the best products or offer the best services on the market.

- There is a danger of pricing oneself out of its market where there is no requirement for extra features provided.

10.3.3 Selling orientation

- The main aim is to sell products due to over-capacity and excess supply or when customers need to be persuaded about the products.

- Aggressive sales and promotion of products and services is used.

- The aim to increase customer share.

- The focus is to sell what is available rather than to provide what customers want.

- Companies may have heavy investment in fixed capital equipment such as building and technology. Thus, the focus is on product rather than the customers.

10.3.4 Marketing orientation

- Rather than ignore the dimensions advocated by the three other approaches to business, the marketing orientation incorporates aspects of each of the others.

- Improvement of product quality just like those which are product-oriented.

- Improvements within product-oriented companies may be internally driven, but within marketing-oriented companies, they are always driven by customers.

- Promotion and price discounting are also used as short-term tactics, solutions or temporary incentives.

- An **outside-in perspective** is adopted as opposed to the **inside-out perspective** favoured by the other business philosophies.

- Focus is on the genuine needs and wants of their target audiences.

10.4 Organisational constraints

No organisation has an endless pool of resources or can easily meet the needs of every single customer group. In reality organisations need to match their resources, skills and competencies to identifiable areas of opportunity.

10.4.1 Resource capability

Resources are tangible and intangible assets which are employed by the organisation to achieve their objectives. Every organisation operates under resource constraints. The typical resources available to an organisation are shown in the table below along with issues to be considered in order to complete an audit of their significance to the organisation:

The Chartered Institute of Marketing

Table 1.11   Typical resources available to an organisation

Resource	Example
Material inputs	Source, suppliers, waste, new materials, cost, availability, future provision
Human resources	Number, skills, wage cost, proportion of total costs, efficiency, labour turnover, industrial relations
Management	Size, skills, loyalty, career progression, structure
Fixed assets	Age, condition, cost utilisation rate, value, replacement, technology up-to-date?
Working capital	Credit and turnover periods, cash surpluses/deficits
Finance	Short-term and long-term, gearing level
Intangible assets	Patents, goodwill, brands, relationships formed with partners
Organisation	Culture and structure
Knowledge	Ability to generate and disseminate ideas, innovation

As resources are rarely in endless supply, we need to be aware of the limitations and constraints faced.

10.4.2 Competency

The speed of change in the business environment has only made the issue of competency more significant. Businesses must be able to continuously evaluate their competencies in many areas:

- Leadership and management skills and how these impact on the direction and effectiveness of the organisation

- Technological competencies in terms of hardware, connectivity, accessibility and management of data

- Technological competencies in terms of process efficiencies

- Access to robust information on markets, customers and competitors and ability to analyse this information effectively

- Ability to use resources such as capital and distribution networks flexibly, to adapt to fluctuating demand and to do so profitably

- Astute financial management and strategies for addressing elements of risk

- Availability of skilled staff and ability to train and develop staff

10.4.3 Internal politics

This can be defined as the informal behaviours within the organisation. Throughout this chapter the factual, published and legislative elements of the organisation are discussed but, as experience will tell us, there may sometimes be a hidden agenda. For example departments with significant influence over forward planning or prioritisation, or a culture of 'quick wins' to satisfy particular stakeholder groups.

Human nature is such that a wholly honest an open culture is virtually impossible to achieve. The role of managers is to develop the appropriate formal processes to limit the negative influences of internal politics, whilst taking advantage of the energy and innovation that they might add.

10.5 Stakeholders

The analysis of stakeholders in the wider context of the micro environment is discussed in detail in Chapter 2. However, the organisation's understanding of its stakeholders' needs and a culture of aiming to satisfy those needs are critical elements of the internal environment. The table below identifies some stakeholders' needs but the identification and satisfaction of stakeholder needs will be unique to every organisation. It will be heavily influenced by the many factors in the internal environment already discussed in this chapter. Consider a charity and how they may wish to satisfy the needs of donors, a government satisfying the needs of voters or a major sporting event satisfying the needs of its sponsors.

Table 1.12   Stakeholder needs

Stakeholder	Needs
Shareholders	Growth in value of shares and return on investment in the form of dividends
Directors	Detailed information on performance and ability to make strategic decisions for the organisation
Employees	Job security, remuneration, recognition and career progression
Customers	Satisfactory products and services and a recognition as a 'valued' customer
Pressure groups	Freely available information on critical issues and a route to communicate and influence
Banks	Minimal risk and a good financial return
Society	Responsible actions in relation to immediate neighbours and the wider community
Suppliers	Continuity of custom and prompt payment

Corporate objectives, marketing objectives and marketing communication tactics therefore revolve only around much more than just satisfying customers; the ability of the organisation to succeed will be driven by a carefully balanced and prioritised approach to identifying and satisfying the needs of all stakeholders.

▶ **Key term**

Stakeholders: Any individuals or organisations that have an interest in, or an influence over, your organisation. This will include people within the organisation as well as individuals or groups in the micro and the macro environments.

ACTIVITY 1.7

Consider the following questions in relation to your own organisation or to the case study organisation:

- Are all stakeholders clearly identified?

- Is research used to identify the needs of all stakeholder groups?

- How does the organisation aim to satisfy the needs of a range of stakeholders?

11 Managing the marketing environment: a contingency approach

There is no one best means of managing organisations to meet objectives in an uncertain environment. Marketers must therefore identify and then adapt continuously to the conditions that are found to prevail in the present and the future. Successful organisations will tend to be those that operate in a way that suits today's **new economy** and fast changing marketing environment.

The Chartered Institute of Marketing

Table 1.13   Old versus new economy organisations

Old economy organisation	New economy organisation
Stable bureaucratic structures	Flexible dynamic structures
Mechanistic and hierarchical	Organic and fluid
Formalised relationships	Lateral, informal, networked relationships
Job and position focused	Task, skills and relationship focused
Permanent 9–5 jobs	Flexitime, as task completion demands
Production orientated	Market and customer orientated
Centralised decision-making	Employee involvement and participation
Salaried	Shared benefits and shared ownership

Greater innovation, more comprehensive service solutions and better value are sought by multifaceted environmental changes.

11.1 Influential trends

> ▶ **Key term**
>
> **Electronic** and **mobile commerce** have already reshaped many organisations' objectives and operations, and they will continue to do so. Successful organisations can adapt quickly to develop electronic services as part of meeting customer needs.

A number of key trends and changes have transformed the structure of organisations. The main ones are:

- **Digitalisation**
    - E-commerce affects the whole organisation. It involves radical restructuring for many organisations combined with fundamental shifts in business culture. Seamless adoption and integration of information technology is needed.
    - The mobile phone is fast becoming a critical instrument in marketing at the individual level (M-advertising and M-commerce).
    - The emphasis is increasingly on flexibility; adapting quickly to digital opportunities across the marketing mix.
- **Knowledge workers**
    - Information is captured, processed, stored and then made available in the right form to the appropriate decision-makers and at the right time to achieve maximum competitive advantage.
    - Organisations reinforce this decision quality by de-layering ie having flatter structures. This involves compressing the hierarchy by reducing the number of reporting levels. This speeds up the flow of information to the decision-maker, and the decisions to those who implement them at the customer interface.
- **Networks and relationships**: developing formal and informal networks to support knowledge sharing, best practice and adding value through involving customers in decision-making, growth and development
- **Organisational adaptability**: having the ability to change quickly and efficiently to meet changing customer needs
- **Globalisation**: the global integration of societies, cultures and economies, facilitated by advances in worldwide communications. Features of globalisation include the divergence of cultures, a reduction of the importance of global manufacturing and a rise in the financial interdependency of markets.

11.2 Globalisation – impact on the organisation

Economic globalisation refers to the growing economic interdependence of countries worldwide through increased international trade, increased capital flows and the rapid diffusion of technology. The term globalisation is now used in a wider context that encompasses the global integration of societies, culture and economies, facilitated by advance in worldwide communications.

The review of the internal environment necessitates an analysis of the comparative strengths and weaknesses of these organisational structures.

Table 1.14   Strengths and weaknesses of local organisations

Strengths	Weaknesses
Intimate knowledge of the market	Limited ability to expand to meet growing need
Ability to adapt quickly to changing conditions	Lack of economies of scale in production, distribution and media buying
Opportunities to develop products for niche markets	Relatively high cost of developing new products
Contained distribution networks	Lack of specialist skills

Table 1.15   Strengths and weaknesses of global organisations

Strengths	Weaknesses
Significant returns from investment in new products	Can be perceived as impersonal; poor customer relationships
Substantial buying power	Failure to adapt adequately to meet local needs
Global brand awareness and strength	Vulnerable to criticism for economic leakage (see Chapter 7)
High levels of expertise across the organisation	Potential of high risks in unstable markets

Issues relating to global versus local strengths and weaknesses are decreasing over time as new breeds of organisation are emerging; organisations with the core competency of an ability to investigate, analyse, enter and develop new markets in way that is tailored to the needs of each market.

Through technology, global organisations are increasingly able to adapt service delivery to the meet the needs of national or local markets and indeed the needs of individual customers. Consider Starbucks and its approach to adapting stores to sit well within a local community. Consider Amazon, a global company but one that uses technology to meet the needs of individual customers, thus achieving extremely high customer service ratings.

Customers will generally therefore ask 'does this product meet my needs?' rather than 'is this product local?

▶ **Exam tip**

As you read the specific sections of this Study Text, try to identify examples from the marketing environment and monitor quality and business press for current news. How are organisations adapting to the changing marketing environment? Websites can help you extend your knowledge about marketing environment (http://www.ft.com, http://www.thetimes.co.uk, http://www.businesscasestudies.co.uk, http://www.economist.com, http://www.corporateinformation.com).

Your exam will be three hours long and is based on a previously seen case study, which is published online eight weeks before the exam date. You will need to review and discuss the case and prepare your (individual) PESTEL and SWOT analyses, which you bring into the exam and submit with your exam paper. A clean copy of the case will be provided in the exam.

The exam will consist of five questions in Part A. Each question will be worth eight marks. There will be three questions in Part B. Each question will be worth 20 marks.

The Chartered Institute of Marketing

CHAPTER ROUNDUP

In this chapter, we have seen that

- A diversity of organisations exists within a mixed economy.

- The public, private or third sector nature of an organisation will shape their status and aims.

- The legal status of the organisation is evident and will also significantly affect how it operates.

- The strengths of one form of organisation are often the weaknesses of an other.

- Organisational objectives are stepping stones along the road to achieving the corporate mission.

- Business objectives are varied and reflect different organisational or personal motivations.

- Strengths and weaknesses can be shaped by internal resource and competency.

- Objectives pursued reflect internal cultures and values as well as external influences and constraints.

- There is an important distinction between organisations that are satisficing and those that are maximising.

- Businesses are open systems which rely on interaction with their environment for survival/growth.

- A major part of the work of the marketer is to manage the internal and external relationships.

- The marketer should respond flexibly to the realities of the changing situation.

- A marketing-oriented structure and ethos is the key to effective achievement of objectives.

FURTHER READING

Palmer, A. and Hartley, B. (2012) *The business environment*. 12th edition. Maidenhead, McGraw-Hill. Chapters 1 and 7.

Worthington, I. and Britton, C. (2009) *The business environment*. 6th edition. Harlow, Pearson. Chapters 2, 3 and 10.

Annual reports published online by most organisations will clarify legal form and structure of the organisation as well as describing its culture and ethos.

REFERENCES

British Airways (2012) 2009/10 Annual report and accounts. http://www.britishairways.com/cms/global/microsites/ba_reports0910/our_business/strategy.html [Accessed on 14 February 2012].

European Commission (2012) Small and medium-sized enterprises (SMEs). http://ec.europa.eu/enterprise/policies/sme/facts-figures-analysis/sme-definition/index_en.htm [Accessed on 4 February 2012].

Johnson, P. (2012) Prospect, http://www.prospectmagazine.co.uk/2012/01/cover-story-grown-up-conversation-paul-johnson-cuts-austerity-deficit/ [Accessed on 10 February 2012].

Marks and Spencer (2012) Company overview. http://corporate.marksandspencer.com/aboutus/company_overview [Accessed on 4 February 2012].

Met Office (2012) Management of the Met Office. http://www.metoffice.gov.uk/about-us/who/management [Accessed on 23 May 2012].

UPS (2012) Our mission. http://www.ups-psi.com/about/mission.asp [Accessed on 4 February 2012].

Worthington, I. and Britton, C. (2009) *The business environment.* 6th edition. Harlow, Pearson.

Zuckerberg (2012) BBC, http://www.bbc.co.uk/news/technology-16859527 [Accessed on 10 February 2012].

QUICK QUIZ

1   True or false? The internal environment refers to the environment of the industry.

2   Which statement most closely resembles a closed system?

    A   Self sufficient
    B   Interacts with the environment
    C   Disallows new members

3   The competitive environment is best described by the term macro or micro?

4   Which of the following are merit goods and which are public goods?
Policing/street lighting/private schooling/flu jabs/free to air TV/solar panels

5   What are the disadvantages associated with being a sole trader?

6   True or false? Stakeholders are owners of a business.

7   Match the correct terms and definitions

    (i)   Goals
    (ii)   Objectives
    (iii)   Aims

    A   What you are trying to achieve; the intention behind any action

    B   Goals which cannot be expressed in quantifiable terms, eg customer satisfaction or loyalty

    C   Goals which can be quantified, eg increase profits by 30% over the next 12 months

8   What is the purpose of a mission statement?

ACTIVITY DEBRIEFS

Activity 1.1

For the three selected companies you should have defined sector as public, private or voluntary. Describing the organisations' activities in one sentence is a good discipline and you can describe size by turnover, number of staff, countries of operation and number of outlets. Most organisations will publish this information on corporate websites. For example, Marks and Spencer is a private sector plc which describes itself as follows

'We are one of the UK's leading retailers, with over 21 million people visiting our stores each week. We offer stylish, high quality, great value clothing and home products, as well as outstanding quality foods, responsibly sourced from around 2,000 suppliers globally. We employ over 78,000 people in the UK and abroad, and have over 700 UK stores, plus an expanding international business.'

Marks and Spencer (2012)

The Chartered Institute of Marketing

Activity 1.2

1   d

2   e

3   a

4   b

5   c

Activity 1.3

Sole traders tend to operate in sectors where entry barriers are low and where capital requirements are limited. They tend to be financially weak, limiting their ability to expand, and can be risk averse and liability is unlimited. This status can be a first stepping stone as a small business becomes established.

Activity 1.4

The merits and drawbacks of partnerships may seem to point to greater risk for the partners and investors but it tends to be favoured in professions where assets may be insignificant but there is a high value on the expertise of the individual partners. It remains a popular legal status for professions such as doctors, lawyers and accountants. They retain a degree of independence but, by working together, can share overhead costs marketing expertise.

Activity 1.5

Public flotation can draw in new finance and enable private owners or founders to liquidate their holding. The company must declare a great deal of information ahead of the flotation and its success will be vulnerable to fluctuating market conditions.

The vast majority of shareholders will never attend an AGM unless they hold a substantial amount of shares. With a limited number of shares in a given portfolio, the set timing and venue of an AGM, and with little or no real influence over proceedings, the incentive to attend can be very small.

Activity 1.6

http://www.uk.coop lists many of the established co-operatives in the UK including customer owned co-ops such as the Co-operative Group and staff owned co-ops such as John Lewis. Customers and workers, as owners, are more likely to be committed to corporate objectives. It is also significant to note that, although the movement started in the UK, there are large numbers of members of co-operatives in the world's emerging economies.

Activity 1.7

- Larger organisations may not publish a list of stakeholders but, through information such as annual reports, there may be evidence of relationships with a wide range of stakeholders.

- Researching the views of customers but also the views of staff, shareholders, neighbours or other key influencers

- Setting objectives in relation to staff welfare, community relations, and shareholder relations as well as profit

1   False. The internal environment refers to the environment within the organisation.

2   A

3   Micro

4   Merit goods are flu jabs; private schooling; solar panels.

    Public goods are policing; street lighting; free to air TV.

5   You are personally liable for all debt; large sums of capital are less likely to be available; you may require enormous investments in time without the normal employee benefits.

6   False. Stakeholders have an interest or a stake in the business but they do not necessarily own it.

7   Goals: What you are trying to achieve; the intention behind any action

    Objectives: Goals which can be quantified, eg increase profits by 30% over the next 12 months

    Aims: Goals which cannot be expressed in quantifiable terms, eg customer satisfaction or loyalty

8   To help articulate the primary aim of the organisation and to help members work towards a shared goal. It is not simply a piece of paper but a living document within the organisation.

CHAPTER 2

The micro environment and stakeholders

Introduction

Having considered the detail of the organisation, its sector, legal form, culture, history and traditions, we now need to begin to investigate the influences that the organisation faces. This chapter introduces the external marketing environment and identifies some implications for marketing strategy and planning. The micro environment may be defined as including the groups and organisations that have a two-way operational relationship with the business, and which are controlled and influenced by it to some degree. This environment is the work-a-day operational context for the organisation. We saw in Chapter 1 that the organisation is an open system with boundaries to its immediate environment. Relationships must be established across these boundaries if supplies or credit, for example, are to be obtained. Similarly, the organisation must have effective linkages, through intermediaries, to the marketplace, or directly to the final customers themselves. Competitors also inhabit this environment and the marketer must understand the significance of relationships that prevail within the industry setting. This will be discussed in depth in Chapter 3.

Topic list

The business as a resource converter	1
The environmental context of the organisation	2
Conditions in the marketing environment	3
The micro environment	4
Significance of stakeholders within the micro environment	5
Pressure groups	6
Consumerism	7
The negative impact of poor stakeholder management	8

Syllabus references

1.3	Explain how organisational objectives differ across a range of different sectors and consider the influences upon setting these objectives and the challenges they represent:
	■ Identifying stakeholder needs
	■ Satisfying stakeholder needs
	■ The increasing need to address corporate social responsibility issues
2.1	Evaluate the stakeholders that constitute the micro environment within which organisations operate and their importance to the marketing process:
	■ Company
	■ Customers
	■ Competitors
	■ Suppliers
	■ Distributors

Figure 2.1   The marketing environment – the micro environment

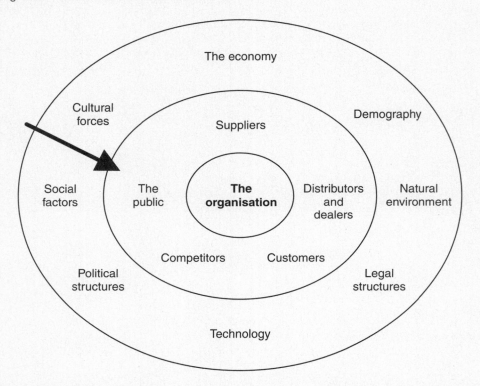

> **▶ Exam tip**
>
> As you approach the exam case study you should become adept at relating the syllabus directly to your own experience. You are a consumer within the market environment. You supply labour for your employer. You are aware of the competitors operating in your industry. You may deal with distributors or consumers. Marketing promotes profitable relationships across boundaries. Hence, you are ideally placed to appreciate the micro environment as both a consumer and as part of a provider mechanism.

1 The business as a resource converter

No organisation operates within a vacuum. All of the factors discussed in Chapter 1 start from the internal perspective. What are the organisation's aims and objectives? What orientation drives it and what is the

The Chartered Institute of Marketing

internal culture? Beyond the internal perspective it must be recognised that the organisation faces many influences and the first step is to view the role of the organisation as a resource converter.

- Resources are scarce and competed for.
- Resources are converted to create utility, value and satisfaction for consumers.
- Resource providers may also be viewed as stakeholders in the business.
- Organisations are coalitions of stakeholders.
- Management must achieve balance between claims and interests of the various stakeholders.

2 The environmental context of the organisation

Figure 2.2   The variety of environmental factors confronting organisations

New government elected	Cloud computing	Competitor enters market
Digital network established	Supplier cartel uncovered	Uncertainty in Middle East
£-$ exchange rate rise	Recession in manufacturing	Euro instability
Japan in recovery	**The organisation**	Trade war threat
Concerns over GM foods		Duty Free concessions go
Distributors merge	Social media	Congestion charges
Minimum wage raised	Supplier cartel uncovered	Pledge to meet emission targets
Life expectance rises	Recession in manufacturing	Growth of mobile internet
		Tax rises

All businesses face the challenges and opportunities posed by the political, economic, social and technological environment.

- These impact organisations differently (size and situation).
- They create opportunities and threats which organisations cannot control.

ACTIVITY 2.1

Look at the factors identified in Figure 2.2 and use different colour pens to highlight or underline those factors that are in the macro environment and those that are in the micro environment. If you are unsure, consider if the factor affects any business or sector.

The external marketing environment comprises the micro or competitive environment, and the macro environment. The key distinction between the two is that the macro environment consists of those factors, affecting any industry, over which the organisation has no control. The micro environment refers to the immediate operational environment and includes all factors which impact directly on an organisation and its activities in relation to the particular market in which it operates.

The micro environment includes the groups and organisations that have a two-way relationship with the organisation, and which the organisation can control or influence to varying degrees through the development of a marketing strategy. It includes suppliers, competitors, customers, intermediaries and other stakeholders.

ACTIVITY 2.2

(a)   Produce a summary of the main events and developments affecting a business of your choice over recent months. Use the micro and macro environment as your headings. This is referred to as a business environment brief.

(b)   Take a typical workday of a marketing executive and log occasions and actions that link your organisation to its external environment eg investigate competitor pricing.

3 Conditions in the marketing environment

Marketing environments can be both complex and dynamic. Variables can be interdependent or can interact with one another through both positive and negative feedback loops. Marketers in both emerging and developed economies are faced by a succession of non-routine problems and situations. These may be opportunities for rapid growth, change and development. Change can be turbulent in nature, following conflicting rather than expected patterns and therefore giving organisations the great challenge of dealing with unexpected change.

During dynamic and complex conditions, businesses must:

- Actively and continuously scan and confront the environment
- Use current data and trends to forecast change

ACTIVITY 2.3

A recurring theme in this Study Text is that various environments are in a continuous state of often-turbulent change.

(a)   What do you think this means?
(b)   What evidence do you have from the marketing environment to support your arguments?

4 The micro environment

In general the micro environment is the immediate or operational environment for the marketer. It drives the tactical responses of the market on a daily basis. The marketer can utilise the marketing mix to influence and affect the stakeholders of a business. Remember that the micro environment contains both actual and potential customers – the marketer can use the marketing mix to convert potential customers into actual customers, however, to do this he must be acutely aware of the needs and wants of those potential customers, Thus an important element in understanding the micro environment is the competition between organisations aiming to win customers, obtain supplies or get access to the best intermediaries.

▶ **Exam tip**

It is essential that you achieve a sound grasp of these basic environmental concepts. The generic marking scheme for this unit gives a total of 70% of syllabus coverage to the macro and micro environment. Be absolutely clear of the micro/macro distinction and how it impacts on the businesses you know of and the organisations in the case study. The macro environment refers to a general or contextual environment and includes political, economic, social, technological, ethical/environmental and legal forces (abbreviated to PESTEL). Changes in the macro environment tend to drive the strategic responses of organisations as they respond to wider opportunities and threats over which they have no control. The micro environment is the immediate or operational environment and includes existing and potential suppliers, competitors, customers, intermediaries and interest groups.

 The Chartered Institute of Marketing

5 Significance of stakeholders within the micro environment

Figure 2.3   The micro-firm environment

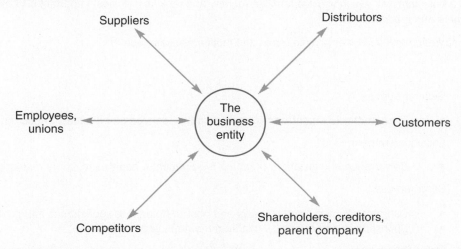

The organisation will have customers or service users as its focus; however, it will be working with and responding to the needs and wants of a range of stakeholders.

Suppliers:

- The power of suppliers depends on size, substitutes and degree of competition.
- The quality of supplier relationship is important.
- If partnership fails, backward integration may be considered.

Competitors:

- Competitors continuously threaten business survival.
- Competitors are varied.
- Organisations must consider threats and opportunities from competitors.

Customers:

- Customers represent the only source of revenue for most organisations.
- Unsatisfied are more vocal than satisfied customers.
- Customer retention is normally more cost-effective than customer acquisition.
- Customer preferences can change quickly.
- Customer knowledge is expanding through internet.

Intermediaries and distributors:

- Effective partners deliver advantages.
- Ineffective ones negatively impact business.
- Distributors have powerful economic leverage.

- Joint ventures and partnerships can be formed.
- E-commerce can encourage direct marketing.

Shareholders and creditors:

- Adverse shareholder perceptions may lead to selling.
- Trade and bank credit are critical to healthy cash flow, so nurture relationships.

Employees and unions:

- Retention of skilled staff is normally more cost-effective.
- Internal marketing in critical departments is central to goal achievement.
- Evolution of virtual companies will make staff much more mobile.
- Increasingly employees are being regarded as internal customers.
- The effect of employees on customers is generally appreciated.

ACTIVITY 2.4

(a) Select a business with which you are familiar. Identify and rank its five most important suppliers, distributors, competitors, customers and creditors.

(b) What marketing mix does it employ to retain and motivate its distributors?

General public:

- They matter to organisations because public concerns and beliefs impact on economic decisions.

Local government:

- Compliance to legislation, planning requirements, health and safety regulations is important.

Communities:

- Can protest, mobilise the media and obstruct planning applications and goals.
- Sponsorship and openness can help maintain good relations.

Financial analysts:

- Can assess past and forecast future performance.
- Shareholders usually tend to listen to them.
- Can help influence a company's ability to raise funds.

Media:

- Can seriously enhance or damage the organisation's public image.

    - Marketers must seek to develop good relationships with representatives.

Central government:

- They often hold a controlling influence over public sector organisations, direct stakeholders.
- They set and enforce the law.
- Dialogue between relevant central and local agencies and marketer is needed.
- The organisation can influence through a variety of actions.

The Chartered Institute of Marketing

> ▶ **Key term**
>
> **Internal, connected** and **external stakeholders**
>
> The importance of stakeholders will be shaped by how 'connected' they are to the organisation. Stakeholders can be grouped as internal, connected or external, as shown in Figure 2.4. This is not a means of identifying power and influence but is does help to evaluate the directness and strength of the relationship the organisation has with each stakeholder group. It can also identify the relationships that may exist between stakeholder groups. For example school teachers and parents of pupils at the school will have a relationship that works informally and formally and is managed through various communication channels and managed processes.

Figure 2.4   Internal, connected and external stakeholders

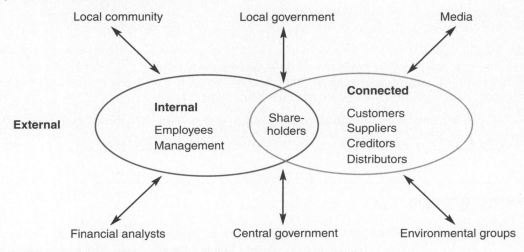

Some key considerations for evaluating the significance of stakeholders:

- They can affect or are affected by the achievement of an organisation's objectives.
- Satisfaction of stakeholders is crucial.
- Connected stakeholders are closely related to business core economic functions.
- Like competitors, they can change goals and organisations unless managed.
- There is considerable potential for conflict of interest between stakeholder groups.
- Stakeholders' expectations must be nurtured while striving for the achievement of objectives, market share and profitability.
- Indirect/external stakeholder groups not directly engaged in business can influence and seriously affect the organisation.
- Not all stakeholders have the same degree of influence and power.
- Stakeholders of any organisation are unique.
- Stakeholders can threaten or challenge objectives and operations or support them.
- Businesses must know their stakeholders.

THE REAL WORLD

US Food giant Kraft was hit by a deluge of criticism when its takeover of Cadbury left staff, neighbouring communities and customers with a very bitter taste. Staff at one of the Cadbury factories felt that their jobs had been guaranteed but once the takeover was complete, Kraft closed the factory, making 400 staff redundant. Two years on, Kraft has been treading more carefully and honoured a commitment to retain all staff at the Bourneville factory. Local MP Steve McCabe was reported saying,

'I think Kraft have behaved quite well in respect of Bourneville, they honoured the two-year agreement about no redundancies, there have been two good pay settlements at a time when some people are taking pay cuts.' (BBC, 2011)

The initial takeover story was front-page news for months but Moeller's case study (2012) published on http://www.ft.com suggested that Kraft recognised that management and their advisers needed 'to stay focused on the deal itself and the real decision-makers – the [Cadbury] shareholders… Other stakeholders may have legitimate concerns that need to be addressed but this can usually be done after the deal is completed, as Kraft did.'

The story of Cadbury's long history and Kraft's hostile takeover was the Assessing the Marketing Environment case study for December 2011/March 2012.

6 Pressure groups

Pressure groups are often the interface between an organisation and the community, since they have a higher degree of interest in the issues and impacts. This may be a problem for the organisation, if pressure groups lobby against them or organise boycotts of their brands, but it may also be a source of marketing advantage, for example by co-opting support from the group; getting products endorsed; using experts in marketing messages; gathering feedback information and ideas; showing willingness to engage in socially responsible dialogue; putting corporate social responsibility on the agenda; and perhaps influencing governing policies and standards which might suit the organisation but not its competitors!

Pressure groups can strongly impact an organisation's activities or goal achievement.

- They represent a subsection of the population.
- They exert pressure on people, organisations or government for a specific purpose.
- They can exert pressure about welfare, recreation or cultural, environmental and political.
- They can be national or international.

The formal channels through which pressure groups function are:

- Pressure through government
- Pressure through the legislature
- Pressure through public campaign

Table 2.1   Cause related pressure groups

Cause	Pressure Group
Welfare	Age UK, Royal Society for the Prevention of Cruelty to Animals (RSPCA), Action on Smoking and Health (ASH), NSPCC
Recreation	National Cyclists' Union, Ramblers Association
Cultural	Citizens Advice Bureau, Lord's Day Observance Society
Environmental	International Fund for Animal Welfare (IFAW), Noise Abatement Society, Greenpeace
Political	Amnesty International, Campaign against Racial Discrimination
International	Oxfam, Médecins sans Frontières, Save the Children, Red Crescent Society, Red Cross

The main pressure groups reflecting economic interests are as follows:

- **Business**: employers' organisations such as the Confederation of British Industry, Federation of Small Businesses, or sectoral groups such as the British Hospitality Association.

- **Professional associations**: groups of people who do the same type of job or use similar skills, such as accountants and doctors. Membership may be an essential requirement for holding the position or it may be a tool for support and continuing professional development (such as The Chartered Institute of Marketing).

- **Trade unions**: represent people in the workplace and use the ultimate power of encouraging workers to strike to achieve improved terms and conditions of employment for their members.

- **Consumers associations**: represent consumers and campaign for the interests of consumers on issues such as product pricing, safety and quality. Recent campaigns have included improved labelling on food and control of processes selling financial products for example.

ACTIVITY 2.5

(a) Draw a mind-map showing the stakeholders for an organisation with which you are familiar, using the list shown to prompt ideas. Consider the criteria you are using in assessing the relative power and influence of each.

(b) Now describe your position as a stakeholder of CIM. How well does it understand your needs? How much influence do you have over its activities?

THE REAL WORLD

The changing financial and demographic environment has brought huge pressures on the public sector pension commitment and in 2011 more than 20 unions representing 3 million workers combined on a joint day of action. As the dust settles and wider public sector cut backs kick in, it seems that, despite the challenges of the work market, some unions will have achieved some valuable concessions for their members.

7 Consumerism

Organisations should be very aware of consumer issues and take time to monitor what customers and other stakeholders are saying:

- Consumer organisations aid and protect the consumer by exerting legal, moral and economic pressure on business.

- Companies should listen to their consumers and address complaints and solve the problems before they turn to the competitors.

It is particularly the case now that organisations much continuously monitor user generated content online to ensure that it is proactively responding to negative and positive comments on open websites, interest groups or user forums.

THE REAL WORLD

UK Uncut is a 'grass roots movement taking action to highlight alternatives to the government's spending cuts' (UK Uncut, 2012). They are using consumer power to campaign against large companies using tax avoidance techniques, and their current campaigns are putting the spotlight on organisations including Arcadia group, Royal Bank of Scotland, Vodaphone, supermarkets and top food brands, such as Walkers Crisps. Through proactive use of the media, their high profile campaigns may to some extent be influencing the wider market place.

Tripping Up Trump, is the entertaining name of a group campaigning against the development of a golf resort next to highly protected sand dunes in Scotland. Global property magnate, Donald Trump, is getting his development but the group has made itself heard amongst the complex range of stakeholders. See http://www.trippinguptrump.com.uk.

Mumsnet is an online forum for new mums and it has been a powerful force in raising issues with both public and private sector organisations. Prime Minister David Cameron has proactively used Mumsnet to generate conversation on relevant policy issues, gaining valuable feedback from this significant group of the electorate. See http://www.mumsnet.co.uk.

▶ **Exam tip**

Remember you are a consumer of CIM and your study centre. You have a 'right' to expect a relevant syllabus, an applied approach, comprehensive information on examination requirements and a feedback on performance. Take advantage of your consumer rights and do not forget to regularly access http://www.cim.co.uk.

The Chartered Institute of Marketing

8 The negative impact of poor stakeholder management

Cost benefit analysis is a standard tool used across many areas of business to evaluate the impact of an action. It is a tool that can be used to evaluate the impact on the organisation of relationships with various stakeholder groups. Costs may include the cost of not acting, such as the cost to Kraft of failing to be absolutely clear in its dealings with Cadbury's stakeholders following the takeover in 2010. Kraft found itself subject to very damaging criticism from staff, the media, consumers and the government when it reneged on a promise not to close a plant. Facebook campaigns and blogs were used to try to persuade UK consumers to stop eating Cadbury's products.

Benefits can also be much more than just financial, such as suppliers being encouraged to adapt to new procurement regimes or staff being passionate about new market initiatives.

▶ **Key term**

Costs and benefit analysis is a tool that is widely used in business to evaluate the impacts, financial and non-financial, of any activity. It is a term that can be used in analysing stakeholders, for example evaluating the costs and benefits of maintaining strong working relationships with a particular stakeholder group. In this chapter's real world case study, Cadbury would be able to evaluate the costs and benefits of improving staff relationships under the new Kraft regime.

In June 2011 the exam included a task. 'Identify two benefits that an employee share scheme could offer those employees working for Royal Mail.'

Possible threats can arise if a business fails to manage stakeholder relations.

- Corporate image may deteriorate in the eyes of stakeholders.
- Consumers may select alternatives.
- Shareholders may prefer to invest in ethically sound companies.
- Recruitment and retention of quality staff becomes more difficult.
- Unnecessarily strict legislation may result due to lack of action (EU penalties).
- Loss of community support, hardening attitudes from authorities.
- Worsening competitive disadvantage compared to proactive competitors.

▶ **Exam tip**

Success in the exam is predominantly dependent on four things:

1 A solid understanding of the syllabus and the relevant models and terminology

2 An in-depth understanding of the case study, and here your PESTEL and SWOT analyses will help you to identify, explain and evaluate the importance of key factors

3 A good awareness of the marketing environment.

4. A good understanding of economic trends and topical issues

As you work through this unit you must therefore ensure that you fully understand the elements within each chapter. This Study Text will also point you towards activities and further reading that will add greater depth to this knowledge. What are the marketing environment factors affecting a range of organisations? How do they monitor the environment? Who are their key stakeholders?

When the case is published you can then start jotting down notes that will support your SWOT and PESTEL analyses. There is no expectation that you need to investigate the case organisation further (and CIM expressly forbid contacting them) but keep your eyes and ears on general national and international business news, discuss the case and its challenges with study groups and compare these challenges with those of other organisations in this sector or indeed other sectors.

In this chapter, we have seen that

- An organisation ignores its environment at its peril.

- Marketers have a key role in identifying environmental change.

- Organisations have a number of primary stakeholders and the influence is two way.

- A business must account/respond to wider opportunities and threats over which it has no control.

- Pressure groups are increasing in importance and can be classified as interest or cause groups.

- Pressure groups employ various means and channels to bring pressure to bear.

- Consumerism has become a force for companies to reckon with, especially as the causes pursued have broadened out from just narrow consumer protection issues.

- The scope of environmental concerns and the specific threats posed to businesses are potentially serious (eg sport utility vehicles have emission, fuel use and road safety concerns).

- The constructive response is not necessarily to confront pressure groups but, where possible, to understand their interests, listen to their point of view and work towards a common solution.

- Consumerism has provided many customer-orientated businesses with an opportunity to achieve competitive advantage. Its concerns now extend far beyond consumer protection to issues such as pricing, design obsolescence and, increasingly, ecology, to which marketers must positively respond.

- Pressure groups' activities and influence are increasing. They are becoming more organised and professional in approaching both government and companies. They are now more adept at marketing their causes and highlighting the deficiencies of companies towards their stakeholder groups.

- Companies must be aware of the threats and opportunities of enhancing their reputation in the eyes of stakeholders through effective and well-managed policies towards the marketing environment.

FURTHER READING

Egan, J. (2008) *Relationship marketing: exploring relational strategies in marketing*. 3rd edition. Harlow, Pearson. Chapter 12.

Palmer, A. and Hartley, B. (2012) *The business environment*. 12th edition. Maidenhead, McGraw-Hill. Chapters 8 and 10.

Websites:

Business pages of quality dailies including:

http://www.thetimes.co.uk

http://www.ft.com

http://www.guardian.co.uk

http://www.telegraph.co.uk

http://www.businesscasestudies.co.uk – *The Times* 100 business case studies

http://www.ft.com/management – case supported by links to relevant news stories

The Chartered Institute of Marketing

In addition all large plcs will publish appropriate detail on their current performance, factors affecting performance and information on key stakeholders. These may be within annual reports but most websites will have a corporate section with general information about the company and how it operates.

http://www.greenpeace.org for coverage of a host of environmental issues and links with other pressure groups.

http://www.webdirectory.com/ is a directory of environmental organisations with a search facility.

http://www.tradingstandards.gov.uk take up consumer complaints over bad service.

http://www.fsa.gov.uk publishes fee and performance comparisons of financial providers.

REFERENCES

Anon (2011) Kraft and Cadbury: How is it working out? BBC, http://www.bbc.co.uk/news/uk-england-birmingham-16067571 [Accessed on 10 February 2012].

Moeller, S. (2012) FT.com/management. FT, http://www.ft.com/cms/s/0/1cb06d30-332f-11e1-a51e-00144feabdc0.html#axzz1v7xQ3ozL [Accessed on 23 May 2012].

UK Uncut (2012), http://www.ukuncut.org.uk/ [Accessed on 11 February 2012].

QUICK QUIZ

1   Give five examples of connected stakeholders.
2   What are the main requirements of distributors as connected stakeholders?
3   The micro environment includes which of the following:

Suppliers
Customers
Political forces
Government
Intermediaries
Shareholders

4   True or false? Pressure groups will always represent a negative force for organisations.
5   What is turbulence in the marketing environment?
6   Which term is correct?

Consumerism is the term describing the demand for good and services by today's consumers.

Consumerism is the movement through which consumers use their power to shape the activities of organisations.

ACTIVITY DEBRIEFS

Activity 2.1

Remember that macro factors are those over which the organisation has no control. In Figure 2.2 these include new government elected; £-$ exchange rate rise; Japan in recovery; minimum wage raised. Micro factors are those within the direct network of the industry and include customers, competitors and suppliers. Therefore the

micro factors here include supplier cartel uncovered; congestion hit delivery times; distributors merge; competitor enters market place.

Activity 2.2

(a)   You will be the best judge of this but try to aim for at least 20 different factors. Micro factors might include competition, geographic spread of customers, a new supplier becoming available to you or a change in employees' expected terms and conditions. Macro factors might include global economic conditions, the ageing population and greater demand for environmental awareness.

(b)   Again there is no fixed answer here but by taking a few minutes at the end of each day you can begin to reflect on how you are linking with stakeholders, taking their needs into account when planning activities or proactively gathering information on their activities.

Activity 2.3

Turbulence in the marketing environment means that changes in the marketing environment can be dramatic, conflicting and extreme and can introduce disorder rather than order to the market. Stock market performance and trends can often be seen as turbulent and in 2012 the European economy continued to struggle to reach a period of calm, presenting a significant marketing environment challenge to many organisations.

Activity 2.4

(a)   Use a table to identify these and consider the factors that you are using to identify what's most important. For example are the top distributors those with the greatest, volume, profit or reliability and flexibility?

(b)   The marketing mix is used not just with consumers in mind. Products will be packed to suit distribution facilities; pricing strategies may reflect not just costs but also volume and speed of payment; promotion may be used to attract new distributors or to develop relationships with existing distributors, place or distribution may be developed in partnership with distributors, for example if they agree to invest in a new depot.

The service mix elements of people, process and physical evidence will also apply.

Activity 2.5

(a)   You should have at least 12 stakeholders identified. If you have fewer then think again. There may be some with which your organisation has a weaker relationship but where their power over the organisation's success is still significant. For example the closure or addition of a new 'anchor' store may completely change the fortunes of smaller retailers around it. The organisation may have little influence over the anchor store but the anchor store has significant power to bring or take away business.

(b)   CIM researches member and study centre needs and is in regular contact with both through various communication channels. However with tens of thousands of members it will be challenging to meet all needs. One member may have limited ability to influence activities, however through member forums and online groups such as Linkedin, members can work together to highlight problems and influence change.

1   Shareholders, bankers, customers, suppliers, distributors
2   Reliable supply, quality improvements, support in marketing

3   Suppliers Y
    Customers Y
    Political forces N
    Government N
    Intermediaries Y
    Shareholders Y

4   False – positive relationships with pressure groups can benefit the organisation.
5   Conflict, dramatic change and unpredictability
6   Both are correct, the term has two recognised meanings.

Assessing the Marketing Environment

CHAPTER 3

Market structures and competition regulation

Introduction

In the preceding chapters we considered the organisation itself – its culture and legal form – and analysis of the organisation's stakeholders. Before analysing the competitive environment and its complex dynamics, it is important that we review the legal context that can support competition or protect market advantage. This chapter will focus on competition legislation and policies, fair trade policies, patents and trademarks and considers how all of these can impact on a firm's pricing and production levels.

Topic list

Market structures (1)

Competition policies (2)

Other areas of legislation which affect the market position (3)

2.5	Examine the nature, scope and impact of competition policies on the organisation and its marketing environment:
	■ Legislation, regulatory bodies and watchdogs
	■ Monopolies and mergers
	■ EU Competition Policy
	■ Bilateral international competition relationships (Europe, Japan and the USA)
	■ Fair trade policies (local versus international)
	■ Patents
	■ Trademarks

1 Market structures

▶ **Key term**

Market structure: The term market structure is used to describe the number of buyers and sellers operating in a market and the extent to which the market is concentrated in the hands of a small number of buyers and/or sellers.

The number of main players, type of competitors and their offerings are inherent to the level of competition within a marketplace. Marketers must appreciate the general structure of the market as well as the dynamics of markets, the behaviour of rivals and the realities of customer preferences and customer behaviour.

The relevance of the monitoring of competitors will vary according to the structure of the industry. The structure of a market will be shaped by the number of organisations in a sector, their size, and therefore their levels of influence over the markets. At one end of the scale are sectors in which there are many players. These can be described as fragmented industries and, at a theoretical level, are said to display perfect competition. At the other end of the scale is the pure monopoly where the organisation has complete and sole control over the market. Very few businesses exist at the extreme ends of the scale and the role of policies regulating monopolies is to give customers the protection from unfair control of supply while not compromising the benefits that monopolistic conditions can offer.

1.1 Fragmented industries

Although fragmented industries cannot be completely generalised, there are a number of underlying common characteristics:

- The number of participants is very large, but their average size is relatively small.

- The monitoring of the main players/the closest competitors should be conducted. Some industries are characterised by businesses competing for market share rather than random selection among identical providers.

- The market is underlain by a diversity of incomes, attitudes, tastes and preferences so sellers must discover what best satisfies their targeted customers.

- Companies must make the most of their product's unique selling points before their competitors impede them from doing so.

- Market leaders in fragmented markets are flexible and adaptable.

- Innovation or differentiation creates competitive edge

  - Differentiation is difficult and costly to sustain in a saturated market.

  - Competitors who supply close substitutes are in a strong position to win customers by offering better value for money.

A global online market place

The online sales world has changed significantly with the considerable role played by online auction sites such as eBay.com These sites give the consumer direct access to large numbers of (often small) potential suppliers. A sole trader can be in a level playing field competing against larger and more established businesses. eBay itself, while not a monopoly, is now a significant market leader in this field. Its large share of the market acts as a significant barrier to entry for smaller auction sites. Those that are thriving are doing so by finding a niche that suits their customers, their products and their ethos. For example http://www.winebid.com or http://www.mastronet.com which specialises in sports collectables.

1.1.1 The concept of perfect competition

Market forms can be classified as follows:

- Perfect competition – a large number of small firms share the market

- Monopolistic competition – many firms compete in a market but the products are differentiated and cannot be replaced by exact substitutes. For example in the fashion industry.

- Oligopoly – several firms share the majority of the market

- Duopoly – two firms share the market

- Monopoly – a single firm supplies the whole market

Most governments believe that the ideal market structure is perfect competition. The more fragmented a market it, the more it will demonstrate the characteristics of perfect competition including many suppliers, limited ability for single suppliers to dictate price, information being freely available, the product is homogenous and there are no barriers to entry.

Once dubbed 'a nation of shopkeepers' the UK was renowned for its characterful and successful small retailers. The retail sector is undergoing significant changes and during 2011, the Local Data Company (LDC) figures revealed in *The Telegraph* stated that '14.3pc of all shops stood empty, equating to 48,000 units on shopping centres, retail parks and high streets.' (*Telegraph, 2012*). Internet retailers and large out-of town malls are seen as the culprits, representing a move away from perfect competition, towards a market controlled by larger players.

ACTIVITY 3.1

(a) Which of the following would you identify as fragmented industries?

- Health and fitness centres
- Restaurants
- Fast-food outlets
- Food retailers

(b) What factors account for the fragmentation?

(c) Are there forces leading to consolidation in the fast food sector?

1.1.2 Strategies and tactics in a fragmented market

Possible strategies for marketers could include any of the following courses of action:

- Invest in relationship marketing to build long-term mutual benefits.

- Build other barriers to protect the market.

- Create the equivalent of a habitual or monopoly good by niche marketing and product differentiation.

- Effective branding

- Buyout or collude with the competitor.

- Cut unnecessary costs in order to offer keener prices.

- Innovate to continuously distance your product or service offering from rivals.

The areas along which differentiation could be applied are varied. But, some tactics may include any of the following choices:

- **Product:** Permutations of the **core, tangible** (eg design, quality, packaging) and **augmented** product (eg brand name, delivery, after-sales service).

- **Price:** Credit and payment terms may vary, as can allowances and trade-in values.

- **Promotion:** To support the differentiation (eg strong emphasis on the sales force building strong customer relationships, distinctive advertising that reinforces unique selling points).

- **Place:** Flexibility to take advantage of opportunities through location adopted, coverage and, most importantly, service provided.

Differentiation of companies is very important. This can create consequences:

- Returns associated with successful differentiation usually attract imitation from existing firms. Customers can benefit from rapid diffusion of superior product/service.

- New entrants also provide extra choice although there is a tendency to excess.

- Extra costs can be incurred due to extra promotion or discounting adds.

1.2 Concentrated industries

Concentrated industries can be characterised as follows:

- The number of competing firms is generally small but economic size is large.

- In economic terms, this is known as high seller concentration and is typical in oligopolies.

1.2.1 Oligopoly

Oligopoly is a market dominated by a few suppliers. It can be explained as follows:

- This is the typical market structure in mature economies.

- There is competition among a few main players. The largest four or five firms account for perhaps 70% or more of total sales.

- Monitoring competitors is critical in this situation because the marketing actions/decisions of any one player depend crucially upon reactions of the others.

- Any substantial change in market share of one firm will positively or adversely affect others.

In brief, the key features of an oligopoly market may be summarised as follows:

- Economies of scale and entry barriers tend to be significant.

- Customer needs are standardised and integrated through effective marketing and mass distribution systems.

- Dominant market leaders may emerge.

- Top companies have a large share of the market but there is a tail of small firms, for example, grocery retailing.

- Demand is uncertain because it is dependent on how rivals react.

- Outcomes are unpredictable when oligopolists have multiple competitive options.

Despite the variety of options available to companies operating in an oligopolistic market environment, a number of generalisations are however possible. For instance:

- Companies operating in an oligopoly tend to avoid the use of price as a competitive weapon.

- Non-price competition, promoting carefully differentiated branded products, is preferred.

- There is a tendency to occasional price war when a restructuring of market shares is in progress.

- Collusion is an attractive option but normally illegal.

- Price leadership often occurs to reflect underlying cost changes (eg retail petrol).

- New product development is the best strategy to achieve sustainable competitive edge.

ACTIVITY 3.2

UK supermarkets are an often quoted oligopoly.

(a)   Investigate online to find out their current market shares.

(b)   Describe examples of current campaigns. How are these aiming to grow or protect market share?

1.2.2 Monopoly

In a monopoly the firm can earn supernormal profits in the long run as well as in the short term because there are barriers to entry which prevent rivals from entering the market. The monopolist can determine the market prices and get away with continually increasing prices to increase profit. Much of the thrust of competition policies in recent decades has been to open monopolistic markets to competition. Pure monopoly is rare but some markets are said to exhibit monopolistic tendencies. For example OPEC, the cartel of oil producing countries, holds considerable sway over global oil prices.

Firms facing intense competition may seek to form cartels and associations as a means of restricting output to raise prices and profitability. Firms in concentrated industries may find collaboration and collusion more rewarding than rivalry.

2 Competition policies

Governments formulate competition policies for a number of reasons:

- They fear that market forces may be insufficient to prevent anti-competitive behaviour.

- They see a level playing field as fair and just and aim to protect consumers.

- They desire efficient and effective use of scarce resources.

- Monopoly must be controlled as the natural outcome of the competitive process.

- They do not wish to see economic power abused at the expense of the consumer/taxpayer.

Making markets more competitive means creating the conditions associated with it. Policies have, therefore, attempted to achieve the following:

- Resist mergers and acquisitions which threaten to reduce the number of sellers to the point where consumer choice is restricted

- Keep entry barriers low so that supply, through new entrants, can respond

- Deregulation of markets (eg domestic energy market and telecommunications)

- Encouragement of SMEs

- Use of regulators in natural monopoly and the law against anti-competitive behaviour

- Improve the knowledge of the consumer through prevention of misleading advertising/promotion

2.1 Monopolies and mergers legislation

2.1.1 UK legislation

The Competition Act 1998 strengthened the UK's competition legislation prohibiting anti-competitive behaviour. The object of UK competition law is to protect the public interest by ensuring that the beneficial effects of competition can be exercised and to regulate anti-competitive practice. In the UK, it is regulated by the Office of Fair Trading (OFT) and the Competition Commission.

The methods adopted in Britain involve the following:

- A case-by-case judgmental approach

- A cost-benefit framework to compare good and bad effects

- A loose presumption that monopolies are against the public interest

- A recognition that market dominance might reflect superior efficiency

- Removing barriers to entry is preferred to preventing firms getting larger

- Investigating horizontal mergers

Both the Secretary of State and the DGFT (but not for mergers) have powers to refer a case to the Competition Commission.

The legal definition of a referable monopoly is a 25% market share, proposed mergers involving assets in excess of £30 million, or where they would create a legal monopoly or add to it. In practice, only a very small proportion of qualifying monopolies or mergers are referred.

The Competition Commission reports or makes recommendations about referrals. The Secretary of State makes the final decision and can overrule the Competition Commission recommendations. The competition can seek appropriate undertakings, regulate prices, require the sale of controlling interests or prohibit the continuation of a practice. Offences are punishable under criminal law.

The Chartered Institute of Marketing

Competition Commission latest…

In 2011 the Competition Commission ruled that the British Airports Authority (BAA) had to sell Stansted Airport. The airport operator's legal challenge was the latest step in a long legal battle to retain its strong market position. BAA has already sold Gatwick Airport and has plans to sell Edinburgh Airport. A spokesman for one of the airlines using Stansted, the ever-controversial Ryanair, was quoted in the *Daily Telegraph* saying 'Ferrovial [BAA's owner] and the other owners of Stansted are unfairly enriching themselves at the expense of UK passengers/visitors who are suffering higher charges and third-rate service at Stansted while the CAA's "inadequate" regulatory regime does nothing to protect airport users.' (*Telegraph*, 2012)

Supermarket giants Asda, Morrisons, Sainsbury's and Tesco dominate the groceries market in the UK. This market has been the focus of two major competition enquiries in recent years. The main thrust of these enquiries has been the fairness of dealings with suppliers rather than a fair price and good service for customers. The practice of the big four holding 'land banks' – large tracts of development land held to prevent competitors from expanding in certain areas – has also come under scrutiny as its impact is perceived to be damaging to wider investment and development.

Other enquiries currently being investigated by the Competition Commission in 2012 include the takeover of a water company; the market for aggregates, cement and ready-mixed concrete and an investigation aimed at opening up the UK bus market to greater competition. Other enquiries pass peacefully under the radar, enabling acquisitions to go ahead, such as the purchase of Headland Foods Ltd by Kerry Foods Ltd in 2011.

ACTIVITY 3.3

(a) Go to the UK Competition Commission's website http://www.competition-commission.org.uk and view current cases. What are the key issues? How long has the enquiry been running for? How might consumers benefit from Competition Commission's rulings?

(b) List the market sectors that you believe are most likely to be under the competition spotlight. Now compare this with the list of sectors currently featured on the website of the European Commission http://ec.europa.eu/competition.

2.1.2 EU competition law

▶ **Key term**

Competition policies refer to the government's stance on open competition for businesses and for consumers. Competition legislation refers to the national and EU laws that regulate competitive practices. Consumer protection laws are a wider base of laws that support the consumer's right to safety, right to information (eg labelling), the right to be heard and the right to choose.

The promotion of free competition between member states of the European Union (EU) is fundamental to the success of the single market. Its legislation therefore overrides the national legislation of member states.

EU rules come into force when anticompetitive practices may affect free trade between member states.

The European Commission states:

'Competition is a basic mechanism of the market economy and encourages companies to provide consumer products that consumers want. It encourages innovation and pushes down prices. In order to be effective, competition needs suppliers who are independent of each other, each subject to the competitive pressure exerted by the others.'

The two Treaty Articles that support this aim are:

Article 101 – anti competitive agreements (replaces Article 85)

Prohibits arrangements and agreements (formal or verbal) that could restrict or distort competition, for example by price fixing or by limiting production. Fines for contravention can be up to 10% of turnover. Price fixing and control of supply by cartels is seen as a serious form of breach of Article 101 and is punishable by imprisonment. When investigating anti-competitive agreements the EC will evaluate benefits and can create exemptions eg to enable two pharmaceutical firms to work together to bring a beneficial new drug to market.

Article 102 – market dominance (replaces Article 86)

Prohibits businesses with significant market share from exploiting their position in the market. Again firms can be subject to fines of 10% of turnover. This does not prevent businesses from having for example, a 50% market share however it does prevent them from abusing that position by predatory pricing, retaining exclusivity or refusal to supply essential services.

2.1.3 Bilateral international competition relationships

The USA has some of the strongest laws on competition in the industrialised world, reflecting the practice in the USA of resolving many conflicts in the courts.

Bilateral agreements on competition issues exist between the EU and the USA, the USA and Japan and the EU and Canada whereby each side shares its information on competition issues. Each side has agreed to consider the significant interests of the other when adhering to competition rules.

3 Other areas of legislation which affect the market position

In most countries it is deemed to be in the public interest that ideas in general should be allowed to be exploited. However, the law has developed to provide protection to certain specific categories of industrial and intellectual property.

- **Patents**: the monopoly right to exploit an invention for a stated period of time
- **Trade marks**: distinctive word, name or other mark used to indicate a connection in the course of trade between good and services and their owner
- **Copyright**: protection for authors, artists, composers etc from being deprived of their rewards by unauthorised copying for their works

> **▶ Exam tip**
>
> Be aware of the competitive structure of the market of the case organisation and if it has been, or could be, subject to investigation by the relevant competition regulator. How will this impact on consumers and customers?

CHAPTER ROUNDUP

In this chapter we have dealt with the following important aspects:

- The nature and implications of competition in fragmented and concentrated industries

- The concept of perfect competition

- The terminology of oligopoly, duopoly and monopoly

- Large firms predominate in concentrated industries due to the importance of barriers to entry in which economies of scale figure importantly.

- Smaller firms are the product of more fragmented structures, although profitable niches can be found in most markets.

- Concentrated and fragmented industries also interact.

- The regulatory framework relating to competition

FURTHER READING

Jobber, D. (2010) *Principles of marketing*. 6th edition. Maidenhead McGraw-Hill, Chapter 19: Analysing competitors and creating competitive advantage.

Johnson, G. *et al.*(2010) *Exploring corporate strategy: text and cases*. 9th edition. Harlow, Pearson Education Ltd, Chapter 3.

Palmer, A. and Hartley, B. (2006) *The business environment*. 5th edition. Maidenhead, McGraw-Hill, Chapter 10.

Worthington, I. and Britton, C. (2009) *The business environment*. 6th edition. Harlow, Pearson, Chapter 17

Websites:

http://www.ft.com

http://www.economist.com

http://ec.europa.eu/competition – The European Commission's policy information on competition regulations

http://www.competition-commission.org.uk – latest news of current anti-competition enquiries

http://www.ftc.gov – the USA Federal Trade Commission

http://www.globalcompetitionforum.org – bringing together experts to discuss competition policy and global trade

REFERENCES

European Commission (2012) Competition. http://ec.europa.eu/competition/antitrust/overview_en.html [Accessed on 21 May 2012].

Millard, D. (2012) BAA appeal against Stansted sale fails. The Telegraph, http://www.telegraph.co.uk/finance/newsbysector/transport/9054203/BAA-appeal-against-Stansted-sale-fails.html [Accessed on 13 February 2012].

Wallop, H. (2012) 48,000 empty shops blight UK high streets. The Telegraph, http://www.telegraph.co.uk/finance/newsbysector/retailandconsumer/9064471/48000-empty-shops-blight-UK-high-streets.html [Accessed on 13 February 2012].

QUICK QUIZ

1   What are the four basic consumer rights?

2   Which of the following would a government consider to be ideal?

    A   Monopoly
    B   Oligopoly
    C   Perfect competition
    D   Imperfect competition

3   Who regulates competition in the UK?

4   In what case would EU rules on competition come into force?

5   Economies have a tendency to develop anti-competitive practices which undermine the power of markets to produce more output at a lower price. Is this true or false?

ACTIVITY DEBRIEFS

Activity 3.1

All are possibly highly fragmented. However in the UK, fast-food is increasingly franchised and therefore linked with larger conglomerates. Small food retailers remain, however, the majority of the market is held in oligopolistic conditions by the big four retailers.

Activity 3.2

The big four, Tesco, Morrisons, Sainsbury's and Asda hold around two thirds of the market. They are in constant battle to retain customers through loyalty schemes and to attract new customers through development of distribution networks and products.

Activity 3.3

(a)   The Competition Commission website describes current cases but also has a consumer section describing the complex issues for this stakeholder

(b)   In 2012 the list comprised: energy, financial services, ICT, media, motor vehicles, pharmaceuticals, postal services, professional services, telecommunications, transport, agriculture, consumer goods and sports.

The Chartered Institute of Marketing

1 The right to safety, to be informed, to be heard and to have choice.

2 C – Perfect competition. One of the ideas behind perfect competition is that market forces alone determine the price at which products can be sold. Not **all** governments would consider as ideal.

3 The Office of Fair Trading and the Competition Commission.

4 When anti-competitive practices may affect free trade between member states, the EU rules on competition come into force.

5 True. This is the reason why competition policies have been developed to counteract anti-competitive practices.

CHAPTER 4

Analysis of the competitive environment

Introduction

We are gradually building on the framework of the existing organisation, its internal strengths and weaknesses, its stakeholders and where it fits in to the competitive marketplace in terms of the structure of that market or sector and how it is impacted by competition laws. Now we move on to a deeper analysis, investigating the dynamics of competitive advantage; how an organisation competes and how it can monitor the activities of its competitors.

Topic list

Evaluating stakeholder power	1
Corporate social responsibility	2
Nature of the customer relationship	3
Monitoring the micro environment	4
Main sources of information	5
Competitor analysis	6
The Marketing Information System (MkIS)	7
The need for continuous market research	8

2.2	Evaluate the micro environmental factors that have a bearing on an organisation's ability to meet customer expectations and generate customer satisfaction.
	■ The importance of continuous marketing research
	■ Product/service portfolio analysis
	■ The link between service quality and customer satisfaction
	■ Extended marketing mix
2.3	Explain the nature of the interactions between the organisation and its various stakeholders including shareholders, employees, customers, local communities, suppliers, channel members and competitors:
	■ Understanding and managing stakeholder power and interest
	■ Developing relationships with partners, pressure groups, consumer groups etc
	■ Competition for customers
	■ Consumer protection legislation
2.4	Evaluate the different types and sources of information required to gain an in-depth understanding of the micro environment:
	■ Company reports
	■ Department of Trade and Industry (now called Department for Business Innovation & Skills (BIS))
	■ Central Office of Statistics Office
	■ Research organisations eg, Dunn and Bradstreet, MINTEL, etc
	■ Industry journals
2.6	Explain the process for undertaking a detailed competitor analysis and how the analysis influences the marketing decision-making process:
	■ Competitor identification
	■ Competitor strengths and weaknesses
	■ Competitor strategies
	■ Competitor response patterns (tactics)
	■ Key success factors (KSF)
	■ Company capability profiling

1 Evaluating stakeholder power

Further to identifications of stakeholders and classification as internal, connected or external (as discussed in Chapter 2) it is important for organisations to evaluate the power and interest of stakeholders. This forms the foundations for effective stakeholder relations. Mendelow (1991) classifies stakeholders on a matrix whose axes are power held and likelihood of showing an interest in the organisation's activities. These factors will help define the relationships the organisation should seek with its stakeholders.

Figure 4.1 Stakeholder power/interest matrix

		Level of interest	
		Low	High
Power	Low	A	B
	High	C	D

(Adapted from Mendelow, 1991, cited in Johnson *et al*, 2010)

- **Engage closely**. Key players are found in segment D: strategy must be acceptable to them. An example would be a major customer.
- **Keep satisfied**. Stakeholders in segment C must be treated with care because of their power. While often passive they are capable of moving to segment D if their interest is aroused. Large institutional shareholders might fall into segment C.
- **Keep informed**. Stakeholders in segment B do not have great ability to influence strategy, but their views can be important in influencing more powerful stakeholders, perhaps by lobbying. Community representative and charities might fall into segment B.
- **Monitor** (minimum effort). This could include small shareholders, insignificant competitors or the general public. However, by monitoring these stakeholders the organisation is always informed if their power and interest changes.

ACTIVITY 4.1

You now have a chance to put Mendelow's classification into practice. Select an organisation (or refer to the organisation featured in the case study), list the stakeholders and assess their relative power and interest. Justify your measures of power and interest.

Waitrose

As the UK's big four supermarkets do battle, employee-owned Waitrose (part of the John Lewis group) has been quietly growing sales and building loyalty in its customer base.

A key selling point for Waitrose is its strong ethical stance in terms of its dealing with suppliers. Compared with their competitors, Waitrose are effectively evaluating their suppliers as having a higher power and interest, enabling the business to achieve its aims. Their Small Producers' Charter aims to reassure producers that they will be treated fairly. Some of the key points in the charter are:

- 'We want to encourage the production of good quality food, regardless of scale and whether those who are producing it wish to supply us.

- We take the long term view and will work with producers to help them reach their objectives, not just ours. We do not want to dilute the integrity or quality of their products...

- We want to help producers reach more consumers, and introduce more people to great food from their neighbourhood.

- As co-owners of our own business, and as part of the John Lewis Partnership, we believe in treating one another with decency and respect. We also believe in extending that same courtesy to our suppliers and producers...

- We guarantee that our producers can enter partnerships with us in full confidence, founded firmly upon integrity and trust.

- What we don't have are shareholders demanding quick and constant change. But we do have a demanding customer base, who expects great things from us.

- We want to build on our levels of traceability; the quality of our products and levels of service in branch; and our long term relationships with producers.

- Only by working together with the right producers and best quality produce, can we build consumer confidence and celebrate the rich variety and splendour of our country's food...'

(Waitrose, 2012)

2 Corporate social responsibility

The macro environment trends that are shaping the need for more sustainable and ethical approaches to marketing will be discussed in Chapter 10. However corporate social responsibility (CSR) is a strong force shaping both the culture and behaviour of the organisation and its relationships with stakeholders. Its role within the competitive environment is becoming more and more critical as customers, suppliers, regulatory bodies, funders and investors are all using CSR issues as criteria for buying from or backing particular organisations.

Particularly in the private sector there is a journey to be travelled as organisations are increasingly being measured not just on the traditional measures of profit, market share, dividends and share value, but against a triple bottom line that measures:

- **Economic sustainability**: a long term view of profit and employment.

- **Social sustainability**: a positive approach to employment, training and development as well as to other human stakeholders in producer and market communities.

- **Environmental sustainability**: responsible use of natural resources and mitigation of any negative impacts on the natural environment.

Figure 4.2 Sustainability

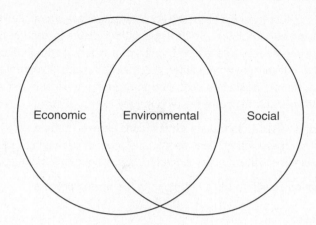

CSR aspirations and actions

Organisations may have two positions on corporate social responsibility; first the one they use to describe their policies and ethos, or their aspirations to contribute positively to their communities; second the one that details the specific procedures in place or actions taken to meet those aspirations. Investigate the CSR policy of an organisation and critically analyse the extent to which policies and actions impact upon stakeholders.

3 Nature of the customer relationship

> ▶ **Key terms**
>
> **Customers** are the persons or organisations who purchase the goods or services (not necessarily the end user).
>
> **Consumers** are defined as the individuals who buy and use a product or service.
>
> **Consumer behaviour** can be defined as the behaviour that consumers display in searching for, purchasing, using, evaluating and disposing of products. It provides the underpinning knowledge which guides subsequent marketing strategy.
>
> Consumer groups represent consumers' interests. They exist to ensure that products give good value. They promote safeguards for consumers against unethical business practice.

When analysing stakeholder groups we need to be sure that we are clear about to whom we are referring. Frequently the terms customer and consumer are used interchangeably, yet in practice we mean two very different groups in terms of their relationship to the organisation, their needs, expectations, influence, power and behaviour.

The needs of each of the parties varies considerably and so it is important to be clear about who is being referred to. Dibb (2006) says, the study by an organisation of consumer buying behaviour is important to the marketing manager for a number of reasons:

- The buyer's reaction to the organisation's marketing strategy has a major impact on the success of the organisation.

- If organisations are to truly implement the marketing concept, they must examine the main influences on what, where and how customers buy. Only in this way will they be able to devise a marketing mix that satisfies the needs of the customer.

- By gaining a better understanding of the factors influencing their customers and how their customers will respond, organisations will be better able to predict the effectiveness of their marketing activities.

3.1 Meeting customer expectations

Customers' expectations will be based on past experience, the knowledge derived from it and the social and cultural influences associated with it. Expectations create in each individual a readiness to respond in a learned/accustomed way to a given stimulus or a group of stimuli. Expectations can affect perception in various ways that are relevant to the marketer. If someone expects something to be so, on the basis or past experiences or on the say-so of a trusted person, then they are more likely to perceive it to be so. Their mind will filter out any inconsistent data, to create the picture they expect to see.

The information used to formulate expectations derives from personal sources such as friends and family, commercial sources such as sales people and product packaging, public sources such as mass media or customer review websites and experiential sources, perhaps trialing or examining the product.

The information search forms a key stage in the buying process.

Figure 4.3   Buying process

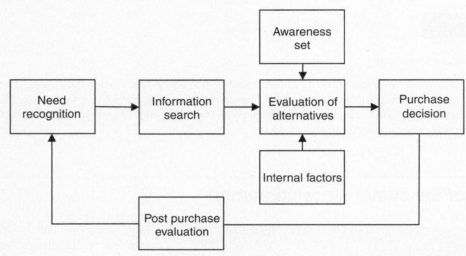

3.2 Service quality and customer satisfaction

> ▶ **Key term**
>
> **Customer retention versus recruitment**
>
> As a general but very significant rule the cost of acquiring new customers will be greater than the cost of retaining an existing one. High customer retention or loyalty can be achieved through continued management of the customer relationship and seamless delivery of customer satisfaction.

Quality of service is an important issue for marketers because it is one of the most significant ways in which customers differentiate between competing products and services. An organisation can improve the quality of service in a range of ways such as improving the product's reliability, opening for longer hours, giving information readily, refurbishing stores or processing orders more quickly. But the main way is through its people.

There are two ways that organisations can gain from improving their quality of service to customers.

- Higher sales revenue and profits and improved marketing effectiveness may come through improved customer retention, positive word of mouth recommendation and the ability to increase prices. Customer retention is normally more cost effective than recruiting new customers – it costs more to attract a new customer or to re-awaken a 'dormant' one.

- Better quality improves productivity and reduces costs because there is less rework, higher employee morale and lower employee turnover.

Organisations manage customer relations in a number of ways. Palmer (2009) described four key methods of building customer relationships to optimise levels of loyalty:

The Chartered
Institute of Marketing

- Achieving high levels of **customer satisfaction** by meeting their needs

- Gaining the **trust** of customers by reliably achieving the desired and expected levels of service quality

- Adding value to the relationship perhaps by offering privileges eg priority booking

- Creating barriers to exit with service contracts that are hard to leave. This however is a false loyalty and one that cannot replace a sustainable business-customer relationship.

3.3 The extended marketing mix

Study of the marketing mix is an element of the unit Marketing Essentials, however, in this unit, its significance as a tool for achieving competitive advantage is an important factor. How might the extended marketing mix be used to evaluate the micro environmental factors that impact the organisation's ability to satisfy customer requirements?

Table 4.1   The extended marketing mix; a micro environmental perspective

Product	Competitor product portfolios and brands and their position in various markets
	Products and services evolving to meet changing customer demands and behaviours
	The core product and additional products and services that meet and exceed customers' expectations
Price	Importance of competitive pricing
	Use of price matching, special offers and promotions to achieve advantage
	Price promises to customers
Place	Availability of distribution networks
	Position and growth achieved through online channels
	Changing customer buyer behaviour
Promotion	Awareness and perceptions – competitor analysis
	Share of voice – media presence
	Maintaining relationships with all stakeholders
People	Meeting the service needs of changing customer profiles
	Managing people to exceed customer expectations
	Communications within the organisation to ensure shared values and goals
	Competitive terms and conditions for staff
Process	Customer relationship management approach to valuing, rewarding and retaining customers
	Management of efficient supply and distribution systems
	Linking suppliers, customers and other stakeholders (eg sharing online customer reviews)
Physical evidence	Competitiveness through eg quality of premises, visible transport and staff uniforms

3.4 Product service portfolio analysis

Products and services have a life cycle and by implication this means that at any time new products are under development and old products are under the spotlight for possible rejuvenation or ceasing production altogether. Organisations need to take a view on their own product/service portfolios and those of their competitors.

- Some products may not follow a typical pattern. For example skateboards, once in decline, have become popular again and most towns and cities in the UK feel they must have a skate park to meet community expectations.

- Portfolio planning is the discipline of ensuring that the firm has a sustainable range of products and services that enable them to continue to meet customer requirements.

- As a tool it is used to inform resource planning – guiding the levels of investment required to ensure maximum profitability.

- Customer demand will shape these decisions, as will factors such as the growth of the overall market and the share that the organisation has of this market.

THE REAL WORLD

The Coca-Cola Company has a portfolio of more than 3,500 beverages including fizzy drinks, fruit drinks, sports drinks and hot drinks. Not all brands are available in all markets, for example Buzz, an energy drink, is only available in Japan.

Every brand will be carefully positioned to meet the needs of its market(s) and will exhibit patterns of growth or decline as the needs of customers change and factors in the wider marketing environment make an impact.

(Coca-Cola, 2012)

4 Monitoring the micro environment

▶ Key term

Research terminology

Market research forms a small but important element of this syllabus and you should be familiar with the terminology that may appear in the exam.

Sources of information refers to where the information is hosted or acquired from and could include internal or external sources. Types of research or research methodology will include **primary research** and **secondary research**. Primary data is gathered for the first time, whereas secondary research has been collected by another researcher/organisation for another purpose. Secondary data is usually gathered before primary data as it is often cheaper to collect and is used to guide the primary research. **Quantitative research** is research information that can be expressed statistically. It tells you what, when, when and how. **Qualitative research** is research that aims to understand customers' behaviour and attitudes towards a product, service or campaign.

Collecting, interpreting and presenting information is crucial to marketing practice. Different types of information are required depending on the decisions to be taken. The following types of information can be collected about specific elements:

- Competitors:
  - Goals, capabilities, strategies and view of the future
  - Production capabilities and product portfolio
  - Set prices, discounts, credit terms
  - Sales volumes by segment, product, region and distribution channel
  - Market shares and key objectives
  - Promotional activities, catalogues and distributor incentives
  - New product development, expansion plans and changes in personnel
  - Financial strengths and weaknesses.
  - Relationships with key stakeholders
  - Organisational information – structure, competencies and skills
- Suppliers, distributors and potential entrants into the market:
  - Set prices, discounts, credit terms
  - Sales volumes by segment, product, region and distribution channel
  - Market shares
  - Main objectives (mission statement)

- Activities, catalogues and business-to-business incentives
- New product development, expansion plans and changes in personnel
- Financial strength and relationships with key stakeholders (clients and parties in the supply chain)

■ Industry:

- Sales volumes by product, segment, region and country
- Sales growth and seasonal/cyclical patterns
- Production capacities, levels, plans and stock positions
- Technical change and investment plans

■ Customers in the industry/sector

- Buying patterns and volumes
- Responses to elements of the marketing mix
- Geodemographic and socio-economic analysis
- Trends and forecasts
- Negative and positive perceptions

■ Information gathered through marketing intelligence and market research must be combined with that gathered internally before being classified, processed and analysed. Information databases are central to modern marketing. Processes include:

- Collecting information on customers (**data collection** and **data storage**).
- Processing and utilising the massive amounts of data captured (**data analysis** and **data mining**).

Figure 4.4   Secondary sources for a business

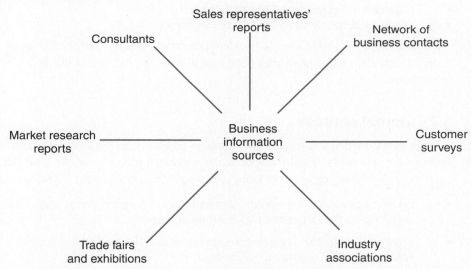

Gathering customer insight through the collection and analysis of information can benefit companies in a variety of ways such as:

■ Create opportunities to explore new ways to create efficient information systems
■ Shape the channels in which organisations communicate internally and externally
■ Individualise and personalise relationships with specific customers and segments
■ Database-related tools can be used to interact with customers

There are three crucial stages in the management of information about customers.

1   Consolidate all the data collected about a customer into a usable set of information.

2   Analyse information about customers.

3   Results of targeting of specific guests must be tracked to determine which customers responded to what campaigns.

In brief, the gathering of information can provide a critical element in the process of:

- Forming or deepening customer relationships and loyalty
- Spotting emerging patterns and trends to provide focus for marketing campaigns
- Segmenting customers for receipt of tailored offers

5 Main sources of information

Information can be sourced externally but there is also a wealth of information available from within the organisation, although it may have been gathered for another purpose, for example as a selling tool or for financial management.

5.1 Internal sources

These might include:

- Sales force records
- Data about inventory
- Production data about quantities produced, materials, labour, faults etc
- Company reports
- Customer Relationship Management (CRM) database
- Users' forum online
- Customer correspondence and complaints
- Financial performance by division or by product

The marketing team should also be tracking data on promotional activity and brand strength and awareness. Such internal information often goes back several years, so that comparisons can be made and trends extrapolated.

5.2 External sources

Sources of information will be discussed again in Chapter 5 as the analysis moves on to the macro environment. There are however a wide range of external sources that can yield valuable information about the organisation's market place and its competitive position in that market. These include:

- Government reports into specific sectors or markets eg the Portas review (see below, The Real World) published by the Department for Business Innovation and Skills

- Companies and other organisations specialising in the provision of economic and financial data (eg Reuters and the Thomson Extel Survey)

- Directories and year books such as Kompass or Kelly's Directory

- Professional institutions such as The Chartered Institute of Marketing, Royal Institute of British Architects and the Chartered Institute of Personnel Development

- Specialist commercial libraries

- Trade associations such as Chambers of Commerce or the Federation of Small Businesses

- Trade and professional journals, newspapers and commentaries

- Commercial organisations such as banks and broadcasters

- Surveys produced by research agencies (Gallup, MORI, Mintel, Euromonitor) Mintel, for example, is a global consumer research company with offices in ten countries. It conducts research for companies and publishes reports on subjects ranging from the food and drink industry to top emerging consumer trends. The depth of its research means it can publish facts such as: 'Results from Mintel GNPD [Global

The Chartered Institute of Marketing

New Products Database] show that at least one new consumer packaged goods product is launched somewhere in the world every two minutes.' (Mintel 2012)

- Company reports including annual reports and reviews, sustainability reports, financial reports, press releases and shareholder information
- Office for National Statistics or international equivalents including reports into specific sectors such as retail, pensions, transport and housing

Today's information society means that marketers can sometimes be swimming in oceans of data. In evaluating the information available from various online and paper based sources, marketers should consider:

- The quality of the source (qualifications of staff and reputation of the publisher)
- The methodology used to gather any original data and appropriate samples used
- Any potential bias, such as the influence of a sponsor
- Currency – how up to date is the data?
- Relevance to the sector or industry

ACTIVITY 4.3

For an organisation with which you are familiar

(a)   List at least three specific sources of information under each type of source described in section 5.2.

(b)   Select one source from each type and explain how it contributes to monitoring the micro environment.

6 Competitor analysis

▶ **Key term**

Analysing the key success factors of competitors is also an important part of competitor analysis. **Key success factors (KSF)** are the factors necessary for success in a market. They are the characteristics of an organisation that most affect that organisation's competitive ability. KSF are what the organisation must be competent at, or concentrate on doing, in order to be completely successful. Analysing KSFs of competitors helps the organisation to develop its own KSFs to distinguish itself and gain competitive advantage.

The relevance of analysing competitors will depend on the structure of the industry in question. For example, in fragmented industries (where the number of participants is very large, but the size of each competitor is relatively small) it will not be worthwhile to monitor the competitive behaviour of all competitors. Instead, the organisation should monitor only its closest competitors, say those that are closest in terms of location or product characteristics. Whereas in an oligopoly, where there are a small number of firms, each of which are large, any changes in the market share of one firm will adversely affect the market shares of competitors. Thus the marketer must analyse competitor behaviour very carefully.

Competitor analysis involves the gathering and interpretation of intelligence from a range of sources regarding key rivals, with the intention of achieving a competitive edge over them by

- Identifying and exploiting competitor weaknesses
- Avoiding actions that provoke aggressive and possibly damaging responses
- Discovering moves that competitors are unable/unwilling to respond to
- Avoiding any surprises that may give rivals a competitive advantage

Actual and potential threats must be accounted for. Threats could be as follows:

- Companies that could overcome entry barriers
- Customers or suppliers who could integrate backwards or forwards
- Possible takeovers of existing rivals or foreign firms benefiting from tariff or regulatory changes

There are literally hundreds of potential intelligence sources but these are useless unless meaningful information can be extracted. Data mining has been developed as a process of analysing and manipulating data so as to provide new and powerful insights into consumer and competitor behaviour patterns.

Key questions for competitor analysis are:

- Who are they?
- What are their goals?
- What strategies are they pursuing?
- What are their strengths and weaknesses?
- How are they likely to respond?
- What are their key success factors?

Strengths and weaknesses of the organisation or its competitors could include:

- Brand strength, customer loyalty
- Intellectual property
- Market share
- Distribution network
- Quality of management team
- Relative cost structure
- Resource, financial and otherwise
- Distinctive competences and key success factors

Dyson hit the world by storm with his bagless vacuum cleaner and in 2010 the business was close to breaking the £1billion turnover barrier. One key success factor is the company's willingness to commit to research and development. In *Management Today* (2011) Dyson noted that R&D may have hit profits that innovation was key to success. The firm had invested £45m in R&D and was recruiting 200 engineers to work at its UK headquarters.

A second key success factor is the company's bold international expansion. Now operating in 52 countries, around 80% of its products are sold internationally with very strong growth in the US and Japan.

KSFs can be related to any aspect of the business, including marketing and tactics, operations, technology, distribution, innovation (as with Dyson above) or to certain skills and capabilities the business has. An effective marketing strategy, or part of that strategy, can be a KSF.

To identify the KSFs of competitors, the organisation needs to look at how customers differentiate between all the organisations offering similar products/services. The following questions are useful:

- What makes a consumer choose this product over another product?
- How do organisations distinguish themselves from the competition in this market?

There are many ways to find out useful information on troublesome rivals. Courses of action could include the following steps:

- Marketing information
- Question job applicants for inside information
- Go on plant tours/monitor aerial maps/monitor staff and transport movements
- Recruit staff from competitors
- Quiz staff at trade shows/conferences/exhibitions
- Commission academic research among relevant suppliers and intermediaries
- Undertake reverse engineering on competitor products to determine performance/costs
- There are of course many more less commendable courses of actions!

6.1 Levels of competitive rivalry

The intensity of competitive rivalry within an industry will affect the profitability of the industry as a whole. Competitive actions might take the form of price competition, advertising battles, sales promotion campaigns, introducing new products for the market, improving after-sales service of providing guarantees or warranties. The intensity of competition will depend on the following factors:

- **Market structure**. How many firms are in the market and what are their respective shares of the market, as discussed in Chapter 3.

- **Market growth**. Rivalry is intensified when firms are competing for a greater market share in a total market where growth is slow or stagnant. For example the major supermarkets in the UK are becoming increasingly competitive in their attempt to increase market share, in the context of the economic downturn which has seen shoppers become more cautious in their spending.

- **Cost structure**. High fixed costs are a temptation to compete on prices, as in the short run a contribution from sales is better than none at all. An example would be hotels selling late rooms at a price that covers cleaning and consumables only.

- **Switching**. Suppliers will compete if buyers can switch easily, for example, energy suppliers who offer little that is distinctive.

- **Capacity**. A supplier might need to achieve a substantial increase in output capacity, in order to obtain a reduction in unit cost.

- **Uncertainty**. When one firm is not sure what another is up to, there is a tendency to respond to the uncertainty by formulating a more competitive strategy.

- **Strategic importance**. If success is the prime strategic objective, firms will be likely to act very competitively to meet their targets.

- **Exit barriers** may make it difficult for an existing supplier to leave the industry, such as the costs of redundancy payments to employees.

7 The Marketing Information System (MkIS)

With markets often changing quickly and dramatically, a formalised information system is required. Most decisions are based on incomplete information; beyond a certain point, the gathering of more information would not be worth the extra time and cost of obtaining and analysing it. The information must be processed into a useful form and distributed to the right people at the right time and in the right format. This is where the Marketing Information System comes into play. MIS as an acronym is commonly used to describe Management Information Systems which would include a wider base of data with metrics from across all areas of the business. The MkIS consists of the people, equipment and procedures to gather, sort, analyse, evaluate and distribute needed, timely and accurate information to marketing decision makers.

- It must incorporate procedures for the co-ordination and communication of intelligence to relevant decision-makers without delay.

- It should encourage participation in the information-gathering process by all organisation members.

Figure 4.5   Marketing Information System

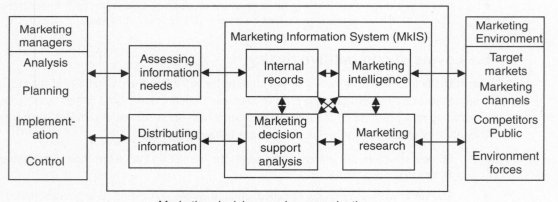

Marketing decisions and communications

8 The need for continuous market research

Too frequently marketers can be accused in practice of collating some of their most valuable information just once a year; generally at the point in time where marketing plans and budgets are being prepared. These marketers have missed the point about assessing their marketing environment; those who keep their 'finger on the pulse' and continuously monitor their environment can gain the greatest competitive advantage. Quality information (timely, sufficient, accurate, relevant,

The Chartered
Institute of Marketing

appropriately formatted) can contribute significantly to competitive advantage. It may enable the organisation to:

- Identify, characterise and target market segments effectively
- Identify new products/market opportunities
- Anticipate and respond to changing customer needs and wants
- Leverage customer and supplier relationships
- Anticipate and respond to threats and competitor actions

8.1 Research methodology

Internal and external sources of secondary information are discussed earlier in this chapter. Primary research is studied in depth in the unit Marketing Information and Research but for this unit a broad knowledge of research tools is needed in order to demonstrate how information gaps can be filled. The table below considers how the competitive advantages identified above could be achieved through use of primary research activities.

Table 4.2   Examples of primary research activities

Competitive advantage	Research options
Identify, characterise and target market segments effectively	Investigating target market attitudes and propensity to buy through focus groups
Identify new products / market opportunities	Product testing or street surveys in selected geographical areas
Anticipate and respond to changing customer needs and wants	Continuous measurement of customer satisfaction through online surveys
Leverage customer and supplier relationships	Survey existing customers' awareness of full product / service portfolio
Anticipate and respond to threats and competitor actions	Lapsed customer research

Key considerations in specifying research projects to fill knowledge gaps include:

- Sample – is the research aimed at existing customers, potential customers or lapsed customers?
- Methodology – in-depth information on attitudes and beliefs will require a more qualitative approach eg focus groups whereas a simple measure of buying behaviour or awareness may be satisfied by a qualitative survey eg an online questionnaire
- Practicality – ensuring that you can reach the sample effectively with the most appropriate methodology and in a timely manner to support your analysis
- Cost – weighing up the costs and benefits of any research methods

> ▶ **Exam tip**
>
> The competitive environment confronts virtually all organisations in some way or another and is a great concern for the marketer. Exam questions could range from the competitive/co-operative relationships between a business and its suppliers or distributors, to assessment of the impact of policies relating to competition.
>
> You must demonstrate not just an understanding of theories and analysis discussed in the chapter but also an ability to relate to your own or a representative industry. You must be very clear as to the contribution of the marketer to shaping marketing forces and sustaining better than normal profitability over time.

CHAPTER ROUNDUP

In this chapter we have dealt with the following important aspects:

- Analysing the power and interest of the organisation's stakeholder.

- How corporate social responsibility influences stakeholder interests and relations as well as competitive position.

- The nature and implications of competition in fragmented and concentrated industries.

- The importance of monitoring the actions and reactions of competitors.

- The nature of the customer relationship and the importance of service quality in achieving customer satisfaction.

- Strategic choice is the key as firms compete on service, innovation and non-price variables.

- Identifying sources of information and evaluating the use of relevant data.

- The definitions of qualitative and quantitative data and primary and secondary data.

- The need for an information system and the important sources of information required for a competitor analysis.

- The need to monitor competitors, while providing some predictions of competitive response, only takes account of rival firms within the market. More thorough analysis requires consideration of several groups in the micro-environment.

FURTHER READING

Egan, J. (2008) *Relationship marketing: exploring relational strategies in marketing*. 3rd edition. Harlow, Pearson, Chapter 7.

Kotler, P. and Keller, K.L. (2009) *Marketing management*. 13th edition. London, Pearson Education, Chapter 3.

Palmer, A. (2009) *Introduction to marketing*. 2nd edition. Oxford: Oxford, University Press, Chapter 4.

Palmer, A. and Hartley, B.(2012) *The business environment*. 12th edition. Maidenhead, McGraw-Hill, Chapters 11 and 15.

Websites:

http://www.ons.gov.uk – Office of National Statistics

http://www.mintel.com – market intelligence in sectors including FMCG, financial services, retail, leisure and education.

http://www.nielsen.com – powerful insights into consumer buying patterns

http://www.euromonitor.com – strategy research for consumer markets

The Chartered Institute of Marketing

REFERENCES

BP (2012) Environmental Expenditure.
http://www.bp.com/sectiongenericarticle800.do?categoryId=9040199&contentId=7067450 [Accessed on 23 May 2012].

Coca-Cola (2012) Product List. http://www.thecoca-colacompany.com/brands/brandlist.html [Accessed on 21 May 2012].

Dibb, S. et al (2006) *Marketing Concepts and Strategies*. 5th Edition. Abingdon, Houghton Mifflin.

Haslett, E. (2011) *Dyson cleans up with £206m profit*. Management Today, http://www.managementtoday.co.uk/news/1084954/Dyson-cleans-206m-profit/ [Accessed on 14 February 2012].

Jobber, D. (2010) *Principles and practice of marketing*. 6th edition. Maidenhead, McGraw-Hill.

Johnson, G., Whittington, R. and Scholes, K. (2010) *Exploring Corporate Strategy: Text and Cases*. 9th Ed. Harlow: Pearson Education Ltd.

Mintel (2012) Mintel company history. http://www.mintel.com/company-history [Accessed on 24 May 2012]

Palmer, A. (2009) *Introduction to marketing*. 2nd edition. Oxford, Oxford University Press.

Portas, M. (2011) The Portas Review: an independent review into the future of our high streets. Department for business, Innovation and Skills, http://www.bis.gov.uk/assets/biscore/business-sectors/docs/p/11-1434-portas-review-future-of-high-streets [Accessed on 16 February 2012].

Waitrose (2012) Small Producers' Charter.
http://www.waitrose.com/home/inspiration/food_issues_and_policies/origin_of_our_food/sourcing_british_food/regional_and_local_sourcing/small_producers_charter.html [Accessed on 14 February 2012].

QUICK QUIZ

1 What strategy does Mendelow propose for engaging with stakeholders that have low power over the organisation but a high level of interest?

2 At what stage in the buying process will a buyer be seeking information?

3 What is a SWOT analysis?

4 Is a government report a primary or secondary source of information?

5 What is the difference between a MIS and a MkIS

6 Why is it often recommended that secondary research is completed before primary research?

7 How does Corporate Social Responsibility relate to stakeholder theory?

Activity 4.1

Stakeholder power can be justified by assessing how dispensable a stakeholder is and what would happen if they walk away or cease support. Stakeholder interest can be justified by what would happen if you walk away – could they simply go elsewhere or do they have a vested interest in your continuance? Relate these positions back to the organisational goals and objectives – how will profit, turnover, market position or reputation be affected?

Activity 4.2

Most large organisations will have a CSR policy and some organisations will share in detail what that means in terms of the day-to-day operation and long-term planning for the business. For example The Body Shop places great emphasis on producer relations, Starbucks aims to reflect the interests of local communities in the areas in which it operates and BP, which has global and site specific environmental policies, spent over $14 billion on the Gulf of Mexico oil spill clean up (BP, 2012).

Activity 4.3

This will vary completely depending on the organisation you have chosen but, for example a hotel group may wish to refer to

- Trade associations – current best practice on quality standards and advice on renewable energy
- Government sources – general economic advice and current tourism initiatives in relevant markets
- Commercial sources such as Nielsen, Mintel – latest reports on leisure and tourism sectors
- Academic sources – journals and papers eg *Journal of Tourism Management*
- General sources – eg articles on up and coming destinations or competitive products

QUICK QUIZ ANSWERS

1 Keep informed. This could include local communities or charities.

2 At the early stage, after need recognition but before evaluation of alternatives.

3 The analysis of the current situation into strengths, weaknesses, opportunities and threats.

4 Secondary

5 MIS is Management Information, which has a wider remit, gathering, managing and dissemination information for all of the organisation's functions. The MkIS, Marketing Information System with have markets and stakeholders as its focus. In reality the MkIS should be an integral part of the MIS.

6 Secondary research, having been already gathered and published, is normally available instantly and cost-effectively. It can also help to further define the requirements for primary research.

7 It recognises that the organisation is responding to the interests of all stakeholders, not just shareholders.

The Chartered Institute of Marketing

CHAPTER 5

An introduction to the macro environment

Introduction

Having analysed the internal organisation and the external conditions within the micro, or competitive environment, we can now extend our investigation to the macro environment – analysing the range of environmental factors that affect all organisations to differing degrees. This chapter introduces the macro environment and the information that we can access in order to monitor it. It also covers the natural environment, the setting for all of society's activities. This section of the syllabus is worth 40% so it is essential to understand all of the factors and to be able to evaluate how these may impact upon an organisation.

Topic list

Understanding the macro environment   (1)

The natural environment   (2)

The challenge of change   (3)

Information for analysing the macro environment   (4)

3.1	Explain the importance of the macro environment to the marketing process: ■ PESTEL market performance indicators ■ Identification and implications of market turbulence, complexity and dynamism ■ Effects of changing markets within the world arena
3.2	Identify key sources of information useful in analysing the macro environment. ■ Government statistics ■ Economic indicators ■ Business confidence indicators ■ Internet ■ Trade publications, etc
3.6	Explain the natural environment and, in general terms, its influence on and implications for marketing: ■ Policies relating to emissions and waste, etc ■ Governmental and pressure group influence on environmental priorities ■ Pollution and waste management ■ Moral and ethical responsibility ■ Green marketing – 5Rs (ROI, Reach, Responsibility, Reputation, Revenue) ■ Social responsibility and sustainability
3.7	Assess the potential significance of environmental challenges to marketing in the future: ■ Globalisation ■ Global warming/emissions/carbon footprints ■ Environmental decline ■ Shortage of natural resources ■ Reducing waste ■ Increasing re-cycling ■ Alternative energy sources (wind power, solar power, electric/gas cars, etc) ■ Alternative transportation

1 Understanding the macro environment

> ▶ **Key term**
>
> **Organisations as open systems**
>
> Organisations gather inputs such as materials and manpower and generate outputs such as goods and services for consumers and returns for other stakeholders. They therefore interact with their environment in a complex web of connections and activities. Much of the theory echoes that found in the natural world where organisms are seen as part of a wider ecological system. Through studying the macro environment in detail, marketers become attuned to the positive and negative impacts that it can have on the fortunes of the organisation.

The organisation lies nestled within the micro environment which in turn lies nestled within the macro environment.

The Chartered
Institute of Marketing

Figure 5.1   The marketing environment – the macro environment

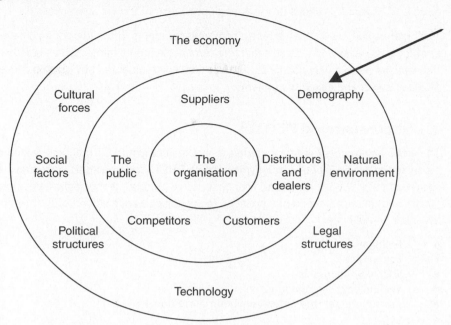

Marketing is actively concerned with anticipating and then responding positively to changes occurring in the external environment. Although an organisation cannot control its micro-environment, it can however do much to adapt to the factors of the micro environment. Organisations can also not control the forces of the macro environment. Notwithstanding, the generally uncontrollable forces of the macro environment can and do create a succession of potential threats and opportunities for organisations.

Figure 5.2   Business as open systems within the macro environment

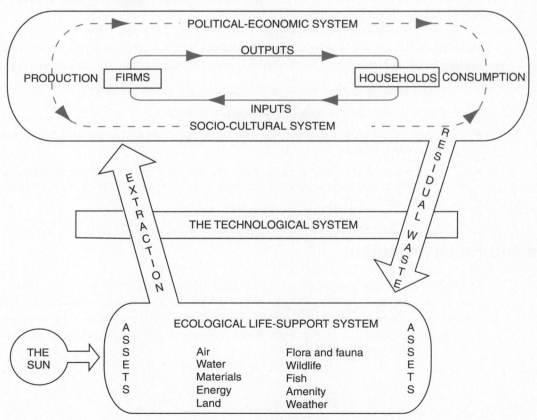

In Chapter 1 the topic of the business as an open system interacting with its external environment was discussed. Figure 5.2 above provides an appreciation of the linkages involved.

The organisation, as an open system, competes for inputs in the form of income or resources from households or other businesses. The organisation converts these inputs into outputs – goods and services. These transactions are not only conducted in the micro environment of any given business, but also within the wider political, social and economic systems.

1.1 Understanding PESTEL

The wider environment is often referred to by the acronym PEST (political, economic, socio-cultural, and technological). Several other acronyms such as DRETS (demographic, regulatory, economic, technological, socio-cultural), PESTEL (political, economic, socio-cultural, technological, environmental, legal) and SLEPT (socio-cultural, legal, economic, political, technological) are also be used. They are all frameworks for analysing the macro environment.

- Political
- Economic
- Social/demographic
- Technological/information
- Environmental (the natural environment)/Ethical
- Legal

> ▶ **Exam tip**
>
> CIM uses PESTEL as a framework for this unit and, as you are to bring a pre-prepared analysis into the exam, you must ensure that you understand all PESTEL elements and are able to relate each one to the case organisation. The cases vary considerably and different elements will carry different weighting within each case. You should however ensure that you investigate all PESTEL elements in preparation for the exam. Your analysis will be of greater use in the exam if you identify the macro environmental factor (eg unemployment rates) and then explain how this factor impacts on the organisation, considering both positive and negative existing or potential impacts.

The political system, explored in Chapter 8, provides for the election of a government on the basis of a declared manifesto. Some fundamental functions underpin most political systems. These are generally as follows:

- Broad policy objectives are set and legislation is enacted to implement it.

- An important political objective is to secure re-election.

- In line with the changing socio-cultural landscape, the number and structure of households are changing as populations alter.

- Firms also operate within a social and cultural system. Patterns of consumption reflect evolving lifestyles, and societal expectations impact on what is deemed to be acceptable behaviour within businesses.

2 The natural environment

As global markets have developed and global organisations have grown to service these markets, the world's natural resources have become part of a global market place. Very few countries can be self sufficient in energy, water, crops, metals and minerals. The exchanges that take place in the global market, combined with the rising world population, has put significant pressure on the world's natural resources.

The natural environment forms the backdrop to our social and economic lives. As such, a growing economy must draw part of its necessary inputs from this life-supporting system. Inputs can be divided into two categories:

- Renewable resources
- Non-renewable resources

While some resources can be renewed, this can only occur due to an input of energy from another system (ie the sun can help trees grow; these in turn will provide softwoods). The environment also receives discharges from the economic system in the form of residual waste. Waste which exceeds what the natural environment can assimilate is referred to as pollution. This can impact air, water and land quality as well as the weather.

The value of the non-renewable fossil fuels is rising as global supply is being overtaken by global demand. The control of these fuels is often seen as a source of conflict as economies seek to control future supply. Peak Oil is a concept that aims to define the turning point in global oil supplies. The secrecy of the Organisation of Petroleum Exporting Countries (OPEC), combined with continued increasingly extensive and innovative exploration and production, mean that forecasting this date is proving to be difficult.

THE REAL WORLD

The United Kingdom's target for 2020 is to increase incineration from 9 to 27%, to reduce landfill from 72 to 25% and to recycle the balance. The European Union's recycling targets are forecasted to cost £10 billion or £400 per household. This said, no private company is likely to make the necessary investments without assurances of a market for recycled material. One seasonal solution to current problems was provided by the Emma Maersk, the world's largest container ship. While it brought 11 000 containers of Christmas goods from China to the United Kingdom, its return cargo was made up of British rubbish. Although UK residents and businesses are encouraged to recycle, most of the recycling of plastic cannot be conducted in the United Kingdom but in China. The real solution requires the United Kingdom's 'throw-away culture' to be revised. Getting households to become involved in recycling is a big marketing challenge. Some countries have however started a positive cycle of change. Ireland now taxes non-recycled waste and plastic bags. In the United Kingdom councils (or their commercial operators) pay a landfill tax of £56/tonne to landfill waste (Business Link, 2012). Supermarkets such as Sainsbury's have started to respond to pressure from consumer groups to reduce packaging. Many companies such as M&S while still producing traditional product ranges, are also offering sustainable and fair-trade products.

It is not only non-renewable energy that is facing a situation of demand exceeding supply; many other natural resources are under pressure. Food sources such as wheat, rice or fish are under pressure from rising global population and changing tastes. This in turn places pressure on land to grow crops or on energy to produce fertilisers.

80% of the planet may be covered in water but fresh water is in short supply in many countries, particularly where irrigation-heavy crops have become an economic necessity. Desalination is an option for some island and coastal states but it appears less attractive when the energy costs are taken into account.

Advances in technology may have been a double-edged sword for the natural environment, opening up the natural world to the ravages of uncontrolled tourism or exploitative cultivation of the rainforests but also facilitating recycling and substitution. This said, reconciling the demand for economic growth with the protection of our natural life-support systems may indeed be considered to be the primary challenge of the twenty-first century.

2.1 Environment Decline

Economic growth has progressively inflicted a significant cost on the natural environment. This has arisen, in part, because of externalities that have been borne by third parties other than the producer or consumer involved.

The negative impact of intensive economic activity can be:

- Loss of natural habitats to development or agriculture

- Degradation of natural habitats through erosion by people or water

- Changes to watercourses both overland and underground

- Pollution of soil, water or air through emissions, run-off or inappropriate waste disposal

- Toxic contamination

- Loss of aesthetic qualities due to over-development

- Loss of ecological diversity through over-development and restriction of natural dispersion of flora and fauna

- The impacts of climate change

Positive impacts of economic activity on the natural environment do exist, for example the protection of wild areas for tourism. However, in most cases, declining environmental quality has been the unavoidable result, unless the state has intervened to legislate or make the polluter pay. Technology and business activity have unquestionably affected the future of the environment.

Three fundamental constraints limit the pace and nature of technological change and the continuity of economic growth:

- Social and institutional factors. These are reflected in customs and legislation intended to curb the appliance of science in ways felt to be undesirable to society. For example in the UK there remains strong opposition to the trials or widespread use of genetically modified crops.

- Depletion of non-renewable resources. This includes fuels, minerals, fertile lands (through overgrazing), tropical rainforests and biological diversity in terms of animal and plant species extinction.

- Pollution of the ecosystem

    - Ecology is the study of plants and animals and their interaction with each other and the environment as a whole.

    - Ecosystems include biodegradation processes that decompose wastes to provide nutrients for renewed growth.

    - Problems arise only when their absorptive capabilities are overloaded due to the volume and/or nature of the wastes concerned. Industrial impact – effluents, emissions, solid wastes are often the result of industrialisation.

2.2 Global warming/climate change

> ▶ **Key terms**
>
> The challenges of climate change are bringing a number of terms into common usage:
>
> **Carbon footprint**. '…the total greenhouse gas emission caused directly and indirectly by a person, organisation, event or product' (Carbon Trust, 2012).
>
> **Carbon neutral**: this is regularly used as a statement of an organisation, product or event that has (or aims to have) a zero net emission of greenhouse gasses. For example a carbon neutral home might produce its own electricity from renewable sources such as solar and wind power.
>
> **Carbon offset** is borne out of the challenges of becoming carbon neutral. For example a transportation company would find it virtually impossible to produce zero emissions but they can mitigate their emissions by buying carbon credits from organisations that fund CO_2–using resources such as forests.

Climate change is 'the major, overriding environmental issue of our time and the single greatest challenge facing environmental regulators' (UNEP, 2012). Climate change is the long term alteration in global weather patterns caused by the steadily increasingly average temperature of the earth ie global warming. Global warming has arisen due to increasing levels of greenhouse gases, (including carbon dioxide – CO2) found in the atmosphere as a result of human activities, particularly the burning of fossil fuels. The potential effects of climate change include:

- Shifting weather patterns – increasing and unpredictable extremes of weather such as droughts, floods and hurricane, resulting in implications for food production and other activities.

- Rising sea levels – due to melting polar ice-caps, causing widespread flooding of currently inhabited coastlines.

- Warming atmosphere – aiding the spread of diseases previously limited to the tropics and changing ecosystems across the globe.

Most countries now recognise climate change as a serious threat to human society and to the natural world. There have been worldwide efforts to try to stem the effect. At the 1997 UN conference in Kyoto, Japan, a significant number of developed nations (excluding the USA) signed up to the Kyoto Protocol and agreed to reduce emissions of greenhouse gases.

The United Nations work in this area is shaped by the annual Climate Change Conferences during which complex limits on or reductions to emissions are negotiated. The latest, in Durban South African in December 2011, introduced a new round of negotiations aimed at ensuring emissions peak by 2020 and are halved by 2050.

2.2.1 Alternative energy

The combined effect of the depletion of non-renewable resources in the form of fossil fuels and the detrimental effect of their emissions on the environment have laid the foundation for significant expansion of renewable energy sources.

Electric and hybrid cars have moved into the mainstream markets. Domestic solar water heating and solar electricity generation, aided by tax incentives, have also grown significantly in the last ten years.

Between 2003 and 2010 there was a 143% increase in electricity generation from renewable sources such as wind, solar, wave and biomass in the UK (DECC, 2011). However, in 2009, this still represented less than 3% of total energy consumption (ONS, 2011).

The European Photovoltaic Industry Association (EPIA, 2012) reports that Europe is still leading the way for this sector with Germany and Italy the top markets for solar power generation. Outside of Europe, the strongest markets have been and are predicted to continue to be Japan, America and China.

2.3 Consumers and the natural environment

Various factors can influence the impact of consumers on the natural environment. The consumer demand for products which claim ecological soundness has waxed and waned with initial enthusiasm replaced by cynicism in a response to 'green wash'. Some of the influencers are:

- **Marketing advantage**. Companies like Body Shop have cleverly exploited environmental friendliness as a marketing tool. Supermarkets now stock cleaning products which are 'kind to nature'.

- **Bad publicity**. Perhaps companies have more to fear from the impact of bad publicity relating to the ecological effect of their activities than positive environmental messages. Negative publicity on tuna fishing methods has resulted in a significant shift in buying behaviour with many consumers now looking for the 'pole and line caught' message.

- **Limits to willingness to change**. Consumers may not want to alter aspects of their lifestyles for the sake of environmental correctness. Consider the continuing growth in aviation as, around the globe, consumers are proving unwilling to relinquish the ability to travel the world for business or for pleasure.

- **Education of consumers**. Finally, consumers may be imperfectly educated about environmental issues. For example, how green is recycled paper? The analysis is complex and balances the sustainability of paper pulp sources against the energy and chemicals involved in recycling paper.

ACTIVITY 5.1

Match the terms with their correct definitions:

1   Effluent

2   Emissions

3   Acid rain

4   Ozone-layer depletion

5   Greenhouse effect

(a)   Carbon dioxide absorbs and radiates back heat that would otherwise escape into space, causing temperature rises.

(b)   Liquid wastes discharged into seas or watercourses.

(c)   Discharges of sulphur dioxide from power stations or vehicle exhaust gases combine with water vapour in the atmosphere.

(d)   Release of gases into the atmosphere.

(e)   Caused by the discharge of CFCs in aerosols, solvents, foam plastics and fridges allowing through dangerous ultraviolet rays.

2.4 Sources of the decline

The natural environment has found no difficulty in coping with the wastes created by our economic development, at least until recently. Natural disasters or acts of God as they are legally referred to, have also been accommodated (at a cost), be they Californian forest-fires, floods in Pakistan or Australia or earthquakes in Japan or New Zealand, because their impacts have been relatively localised and, over time, these areas can re-build. Figure 5.3 shows the main factors responsible. The cause and effect of such natural disasters is the subject of a wide area of study and much impassioned argument but there seems to be little doubt that industrialisation and population growth lie at the heart of the globe's vulnerability to such disasters.

The Chartered
Institute of Marketing

Figure 5.3   Key factors in environmental degradation

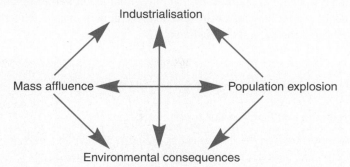

However, although any one of the three elements will cause environmental problems, their combined and interdependent effects are much more serious. The effects of the above are compounded by the pressure of competition, the pursuit of economic gain and the political imperative of economic growth in all countries. Many natural resources are neither privately nor corporately owned but are subject to common exploitation with little regard to environmental costs and benefits.

THE REAL WORLD

British Airways is the UK's largest international scheduled airline and in its annual Corporate Responsibility Report (2011/12) starts by accepting the nature of the problem 'At British Airways we recognise that the key environmental issue facing the industry is climate change. Today the airline industry represents approximately 2% of global CO_2 emissions with this share increasing as the airline industry continues to grow.'

(British Airways, 2012)

In practice the airline is able to identify a number of mitigating measures it has undertaken including:

- Encouraging over half a million passengers to 'offset' their carbon contribution over the last three years
- Altering use of auxiliary power units and reducing fuel waste by £1.5m
- Recycling 45% of all waste and reducing landfill waste by 3%

It also aims to reduce CO_2 emissions from flights, measured in grams per passenger mile, by 25% in the 20-year period to 2025, however some of this is to be achieved through carbon trading – a controversial EU scheme enabling carbon-producing industries to purchase emission reductions made in other sectors.

British Airways operates the One Destination Carbon Fund – enabling passengers to voluntarily donate an appropriate amount which is used to fund projects around the UK for example, solar heating in community swimming pools and energy efficiency measures in housing.

Other organisations offering the general public offset opportunities include:
http://www.climatecare.org
http://www.carbonearth.co.uk

They invite donations and fund projects largely related to woodland and forest management and renewable energies. In reality only a tiny percentage of air passengers will volunteer to donate and air travel remains one of the high-profile CO_2 generators of our time.

2.5 Sustainable development

Sustainable development involves meeting the needs of the present generation without compromising the needs and requirements of future generations. In effect, the objective is to achieve a negative relationship between gross domestic product and pollution through the introduction of viable controls for the achievement of sustainable development. The content in Chapter 4, explains the concept of Corporate Social Responsibility and

its fundamental links with sustainability. The triple bottom line of economic, social and environmental sustainability is one that is driven by macro environmental trends including socio-cultural and demographic trends, political priorities, the desire for economic growth, available technologies and of course the underlying vulnerabilities of the natural environment.

2.6 Reduce, re-use, recycle

Simple economic sense suggests that individuals and organisations should review their use of resources, renewable and non-renewable. Savings can be made in the purchase of materials and reductions in waste disposal costs.

Legislators, responding to pressure groups, have introduced taxes on waste disposal. In the UK this has resulted in segregated rubbish collection but it has also resulted in the challenges of finding both processors and an end use for recycled papers and plastics.

Consumers, with a deeper awareness of the issues, are buying products that can demonstrate their sustainable credentials through:

- Reduced packaging
- Recycled components and packaging
- Recyclable materials
- Verified environmental performance eg of cars or white goods

Fuelled by the growth of eBay, other people's unwanted goods are finding a new life rather than making their way to the dump. A new trend of 'upcycling' has emerged where consumers renovate furniture and clothing for the current fashions.

The Chartered Institute of Marketing

2.7 Implications of the natural environment for marketers

Business is central to the problem of environmental decline, but also to the solution.

- Environmental consciousness is rising, so the evolving green agenda needs to be monitored by companies.

- Few consumers budget on environmental performance alone and all external stakeholders seek reassurance. Therefore, improvement of performance and a risk-free future need to be emphasised.

- Agreed objectives need to be set by top management/trading partners. The latter will prefer to deal with a business applying environmental standards it is committed to.

- Seek a competitive edge via ethically sound practices. This could be achieved by means of the use of cleaner technologies.

- Assess the carbon footprint made by the organisation and assess the possibility of carbon offsets from investment in cleaner technologies and products.

- Offset resource depletion through technical change, redesign, reduction, reuse, recycling and substitution, linked to quality initiatives.

- An environmental strategy needs to be based on sound ethical principles, an audit, impact assessment (see Chapter 10) and action based on benchmarking of best practice.

- Stakeholders must be involved/educated in good environmental practice.

- Pay-off is in an increased sense of security, improved image/relationships, lower insurance premiums and avoidance of fines/litigation.

Heightening concern for society and the natural environment requires that new technology is only introduced with care and foresight as to its likely impacts. While technology can help solve challenges and enable sustainable development through accelerated research and development, it also has shortcomings.

From the marketing point of view, the natural environment is a potentially valuable but not very consistent market as action-awareness gaps arise between what green consumers profess to want and what they actually buy. The Japanese, for example, buy 25 billion wooden chopsticks a year for cultural not environmental reasons. In the UK's supermarkets consumers are conspicuously re-using carrier bags and then filling them with heavily pre-packaged goods. Awareness varies across market segments and even cultures. This however represents opportunities as well as threats for marketers across the marketing environment.

Finally, it should not be assumed that environmental impacts are primarily the concern of large firms and governments. It is in fact the concern of all the stakeholders in a marketing environment.

> ▶ **Key term**
>
> **Green marketing**
>
> Defining this term brings us back to CIM's definition of marketing 'the management process responsible for identifying, anticipating and satisfying customer requirements profitably. **Green marketing** is therefore taking an environmentally sustainable approach to those processes. For example sustainable products, that do not have a negative impact on the environment, distribution systems that do not add unnecessary mileage of fuel use and promotions that reduce wastage and portray messages with integrity.

2.8 The 5Rs of green marketing

Some of the issues touched here were discussed earlier, including the need to avoid accusations of 'greenwash'. The macro environment is shaping green marketing through the general pressures of protecting and managing the natural environment but also the social trends whereby consumer, and the decision-makers in organisations, are increasingly swayed by these issues. The markets can consider options using the 5Rs framework:

- **ROI**: Return on Investment, measuring the costs and benefits of green initiatives such as a move to digital customer relations or banking

- **Reach**: the extent to which green actions are meeting the environmental aspirations of customers or customer segments

- **Responsibility**: relating marketing practices within the wider concepts and policies of the organisation's Corporate Social Responsibility

- **Reputation**: shaping the organisation's reputation through meaningful actions rather than just 'green' messages

- **Revenue**: how all of the above may combine to improve customer satisfaction and retention and also the acquisition of new customers

3 The challenge of change

Unlike the micro-environment, broad natural, political, economic, social and technical trends and changes do not directly impact on day-to-day operations but are extremely important in shaping the competitive situation and the actions and perceptions of relevant stakeholders.

Although the size of an organisation can safeguard it with regard to some factors, size is no longer an automatic defence against the forces of change. Indeed, it is thought that only half of the companies listed in the *Financial Times Top 100 Companies* 25 years ago are still operating today. It is argued that the companies that are missing failed to meet the challenges and so fell victim to a number of misfortunes, which could have included:

- 'Old economy' companies are increasingly replaced by 'new economy' internet-related businesses
- Acquisition by another firm
- Spectacular failure
- Poor relative performance
- The state forced to take ownership

Clearly, the larger business must stay alert to survive changing circumstances. However, the weight of its bureaucracy may make this difficult. Smaller businesses may have the flexibility to adapt more effectively, but only if given access to sufficient resources. In brief, all types of companies must recognise that they are on the equivalent of a moving conveyor; they must therefore be prepared to move fast in line with changes as tastes, technology and competitive forces are evolving rapidly.

Dynamic and complex market environments demand that astute understanding from the marketer. Accordingly, the marketer needs to follow some consistent yet continuous and systematic processes. These would invariably include the following:

- Environmental scanning
- Identify those forces relevant to the organisation/its industry
- Forecast political, economic, social and technical changes
- Respond to threats and opportunities by implementing strategies
- Monitor the outcome of planned action
- Continue to scan their environment

The response to uncontrollable macro forces in terms of strategies requires more explanation. Businesses cannot afford to passively accept change in the macro environment but must adapt or suffer the consequences. This requires the marketer not only to scan and analyse threats and opportunities but also to develop positive strategic responses. This might involve lobbying for political change or managing the media in order to influence critical publics. Being proactive, even where scope for direct influence on events is limited, will always have more effect on the outcome of the 'game' than the pure spectator role. However, one of the first steps in effective environmental scanning is to identify the relevant sources of environmental data and it is to this task that we turn next.

Can you think of any businesses that face **static** market conditions? (This implies no change in both consumer tastes and the state of technical knowledge.)

4 Information for analysing the macro environment

Figure 5.4   Secondary data for a business

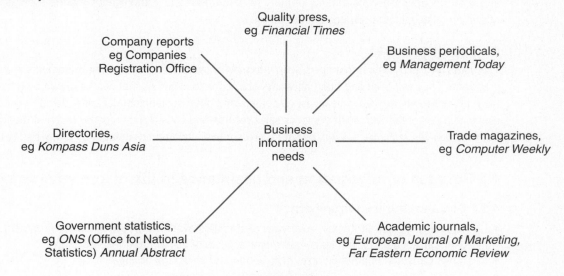

4.1 Information required for marketing

Many different types of information facts, trends and influences in the macro environment are required to support decision-making within the organisation.

Economy

- Main economic indicators – inflation, interest rates, labour market changes
- Business confidence indicators – capacity utilisation and investment
- National income, output and expenditure patterns
- Government taxation and spending plans

Society

- Demographic indicators – birth/death rates and interregional migration patterns
- Household and working patterns – change in cultural norms
- Leisure activities and ownership ratios for homes, cars, mobiles and so on

Similar factors could be identified in other areas of the PESTEL environment underlining the diverse nature of information requirements in modern business today. In an environment of rapid change, where time and delay can cost a company dearly, the ability to obtain a clear and accurate picture of developments can provide the firm with a distinct competitive advantage. Information is power, but to achieve this requires knowledge not just of key sources of information but also of how to access them quickly and effectively.

4.1.1 Published material

Such sources are used regularly or systematically by business decision-makers. However, the diffused nature of many of these sources makes collection, classification and distribution to interested managers an expensive and time-consuming process. The government is one of the main producers of primary data, published through the Office for National Statistics (ONS). Fortunately, many of the more important sources have now been produced on CD or the internet, making access almost instantaneous and far more cost-effective. Increasingly, through intranets and extranets, much in-depth information can be acquired.

As discussed earlier, information and communication technologies are now being applied to search more widely for data and to transform scattered data into quality information available whenever it is required by the appropriate decision-maker. The key skill for a marketer to develop is therefore to know what information is available on a particular issue and, most importantly, where to find it. Published material exists on most topics and is far cheaper than undertaking primary research. Marketing intelligence reports such as Key Note and Mintel are also valuable sources of information.

4.1.2 Trade sources

The usual means by which managers keep informed of internal and external developments is through the grapevine. They establish and build **networks** of information sources that can be drawn on when the need arises. Regular conversations with colleagues, customers and other stakeholder contacts provide a moving tapestry of events supplemented with such things as sales records and consultancy reports. Much of the material gathered from the sources in Figure 5.4 will be sifted, cross-referenced and assimilated on a day-to-day basis.

4.2 Sources of information and assistance in the macro environment

4.2.1 Social-cultural environment

- Guide to Official Statistics – overview of statistics available on the macro environment.
- Annual Abstract of Statistics – all major aspects of government responsibility.
- ONS Census – population size, distribution and structural change.
- Social Trends – annual survey of key societal indicators.
- See http://www.statistics.gov.uk/onlineproducts/default.asp#social (or economy).
- Family Expenditure Survey – annual statistical analysis of spending/lifestyle patterns.
- ACORN/Mosaic – classification of local neighbourhoods for segmentation purposes.
- Journals/quality press society sections, for example, New Society – changing social patterns.
- British Market Research Bureaux – research cases on lifestyle change.
- UN indicators on population worldwide: http://www.un.org/en/index.shtml
- World Bank development data: http://www.worldbank.org/data/data/

4.2.2 Political-legislative environment

- Select Committee reports – monitor and report on political issues of the day.
- JUSTIS online legal database – current legislative developments.
- Legal digests – recent case law.
- European Commission – EU directives and implementation timetables.
- Mainstream media and news databases.
- People's Republic of China Ministry of Commerce site: http://english.mofcom.gov.cn
- Nigeria law: http://www.nigeria-law.org/

4.2.3 Economic environment

- ONS National Income and Expenditure/the Blue Book – macroeconomic analysis.
- Economic Trends – changing economic structure and activity patterns.
- Bank of England Quarterly Review – monitors monetary system/exchange rates.
- Regional Trends – detailed annual data on social and economic changes.
- Employment Gazette – monthly publication covering wage and price movements.
- CBI Quarterly Survey – measuring industry confidence and intentions.

The Chartered
Institute of Marketing

- National Institute Economic Review – quarterly commentary and comparisons.
- Journals and quality newspapers/databases, for example, Economist, Financial Times.
- Bank reviews – articles and economic analysis.
- Datastream provides economic data for Asia, Europe and the Americas.

4.2.4 International environment

- Department for Business Innovation & skills – export credits/advice
- Professional bodies, for example, CIM, Institute of Exporters – networks of contacts
- Embassies and trade missions – on-the-spot advice/promotion/contacts
- Eurostat EU database: http://epp.eurostat.ec.europa.eu/portal/page/portal/eurostat/home/
- Banks, for example, HSBC, provide credit rating/market analysis
- International organisations, for example, OECD/IMF/WTO/UN World Economic Survey
- International trade centre (UNCTAD/WTO): http://www.intracen.org
- Trade blocs, for example, EU/ASEAN/NAFTA/Indo-Sri Lanka FTA-research studies
- Government departments, for example, customs and excise/planning – specific sectoral data
- Quality press, journals and directories, for example, Kompass, Country Reports/Asia Week

4.2.5 Technical environment

- Research journals and conference papers
- Trade press reports
- Channel intermediaries and ultimate customer need surveys
- Technical abstracts and databases
- Professional associations and industry networks

4.2.6 (Natural) environment

- Government sources including the Department for the Environment and Rural Affairs
- Pressure groups including Greenpeace and Friends of the Earth
- RIO+20, the 2012 UN Conference on Sustainable Development, 20 years on from the first conference in Rio de Janeiro.
- The UN Framework Convention on Climate Change – building on the Kyoto Protocol

ACTIVITY 5.3

Investigate the website http://www.defra.gov.uk and summarise the generic areas of advice for businesses that is offered by this government department.

CHAPTER ROUNDUP

In this chapter, we have:

- Introduced the concept of the macro environment and described the use of PESTEL as a framework for analysis

- Described some of the key factors in the natural environment

- Looked at how the macro-environment can cause threats and opportunities

- Discussed the importance of monitoring change in the macro environment

- Considered how and why marketers can draw on information sources to monitor the macro environment

FURTHER READING

Palmer, A., Hartley, B. 2006 *The business and marketing environment*. Maidenhead McGraw-Hill, Chapters 2 and 10.

Jobber, D. (2010) *Principles of marketing*. 6th edition, Maidenhead McGraw-Hill, Chapter 5.

Websites:

http://www.cnn.com for serious international news reports cross-referenced and backed by video clips, photos, audio files and links to relevant websites. It is translated into several languages.

http://www.bbc.co.uk/news is also translated and offers in-depth reports.

http://www.washingtonpost.com has won many quality awards and can be customised to a specific region.

http://www.huffingtonpost.co.uk – global online news community

http://www.newsnow.co.uk provides international news updated every five minutes with a search facility that covers headlines if you wish to trace the origins of a story.

http://www.statistics.gov.uk/instantfigures.asp provides data on latest economic indicators.

http://earthtrends.wri.org/ is an environmental information portal.

http://www.africa.com is a gateway site to the African continent covering business, news and so on.

http://www.allafrica.com provides digests and reviews from 48 national news agencies including special reports on economics, technology and the environment.

http://sd.defra.gov.uk – sustainability in UK government policy.

REFERENCES

British Airways (2012) Corporate Responsibility Report 2011/12.
http://www.britishairways.com/cms/global/pdfs/environment/ba_corporate_responsibility_report_2010-2011.pdf [Accessed on 17 February 2012].

Business Link (2012) Environmental tax obligations and breaks.
http://www.businesslink.gov.uk/bdotg/action/detail?itemId=1074404201&type=RESOURCES [Accessed on 17 February 2012].

Carbon Trust (2012) Footprint measurement. http://www.carbontrust.co.uk/cut-carbon-reduce-costs/calculate/carbon-footprinting/pages/carbon-footprinting.aspx [Accessed on 18 February 2012].

Department for Energy and Climate Change (2011) Renewable Energy 2010.
http://www.decc.gov.uk/assets/decc/11/stats/publications/energy-trends/articles/2082-renewable-energy-2010-trends-article.pdf [Accessed 21 May 2012].

EPIA (2012) Global Market Outlook for Photovoltaics until 2016. http://files.epia.org/files/Global-Market-Outlook-2016.pdf [Accessed 21 May 2012].

Jobber, D. (2010) *Principles and practice of marketing*. 6th edition. Maidenhead. McGraw-Hill. Page 93.

Marks and Spencer (2012) The Shwop Lab: ready to wear challenge.
http://social.marksandspencer.com/fashion-2/the-shwop-lab-ready-to-wear-challenge/ [Accessed 21 May 2012].

Office for National Statistics (2011) UK Environmental Accounts 2011 – Blue Book Update
http://www.ons.gov.uk/ons/dcp171778_240604.pdf [Accessed 21 May 2012].

United Nations Environment Programme (2012) Climate change:
http://www.unep.org/climatechange/Introduction.aspx [Accessed on 18 February 2012].

QUICK QUIZ

1   What is the difference between SLEPT and PESTEL?

2   What is Peak Oil?

3   How is a carbon footprint measured?

4   What are the 5Rs of green marketing?

5   What element of the macro environment would you be investigating with use of ACORN or Mosaic?

6   What element of the macro environment would you be investigating with use of the CB's quarterly surveys?

Activity 5.1

1   b

2   d

3   c

4   e

5   a

Activity 5.2

In these turbulent and challenging times it is challenging to identify industries that are truly operating in static conditions. Think about the phrase 'People will always need…' You may have suggested the funeral sector, baby goods, some insurances and the centre ground of the food sector – although all of these will to some extent be affected by, for example, demographic changes or more sustained economic or political trends.

Activity 5.3

Environment impacts will clearly vary considerable with different sectors (eg agriculture or construction) however the generic advice offered on this site includes:

- Promoting resource/energy efficiency
- Developing environmental management systems
- Advice on materials, innovation and design
- Advice on packaging, marketing and distribution

QUICK QUIZ ANSWERS

1   The differences are insignificant – both are models for analysing the macro environment, however, the model used by CIM is PESTEL.

2   Peak Oil is the term used to describe the point at which the global oil product rate peaks (and begins to fall). It will represent a milestone in global politics and economics.

3   The carbon footprint is measured in CO_2 tonnes and takes into account all direct and indirect emissions resulting from the activity being measured.

4   ROI, Reach, Responsibility, Reputation and Revenue

5   Social/cultural element of the macro environment. These are geo-demographic databases that describe consumer behaviour patterns of specific neighbourhoods.

6   Economic. The CBI quarterly surveys report on growth, employment and projections for the UK's largest employer sectors.

CHAPTER 6

The demographic, social and cultural environment

Introduction

Knowledge and understanding of demography and socio-cultural change is vital if the marketer is to truly appreciate the origins of buyer behaviour. Even though these are uncontrollable by marketers, their appreciation and understanding is essential. Both evolve slowly but their cumulative impact on the market is considerable. Demands for products and services in the longer term are more likely to be determined by population changes than any of the other macro environmental elements. Change in this environment is the most difficult to assess, yet it offers many opportunities to marketers. This chapter addresses demography, the study of population, and then it investigates the impacts of social class and culture on the world's population's behaviours and attitudes. The relevant variables are complex and interrelated and the challenge for marketers is to develop an understanding of these relationships and emerging trends.

Topic list

Trends in population	1
The workforce in employment: some important trends	2
Social class	3
The social and cultural environment	4
Health	5
Lifestyle	6
Geodemographic segmentation	7

3.2	Identify key sources of information useful in analysing the macro environment:
	■ Government statistics ■ Economic indicators ■ Business confidence indicators ■ Internet ■ Trade publications, etc
3.3	Explain the social, demographic and cultural environments and, in general terms, their influence on and implications for marketing including:
	■ Social cultural behaviour and change ■ Demographic/population trends, etc ■ The need for social responsibility and marketing ethics ■ The growth of consumerism

1 Trends in population

> ▶ **Key term**
>
> **Demography** is the study of population and population trends. It is relevant to businesses, as long-range trends in the population affect the demand for goods and services and also the supply of labour.
>
> **Equality and diversity**
>
> UK laws are strict in implementing the principle that goods, services and jobs should be made available to people of all needs. The Equalities Act 2010, replaces all previous anti-discrimination laws and defines the nine protected characteristics of age, disability, gender reassignment, marriage and civil partnership, pregnancy and maternity, race, religion or belief, sex and sexual orientation. The ethos of **equality and diversity** is, guided by this law, becoming deeply ingrained in our personal and corporate lives.

The study of population trends is important to marketers because of marketing's concern with the size, structure, composition and characteristics of the population. Segmentation and the assessment of the market potential of various segments of the population are of utmost importance to the marketer. A responsibility of the marketer is to adequately target products/services to meet the needs of defined market segments. Therefore, an understanding of the breakdown of the population, of the segments and of trends is important.

Nations, regions and local areas will gather statistics on the total population and the natural increase or decrease in population will be shaped by birth and death rates. These rates will be influenced by the significant rise in life expectancy across much of the world. Populations will also change with immigration and emigration, combining to create a net migration factor.

The Office for National Statistics (ONS) is responsible for the collection and publication of official statistics about the United Kingdom's society and economy.

■ It is the principal provider of official statistics about the United Kingdom.

■ This information is also readily available.

■ A ten-yearly census is carried out by the ONS.

    – A census is a survey of all people and households in the country.

    – It is usually conducted by the government of a country.

    – It provides information at national, regional and area levels.

■ Sample surveys are carried out every five years.

    – Timely updates, known as amendments, are conducted.

■ The department is also responsible for the registration of vital events in England and Wales through the General Register Office (GRO).

Collecting and interpreting information

It is important for marketers to appreciate the composition of a given population.

Use the internet or your library to prepare a brief report on the following:

- Total population, current and trend rate of change of the UK population
- Age, gender, marital status and location of population
- Occupational structure and ethnic mix
- Significant trends in structure (eg ageing, urbanisation)

You may find it helpful to browse through the reports in ONS or its local equivalent. You could look at http://www.ons.gov.uk/ons/taxonomy/index.html?nscl=Population or search for latest editions of ONS *Social Trends: Population and Social Trends: Labour Market*. The World Bank and the United Nations also have extensive comparative statistical information on their websites http://www.worldbank.org and http://www.un.org.

Examples of trends uncovered by censuses considered to be significant to marketers are:

- Current population levels and the future size and distribution of any given population.

- The demographic impact on world resources and the physical environment. The growth rates of developed countries versus developing countries and the broad trend of urbanisation.

- The age and gender structure and its distribution by region/locality.

- Ethnicity – Western Europe increasingly has populations drawn from a wide variety of different ethnic backgrounds.

- Migration within national borders and between international borders.

- Marital status and household structure – 27% of UK households are people living alone.

THE REAL WORLD

Towards the end 2011 the world's population was deemed to have exceeded 7 billion, just 12 years after it topped the 6 billion mark, however, population growth is slowing, having peaked in the 1960s. It is projected to peak at around 9 billion but deeper trends lie behind this statistic. Fertility rates (live births per woman) are falling and a generational bulge is working its way through the population. The Economist (2011) described the impact that this can have on societies, 'There are disproportionately more old people depending upon a smaller generation behind them. Population growth stops or goes into reverse, parts of a country are abandoned by the young and the social concerns of the aged grow in significance. This situation already exists in Japan. It is arriving fast in Europe and America, and soon after that will reach East Asia… below the surface societies are being churned up in ways not seen in the much more static pre-industrial world.'

Table 6.1   Features of growing and falling populations

Growing populations	Falling populations
Fast economic growth required	Difficult to achieve economies of scale
Overcrowding	Greater burden on the young
More resources required for capital investment	Changing consumption patterns
Increased market stimulating investment	
Labour mobility	

1.1 The family life cycle

Particular products and services can be targeted at people who occupy specific stages of the family life cycle which represents a package of demographic variables: age, marital status, children, career status and income:

- **Single adulthood**: Individuals may have high disposable income and they are on a low point of a career ladder. They have few financial commitments and may still be staying with parents. This means they can indulge in dining out, travel, music and entertainment. They are however less likely to be planning for the future.

- **Young couples with no children**: A prosperous period with possibly two incomes and no children. Luxury purchases such as fashion or cars may be balanced with a greater propensity to invest in property or pensions. Some may be married but many co-habit.

- **Couples with dependent children**: Disposable income falls as children consume resources of money and time. Spend becomes focused on family and the home.

- **Empty nesters**: These middle-aged people whose children have grown up and left home are the marketer's Holy Grail. Having no responsibilities and mortgages paid off, they still have incomes, perhaps from senior positions and are therefore seen as a wealthy market. Spending on quality durables is high. They have well established tastes and preferences.

Marketers should seek to identify not only who makes the final purchasing decision but also the influence exerted by other family members. Promotional messages can then be precisely targeted.

ACTIVITY 6.2

Scan the advertisements in newspapers and magazines and classify their appeal according to family stages.

1.2 Implications for marketers

Implications of population trends are significant to marketers on several levels, namely:

- An increase in population levels could lead to an increase in the aggregate demand for goods and services.

  - The resulting level of demand will have a direct effect on the distribution of products and services. Regions, localities as well as market segments will need to be considered. Across the globe the patterns vary significantly.

  - Supply becomes an issue as the population levels place a strain on finite resources.

- The ageing of the population structure in mature industrial economies is having a direct effect on consumer demand and spending power.

- Demographic changes have had significant repercussions not only on the marketing environment but also on the general business environment.

- Successful economic development has enabled many developing economies to raise living standards and reduce poverty levels. This has had a direct effect on personal disposable income.

- There is considerable change in many societies due to later marriage, rising divorce rates and remarriages.

  - The traditional marketer's assumption of two adults + two children is now the exception rather than the norm.

- Partners living together and sharing households without being married is becoming increasingly popular in many countries.

- Single households now clearly form a rich stream of potential segmentation.

- Natural increase and net migration is shifting the distribution of population.

- The drift from rural to urban living. There has been a reverse flow from the inner cities to suburbia and ribbons of development along motorways and rail routes away from city centres.

- Many populations are diverse in their ethnic origins. Buying patterns are therefore quintessentially different.

- The changing role of women in work and society. The situation of men and women at work differs dramatically across different societies due to varying cultural norms, education levels and stages of development.

Businesses, particularly in services, have responded positively to economic upturn and labour shortages arising out of lower birth rates and ageing. Initiatives/courses of action have included the following:

- More focused marketing of the business to a more complex range of stakeholders including potential customers and employees

- Building closer links with local educational establishments

- Using the internet

- Tapping alternative workgroups using flexible employment patterns

- Internal marketing for retention, retraining and promotion

- Improving pay and incentives especially for flexibility

- Moving to cheaper labour markets or using selective immigration

One important means of compensating for contraction in the under-25s is by increased employment of married women and the older age groups themselves.

Threats associated with an ageing population that need to be considered by marketers include:

- Risk of focusing too much on the ageing segment of the market and therefore missing demographic changes in other areas.

- Less disposable income of those of working age, due to having to support the ageing population, either directly by supporting elderly relatives, or indirectly by increased taxation or contributions to pension programmes.

- Emerging economies (eg India and China) gaining a competitive advantage due to their younger age structure.

Given current trends, by 2050 the median age in the European Union is forecast to rise from 38 to 49 and there will be some 70 million West Europeans aged 65+, representing over 20% of the population. In Italy there are already more over 60s than under 20s. Only greater longevity is preventing declining populations in many parts of Europe.

As the number of retirees rises, so too does their power as an influential pressure group. More educated and articulate, they will possess the wit, the time and the means to use search and comparison technologies and so constitute a demanding and service-orientated customer.

(a)   Can you think of any change in services that any government has had to offer because of the ageing of the population?

(b)   Within the marketing environment, can you think of any company that has taken advantage of opportunities presented by the ageing population? How has this impacted upon their marketing mix?

> **Exam tip**

You should become competent at investigating commercial research sources such as trade press, Mintel, Key Note and the quality press to look out for examples of industries responding to these demographic changes. For example Mintel reports on the growth of the coach holiday trade or articles on the burgeoning health and social care industries. Multicultural societies present opportunities and challenges for communities and for businesses.

2 The workforce in employment: some important trends

> **Key term**

Work-life balance

Busy lives, juggling roles and flexible working can all lead to real challenges in managing the work-life balance. Generation X, the baby boomers, are more likely to bend to meet workplace requirements, working more hours and prepared to make sacrifices. Generation Y, young adults, will prefer a more flexible approach. However the ubiquitous mobile technologies combined with a culture of 24/7 can mean that the pressure is never switched off. Are we really able to say that we achieve a better balance today than in the post-war years?

A number of important and interrelated developments in employment and education can be identified as economies mature and evolve from industrial into service and information societies. These affect marketers in terms of the human resource demands of marketing and in terms of the impact on demand for products and services. Some of the more obvious features include the following:

- The decline in full-time employment
- The corresponding rise in part-time employment
- Hours are lengthening for full-time workers

- Self-employment is rising
- A rise in contractual and temporary employment
- The growth of older workers as the compulsory retirement age is abolished
- The rise in 'women returners'
- The emergence of flexible organisations
- Employment stress
- The rise of the knowledge worker
- Flexible work lives with career breaks, maternity and paternity leave and home working
- The culture of work-life balance
- Increased mobility
- The self-service economy

Labour shortages are being countered by the use of alternative workforces, such as married women, immigrants and ethnic groups. African, Caribbean and Asian immigrants in England rose 40% from 1991 to 2001 whereas immigration from Eastern Europe reached 600,000 between 2004 and 2006. Marketers need to embrace these changes in population dynamics. New technology, flexible contracts and a culture of continuous learning can help alleviate any skills gap. However, partnerships with educational institutions, tailored and attractive recruitment packages and developing a positive image may help marketers to position organisations as responsible employers.

The Chartered
Institute of Marketing

3 Social class

The social structure of the population can be analysed in a number of ways, on the basis that there is a correlation in the activities of certain groups. Class is not always easy to define but there are significant differences in income, education and wealth in different segments of the population

- Groups within society can be classified according to class or strata.

- For the marketer, it is not always the actual social class an individual belongs to that is significant but rather the class they identify with or aspire to.

- Class and class aspirations are important, since shared values, attitudes and behaviour will be reflected in purchasing preferences. This forms one of the most widely used methods of segmenting markets.

- It is important for marketers to consider the aspirations of their target audiences.

- The JICNAR National Readership Survey's social grade definition below is widely used by marketers.

Table 6.2   National Readership Survey (JICNAR) classification system

Social class category	Occupation
A (upper middle class)	Professional, administrative, top management (eg directors, barristers)
B (middle class)	Intermediate professional, managerial (eg marketing manager, lecturer)
C1 (lower middle class)	Supervisory, clerical and lower management (eg foremen, retail managers)
C2 (skilled working class)	Skilled manual (eg electricians and mechanics)
D (working class)	Semi- and unskilled manual (eg machine operators, cleaners, customer service assistants)
E (lowest level of subsistence)	State pensioners, long-term unemployed and so on

ACTIVITY 6.4

Critically appraise the usefulness of the above classification system.

Is there a more appropriate approach to segmenting socio-economic groups?

Is buying behaviour of a consumer more related to his or her income level or to the social class to which he or she aspires?

4 The social and cultural environment

Culture is a concept which denotes the beliefs, values, rituals, artefacts and habitual ways of behaving which are shared by a group of people (nation, religion, class, organisation etc). It embraces the following aspects of social life:

- **Beliefs and values:** Beliefs are what we feel to be the case on the basis of objective and subjective information. Values are beliefs that are enduring, general and accepted as a guide to culturally appropriate behaviour. They shape attitudes and so create tendencies for individuals and societies to behave in certain ways.

- **Customs:** Customs are modes of behaviour which represent culturally accepted ways of behaving in response to given situations. For example monogamy is a customer that is a strong custom is many societies but not all societies.

- **Artefacts:** They physical evidence that represents our culture such as flags, logos, buildings and symbols.

- **Rituals:** The activities in our societies that represent our cultures such as marriage ceremonies, graduation ceremonies and major sporting events.

Sub-culture groups exist within a society and they will share certain beliefs, values, customs, artefacts and rituals:

- **Class:** People from different social classes might have different values reflecting their position in society. These values might relate to attitudes to work, value of education, dress and relationships across the classes.

- **Ethnic background:** Social trends make a distinction between white ethnic groups and all others (although within white groups there are also many ethnic minorities). Even though most people from minority ethnic backgrounds may have been born in the home country, they can still be considered to be (or prefer to be considered as) a distinct cultural group.

- **Religion:** Religion and ethnicity may be related, for example, most Muslims in the UK come from Pakistan, Bangladesh or Africa. Values and lifestyles are affected by religions (eg the prohibition of eating certain foods). Religious beliefs are protected by UK law (eg Equality Act 2010).

- **Geography or region:** Even in a small country such as England there are distinct regional differences. Speech accents vary but there are also perceived variations in personality, lifestyle, eating and drinking habits between north and south or the east and west. Across the UK the distinctiveness increases with the powerful geographic identities of Scotland, Wales and Northern Ireland.

- **Age:** Age sub-cultures can be influenced by all other sub-cultures to a degree. Each individual progresses through teen or youth sub-cultures, which are the most strongly bonded and identifiable group. The elderly are another distinct sub-culture.

- **Gender:** There are some sub-cultures related to gender, for example the strength of women's friendship groups, as evidenced by the growth in popularity of women's book groups. The homosexual community also might be considered as a sub-culture in its own right.

- **Work:** Different organisations have different corporate cultures, in that the shared values of one workplace may be different from another in the same industry.

The exclusivity of sub-cultures should not be exaggerated, since each consumer is simultaneously a member of many sub-cultural segments and these will form part of their individual set of values, beliefs, customs, artefacts and rituals.

The Chartered Institute of Marketing

4.1 Cultural awareness in marketing

Understanding culture is particularly important to cross-cultural management and marketing in global organisations. Marketers must recognise that:

- Culture is reflected in what people eat, how and where they live, their lifestyles, buying preferences, mannerism, humour, art, religion and music.

  The international marketer must also be aware of diverse social mores.

- The marketer should recognise that while many social mores and customs are deeply rooted, others are in the process of change.

- The following have had particular significance to the marketing environment:
  - Role of women
  - Religious values
  - Healthy living and fitness trends

- Values are more generalised, deep seated and enduring. For example, 'greens are good for you' may be a belief, but vegetarianism a more deep seated value.

- Products can acquire cultural meaning through the marketing process. For example, designer clothes or a BMW could be said to be brands that represent an achiever's lifestyle.

THE REAL WORLD

The worldwide Islamic finance industry is estimated to be worth $750 billion. However, for the marketer of financial services in the United Kingdom, the 2 million plus Muslim population represents a challenging segment. Sharia law forbids riba or usury, making both saving and borrowing difficult. Sharia-compliant Ijara mortgages have to be based on sale and leaseback arrangements while Sharia-compliant savings accounts like that of the Islamic Bank may be operated where the interest is expressed as a share of the bank's profit or given to charity. Credit cards are considered acceptable as long as the monthly balance is cleared thereby avoiding any interest payment. Share dealing is acceptable but not speculation. Permitted investments necessarily exclude shares deriving income from pork products, alcohol and gambling for instance as these activities and products are forbidden by the Islamic religion.

Figure 6.1   Elements of cultural difference

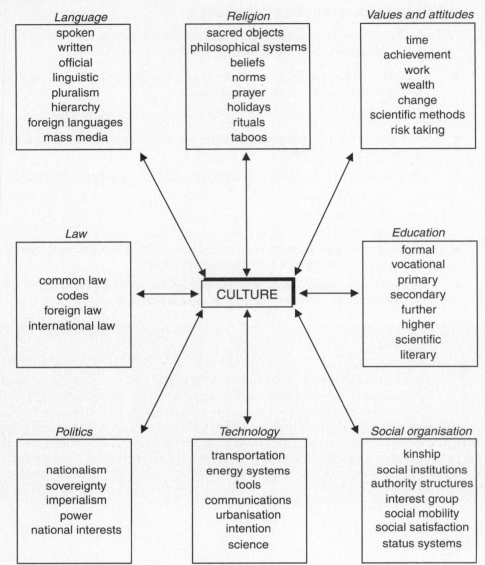

4.2 Reference groups

- The actions and behaviour of a reference group influence the attitudes, behaviour and values of large numbers of others who seek to imitate them.

- They include:

    - The family
    - Student peer group
    - Work colleagues
    - Club members
    - Online peers

- Opinion formers or leaders have substantial influence over what is and is not acceptable. Opinion followers usually follow the lead of opinion leaders.

- Marketers must identify the relevant reference groups in the segments they have targeted. This is required especially where expensive purchases (relative to the group's income) involving conspicuous consumption are concerned.

The Chartered
Institute of Marketing

4.3 The power of the consumer

Do people consume more than they used to?

The first definition of consumerism relates to the global trend of increasing consumption. Behind this trend, however, lies significant disparity between the world's wealthy and the world's poor. The World Bank (cited in Global Issues, 2011) estimates that the world's richest 20% consume more than three quarters of all goods and services.

Do people complain more than they used to?

The second definition of consumerism relates to consumers' sense of control over the organisation and the transaction. The growth of consumer protection legislation and organisations has in part led to this change in customer attitudes and expectations. The explosion in user-generated content online (where the customer's views are publicised to other customers and potential customers) has fuelled the power of the consumer to praise and to berate.

State funded higher education may be seen as a privilege but as the UK introduces annual fees of up to £9,000 a year, are students taking a consumerism approach to their investment, demanding value for money and return on investment?

THE REAL WORLD

Lives are being shaped by immense changes in technology (more of this in Chapter 9) and consumers' reference groups now include complete strangers in the same markets as they are increasingly sharing product reviews and holding conversations online. Industries and markets will vary but marketers need to be very aware of the threats and opportunities posed by consumers' reliance on the views of other product or service users. With 50 million users a month, TripAdvisor (2012) is a travel website hosting 60 million reviews and opinions about hotels, restaurants and destinations. We always knew the power of word of mouth, but now consumers can much more easily access the views of huge numbers of other customers for a wide range of products including travel, book, electronics and even medical professionals. Marketers need to be a part of these online conversations – dealing with negative reviews, encouraging positive reviews and opening conversations, for example, food companies inviting suggestions for new flavours, or politicians and journalists inviting views on issues.

5 Health

There have been significant changes in the UK in attitudes to diet and health. Most obvious have been a decrease in smoking, concern about obesity (particularly in children) and an increased interest in alternative and complementary medicines.

In addition, concern over pesticides and other chemicals used in farming has resulted in an increase in demand for organically grown food. Other shifts in buying patterns due to health concerns have also been seen, such as the increase in demand for poultry over red meat and artificial sweeteners over sugar.

Sport is also a health issue, but has wider significance in achieving wellbeing across communities and societies. The London 2012 Olympics programme became much more than just a celebration of excellence in sport; including the cultural Olympiad, volunteering and initiatives to inspire and engage individuals and communities in sport and the national identity.

Tackling obesity

The World Health Organisation (2011) published statistics stating that obesity had doubled since 1980 and estimating that 1.5 billion adults are overweight including 500 million who are obese. Most frightening of all, they reported that 43 million children under the age of five were overweight. WHO blames this on:

- 'An increased intake of energy-dense foods that are high in fat, salt and sugars but low in vitamins, minerals and other micronutrients; and

- A decrease in physical activity due to the increasingly sedentary nature of many forms of work, changing modes of transportation, and increasing urbanisation.'

In response to intense lobbying, the UK government introduced regulations banning junk food adverts during peak children viewing times in 2009. The traffic light food-labelling system that makes clear which products are unhealthy has also been implemented. However, instead of adopting the unified FSA guidelines for the traffic light system, different supermarkets have adopted their own traffic-light colour codes leading to some confusion amongst consumers.

Change4Life was 'England's first ever social marketing campaign' (Department of Health, 2012) aimed at encouraging the population to eat more healthily and exercise more. Backed by national TV campaigns, health agencies used the brand along with supporting research, guidance and toolkits to try to drive home the messages but, despite the investment and the bold communications, it seems that the campaign has not made much of a dent in this devastating trend.

Surely food producers are trying to encourage healthy eating? Kellogg's low sugar version of Frosties didn't last long on the supermarket shelves and in India Pepsi Max, Pepsi's sugar free cola, sank without out trace less than a year after launching (Economic Times, 2011).

Similarly, Burts crisps developed a lower-fat crisp which was warmly welcomed by parents and by the health authorities but…children hated them and they too disappeared from supermarket shelves.

6 Lifestyle

Lifestyle is the way in which people live in terms of attitudes, preferences, interests and aspirations. It is a manifestation of a number of behavioural factors such as motivation, personality and culture. When the numbers of people sharing lifestyle characteristics are quantified, markets can target products and promotions to the identified lifestyle segment.

- These are defined as the patterns in which people live, spend time and money.
- They are mainly a function of the individual's motivation, prior learning, class and personality.
- They are measured by analysts, using **attitude, interests** and **opinions** alongside demographic factors to establish market segments with clusters of common characteristics.
- The central idea is to identify behavioural patterns to build a picture of how individuals interact with their environment.
    - This allows marketers to segment the market more effectively and tailor campaigns designed to appeal to particular lifestyle types.
    - Different groups will respond to different marketing messages.
    - Marketers must avoid oversimplified categorisation. Individuals may exhibit multiple lifestyle characteristics or evolve from one type to another as time and circumstances alter.

6.1 Green movement

The green movement has become part of many lifestyle segments. Companies segment some market clients according to whether they are pale or dark green in their attitude to the environment and therefore how significantly environmentally friendly product attributes will influence the purchasing decision.

The Chartered Institute of Marketing

6.2 Lifestyle segmentation

Lifestyle segmentation attempts to discover the particular unique lifestyle patterns of customers, which will give an insight into their preferences for various products and services. Strategists who use this segmentation will be better able to direct their marketing energies to meet the future needs of groups identified. Technology and Customer Relationship Marketing have driven lifestyle segmentation forward, for example, Amazon's processes that enable them to advise 'customers that bought this also bought...'

6.3 Lifestyle trends

Table 6.3   Lifestyle trends and their implications

Trend	Implication
Instant gratification	Live now – pay later
Easy credit attitudes	To finance the good life now!
Time conservation	Critical resource constraint on consumption
New work ethic	Working to live, not living to work
Consumerism	Concern for price/quality/service/environment
Personal creativity	Desire for self-expression/improvement
Naturalism	Return to nature but retaining material comforts

An understanding of demography and socio-cultural change is vital if the marketer is to truly appreciate the origins of buyer behaviour. Even though these are unquestionably uncontrollable by marketers, their appreciation is essential. Both evolve very slowly but their cumulative impact on market realities over time is considerable. Real living standards in the longer term are more likely to be determined by population changes for instance than the economic policy-making of governments.

Change in this environment is the most difficult to assess, yet the opportunities it offers must be grasped and exploited by the marketer. The relevant variables are usually interrelated. Therefore, it is often difficult for marketers to assess and understand the contribution of any one element. As most of this is unspoken and unwritten, it poses in actual fact one of the greatest challenges to the marketing practitioner.

7 Geodemographic segmentation

Geodemographic segmentation is based on **neighbourhood and type of dwelling.**

- As a composite index of factors relevant to buying behaviour, this is thought to represent a more accurate assessment than those based solely on one factor such as class or income.

- A well-used example of this approach is the ACORN system (ie A Classification of Residential Neighbourhoods), which classifies households into one of five categories, 17 major groups and 56 specific neighbourhood types and is used by companies such as IKEA, the Swedish furniture retailer, to analyse its customer base.

The data then describes the residents of each neighbourhood in terms of their spending habits, interests, media used, health education etc. Over 400 variables are analysed.

- Other examples of such databases include PIN (Pinpoint Identified Neighbourhoods) and MOSAIC.

- Organisations across the public and private sectors use these segmentation systems to carefully and segments for existing customers and also to reach potential new customers.

For example:

ACORN's Category 3 is labelled 'Comfortably Off' and includes young couples 'starting out', 'secure families', 'settled suburbia' and 'prudent pensioners'. The 'starting out' data tells us for example that this segment has a higher propensity to go the cinema but a lower propensity to buy *The Telegraph* or *The Times*. Details of ACORN can be found at http://www.caci.co.uk.

- It is important for marketers to monitor and understand the implications of demographic changes.

  - Demographic changes occur slowly over time but their cumulative impact over a period can have great consequences for buying patterns.

  - Demography can help marketers predict size and change in target markets by population, age, gender, region, family size or ethnic group.

  - The scope for demographic segmentation is considerable and is a means of adapting marketing approaches and product offerings to match changing needs at the different stages of life.

- Employment trends can and do influence the need for greater business flexibility.

  - Consumer markets can be segmented through geographic factors, lifestyles and demographics (age, gender, race, nationality and religion; income and education; family size and life cycle; occupation and social class).

- The significance of social influences (ie class, occupation, lifestyle, reference groups) can be used as bases for segmentation.

- Geodemographic segmentation is based on **neighbourhood and type of dwelling**.

  - Culture is a complex blend of acquired values, beliefs, attitudes, customs that provide context, conditioning and behavioural guidelines in society.

  - The marketer must recognise the degree to which purchasing behaviour is culturally driven.

- Marketers should take care in classifying people into different groups/segments for marketing purposes, since many of the behavioural assumptions are generalisations and subject to change.

- If it is an individual's perceptions and aspirations that drive purchasing decisions, rather than their objectively defined status, then prediction is much more hazardous.

FURTHER READING

Palmer, A. (2009) *Introduction to marketing: theory and practice.* 2nd edition. Oxford, Oxford University Press, Chapter 6.

Palmer, A. and Hartley, B. (2012) *The business environment.* 12th edition. Maidenhead, McGraw-Hill, Chapter 3.

Worthington, I. and Britton, C. (2009) *The business environment.* 6th edition. Harlow, Pearson, Chapter 6.

Websites:

http://unstats.un.org for UN population data

http://www.worldbank.org for World Bank population data

http://data.gov.uk – government data

http://www.ons.gov.uk – Office of National Statistics

http://www.caci.co.uk – Operators of A Classification of Residential Neighbourhoods

The Chartered Institute of Marketing

http://www.geodemographics.org.uk – the census and geodemographics group of the Market Research Society and links to many other sources

http://www.experian.co.uk – operators of Mosaic geodemographic database

REFERENCES

Anon (2011) A tale of three islands. The Economist. http://www.economist.com/node/21533364 [Accessed on 24 February 2012].

Economic times (2011) Newsby Industry. http://articles.economictimes.indiatimes.com/2011-07-11/news/29761133_1_pepsi-max-sugar-free-fat-free-food [Accessed on 17 May 2012].

Global Issues (2011) Consumption and Consumerism. http://www.globalissues.org/issue/235/consumption-and-consumerism [Accessed on 23 May 2012]

TripAdvisor (2012) About TripAdvisor. http://www.tripadvisor.com/pages/about_us.html [Accessed on 25 February 2012].

World Health Organisation (2011) Obesity and overweight. http://www.who.int/mediacentre/factsheets/fs311/en/index.html [Accessed on 25 February 2012].

QUICK QUIZ

1   What is the meaning of the term 'natural increase in population'?

2   Fill in the blank. _____ is the sum total of the beliefs, knowledge, attitudes of mind and customs to which people are exposed in their social conditioning.

3   What is the JICNAR social classification?

4   What is an empty nester?

5   Which of the following are lifestyle categories?

    A   Upwardly mobile and ambitious

    B   Environmentally aware

    C   Affluent grey

    D   Intermediate non-manual

6   Who produces *Social Trends*?

7   Describe the term 'geodemographic database'.

ACTIVITY DEBRIEFS

Activity 6.1

The ONS sources have a great depth of information on UK social and demographic trends. If analysing the UK, key points might include:

- 61.8 million population, an increase of 23.6m since the start of the 20th century with changes in birth and death rates as the key driver.

- The most common country of last residence for long term immigrants in 2009 was India.

- The average age of the UK population has increased from 36 in 1992 to 40 in 2009.

- There is an upward trend in employment rates for women.

- 70% of UK the population (15-64) is in employment against the EU average of 64%.

Activity 6.2

Your answer will depend upon the advertisements reviewed. Consider the words and images used, the core messages and the relevance of the media to specific life stages.

Activity 6.3

(a)   The strain on pensions and healthcare has been the one of the biggest challenges facing the UK government since the turn of the century. It has impacted on a wide range of service delivery areas as well as policies, such as the abolition of compulsory retirement at 65.

(b)   Quality, service, value for money and greater durability. Over-60s, having planned financially for retirement will have the income to renew household effects after child rearing and will look for design, not functionality.

Activity 6.4

- Classes tend to have distinct/symbolic/recognisable product and brand preferences but this classification is based solely on occupation and ignores the fact that changing wage relativities have altered comparative purchasing power.

  - Some C2s are better off than many C1s and Bs, for example, and this is reflected in purchases.
  - Some may not fit the classification (eg if living on inherited wealth).

- An alternative classification would be to define the households concerned in terms of source and size of income, place of residence, type of work, core attitudes and so forth.

QUICK QUIZ ANSWERS

1   Birth rate minus death rate

2   Culture

3   ABC1C2DE – resulting from the National Readership Survey

4   Middle-aged person whose children have grown up and left home

5   A and B – these are examples of a person's views and aspirations. C and D are objective categories which could be used as social class definitions.

6   Office of National Statistics

7   Databases that describe people by where they live.

The Chartered Institute of Marketing

CHAPTER 7

The economic and international environment

Introduction

Recent years have made many organisations and economies across the globe aware of the vulnerability of their economies. Not everything is predictable but marketers must understand the basic working of the economy and how to evaluate measures of economic activity. These are the macroeconomic conditions over which the organisation has no control but that have significant implications for businesses. It is no longer enough to view conditions in national markets as globalisation is increasingly shaping economic conditions.

Topic list

Key macroeconomic concepts	1
Economic measures	2
The business cycle	3
Government economic objectives	4
The impact of international trade	5
Implications of economic factors for marketers	6

3.4	Explain the economic environments within an international context and, in general terms, their influence on and implications for marketing, including consideration of:

- Interest rates
- Exchange rates
- GDP
- GNP
- Effects of demand and supply
- Economic growth and unemployment
- The effect of changing economies eg,
  - The single European Market (EU)
  - Market driven economies in Eastern European
- European Monetary Union
- Business cycle

▶ **Exam tip**

The economic environment is one area where we can all have first-hand experience. The basic concepts of all syllabus areas will be outlined in this Study Text but you must read more widely to be able to evaluate, with confidence, their impacts on the marketing environment. For all macro environmental elements you should also be aware of current news in relevant national and international quality and business press. However, of all the macro environmental elements, it is the economic environment that will be most volatile so you should be aware of the key economic measures described in this chapter. It is also important that you have a clear appreciation of your country's international trade position. Is its balance of payments in surplus or deficit? What is its pattern of trade with other countries and the composition of its imports and exports? Does your country belong to a trading bloc? If so, what regulations govern its internal and external relationships?

Exam questions on the macroeconomic environment are frequently set to test your knowledge and understanding of current economic conditions. Accordingly, you should keep yourself informed about changes in growth, employment, inflation, the balance of payments and even more importantly about the effects of these factors on businesses, the marketing environment and marketers. You should also prepare for this when you are given the case study in advance for your exam. Reflect upon which of these economic dimensions are relevant to the case study.

1 Key macroeconomic concepts

Macroeconomics is the aggregate behaviour of consumers, businesses and governments within and between the world's economies.

- Concern is with general price level rather than individual product prices.

- Attention focuses on total output, income and spending.

- The rate of economic growth and cyclical fluctuations are of central importance to businesses. Unanticipated movements in interest or exchange rates can convert expected profit into crippling loss.

The circular flow of income (concept 1) and the multiplier effect (concept 2) are two macroeconomic dimensions, which are significant to the economic environment.

1.1 The circular flow of income (concept 1)

- This is a simple model for understanding the workings of the economy.

- Flows between households and businesses, banks, foreigners and governments are either incomes or expenditures and circulate around the economic system. Figure 7.1 displays how households receive a flow of goods and services from firms. It also shows how households receive income from firms who employ them to produce goods and services.

- Economic activity is like a circulating flow of spending power.

- Households pay taxes on income and expenditure. Government spending and exports are injections of purchasing power into the flow, creating demand for domestic firms.

- In reality, there is also an element of saving and this creates leakage (concept 3).

- Unless any leakage is re-channelled into the circular flow, the level of the flow will fall because of lower demand for products and services.

- Equilibrium is achieved by companies responding to excess demand by producing more and vice versa.

Figure 7.1   The circular flow of economic activity

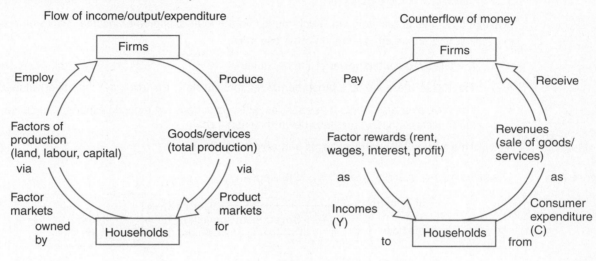

> **Exam tip**
>
> With regard to this syllabus, although all aspects of the environment need to be considered, only an appreciation of economics is expected. Accordingly, you will not be expected to reproduce a detailed analysis. However an understanding is important.

1.2 The multiplier effect (concept 2)

The multiplier effect involves the process of the circulation of income in the national economy, whereby an injection of money leads to a much larger increase in national income. The initial increase has a snowball effect; more jobs are created and these employees spend their earnings, generating more demand and more jobs.

An extra injection from the government or other investment may increase the level of income in the flow by more than the initial expenditure. The injection creates demand for extra output and this in turn requires businesses to employ more resources if available.

- Extra output generates new incomes which are paid to households.

- Households receiving this income pay taxes, buy imports and save, but the rest is spent on domestic consumer goods and services at the second round of the process.

- As affected businesses produce more output to meet this demand, more resources are brought into the equation.

- The resulting incomes are paid out to households, and the process is repeated.

Identify examples of government related spending that could be projected to generate a multiplier effect, resulting in a greater increase in economic activity.

1.3 Leakage (concept 3)

Leakage describes the situation in which money, in the form of capital or income, leaves an economy. For example where profits are diverted to other countries.

- Leakages reduce the power of the multiplier

- The higher these are as a proportion of the circular flow, the lower the multiplier value and vice versa.

- The multiplier also works in reverse, as falling injections (eg reduced exports) can cause a cumulative fall in income, output and jobs down the supply chain.

- This in turn will create leakages and perpetuate the flow.

Figure 7.2   The full-economy model of injections and leakages

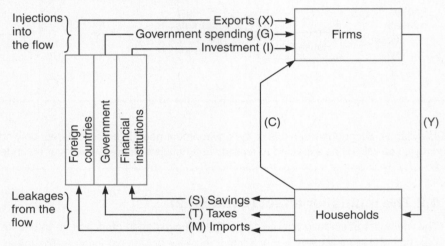

London 2012 Olympic Games

Olympic Games through the 20th and now the 21st century can appear to be an exercise in throwing money into the crowd, as host cities and countries endeavour to stage the 'best ever' games. Many of the venues used for the Athens games are now neglected and underused. Are Greece's current economic problems rooted in the bill of £11bn for the 2004 games; a bill that represented 5% of Greece's GDP?

China invested an estimated $40bn of public money in the 2008 games and as the memories fade the economic impacts will still be the subject of analysis and argument. Host cities will often exaggerate economic benefits and the task of ensuring that a positive legacy of public infrastructure and positive brand awareness can be neglected once the closing ceremony ends.

The Telegraph (2012) reported that '£9.3bn spent on constructing and hosting the London Games is a Keynesian-style boost for the economy. 98pc of the facilities for the Olympics have been built by British companies through contracts worth £6bn. The £300m already spent on tickets also means the economy is guaranteed to grow by 0.1pc during London 2012, while surveys say international visitors will spend around £700m'. However critics stated that the negative impact would be felt by absenteeism, lost productivity as a result of transport problems in London and even a 'stay-away' ethos that could hit tourism.

The UK's international tourism agency, VisitBritain, has set an objective of attracting an additional 4.6 million visitors who would account for additional tourism spend of £2.3 billion. However, this is achieved in the years from 2012 through until 2014 as the impacts should be felt long after 2012 itself. (VisitBritain, 2012)

The legacy of the games has always been hotly discussed and, as the dust settles, the number crunchers will do their sums and reveal the final costs – and estimates of benefits – to the UK's economy.

2 Economic measures

2.1 Gross domestic product (GDP)

▸ **Key terms**

Gross domestic product (GDP) is a measure of the total value of goods and services produced in an economy in a given period. It is the most commonly used measure of the economic activity of a country.

Gross national product (GNP) is the same measure but with the inclusion of 'net income from abroad'. In stable economic times the GDP of western economies might grow at a rate of around 2-3% per annum. Emerging economies such as China and Brazil have enjoyed growth rates approaching 10% per annum.

Gross value added (GVA) is a term also used by the Office of National Statistics. GVA measures the contribution to the economy of individual producers, sectors or industries and, with adjustments for taxation and subsidies, is used to estimate GDP.

The circular flow represents the value of goods and services produced in an economy. This is measured annually in three ways:

1   National income (created from producing the output, ie wages, rent, profit)

2   National output (sum of final output or the value added by each domestic firm)

3   National expenditure (aggregate spending on national output)

Healthy economies traditionally aim for growth in GDP and across the world in recent years growth targets have been missed as many countries entered recession. The International Monetary Fund's June 2011 World Economic Outlook Update projected growth in 2012 of an average of 2.6% in advanced economies but a growth of 6.4% in emerging economies (including Brazil, Russia, India and China). China was, for a second year, predicted to have the highest growth in the world in 2012 of 9.5%.

The cyclical nature of GDP growth is discussed in section 3 of this chapter.

In fact GDP is just one measure of economic activity. Other measures include:

■   Unemployment rates – unemployment tends to rise as economies enter recessionary periods.

■   Output levels of firms as published by the government and by business organisations such as the Confederation of British Industry (CBI).

■   Average earnings – reductions in working hours and pay freezes or even pay cuts have also had a negative impact on average earnings in the current economic downturn.

■   Disposable income – this is a critical measure for marketers to understand as it measures net income after taxation.

■   Confidence levels – again these are measured regularly by the CBI but many industries attempt to measure confidence levels. Key survey questions might include asking if organisations anticipate the coming period to be better, tougher or the same as the last period. Confidence can be shaped just as much by upbeat news or consumer confidence as it can by hard internal performance measures.

■   Inflation – this can guide negotiations on prices, wage levels and also the costs of public services.

■   Interest rates – these are normally lower in recessionary times and higher in boom times, as the national and global supply and demand for money fluctuates.

- Government borrowing – lower levels of economic activity will tend to cause taxation income to fall and the burden on the public purse to rise. The government then borrows to cover the shortfall and so this is a clear measure of economic activity within an economy.

2.2 Inflation

▶ **Key term**

Disposable income: technical definitions describe disposable income as the individual's net income after taxation. However a more commonly used interpretation is the income available for discretionary spending once allowances have been made for non-discretionary items such as food, housing and energy.

Inflation is a general increase in the average price level as sustained over a period of time. It is usually calculated by changes in the consumer price index (CPI). The consumer price index (CPI) is measured by a basket of representative products and services typically used by the average household, with products and services are weighted according to their importance in total spending.

In some countries, a distinction is made between the so-called 'headline rate' and the 'underlying rate'.

- The headline rates include all elements of expenditure.
- The underlying rates exclude exceptional influences such as mortgage interest as these tend to inflate the index in times of rising rates.

From the late 1970s inflation and unemployment tended to rise together to unacceptable levels.

- This is considered to be very detrimental to the economy.
- This economic situation is referred to as **stagflation**.

Creeping inflation, when associated with buoyant high demand, can generate buyer confidence and business investment.

- Since borrowings are repaid in gently depreciating currency and the value of stocks appreciate, it tends to enhance profitability.

Once inflation exceeds a critical rate the costs outweigh any possible benefits. This is because of a variety of reasons such as:

- A rapid fall in the value of money affects consumer confidence.
- Uncertainty over future price levels deters companies from entering long-term contractual commitments.
- Arbitrary and unintended redistribution of income occurs as:
  - Debtors gain
  - Fixed income groups like pensioners suffer
  - Weak bargaining groups are unable to keep pace.
- Rising nominal income means higher tax brackets but tax allowances can be eroded.
- Domestic marketers face competitive imports/rising export prices affect international sales.
- Frequent price rises upset customers.
- Prices no longer accurately reflect 'relative' values. Consequently, the consumer is confused and increasingly price sensitive.
- Investment moves to 'unproductive' inflationary hedges such as gold, antiques, property.
- Wage groups fight for income shares hence can strike or complain.
- Price wars due to misinterpretation of rival intentions could be triggered.

Marketers must be aware of the significance of inflation within economic cycles.

- As inflation accelerates, so governments will be forced to drastically reduce demand pressures to restore stability.

The Chartered Institute of Marketing

- Attempting to overcome inflation, with limitations on spending, is often worse in its effects than the inflation itself.

- Zero inflationary expectations also challenge marketers due to their effect on cost increases.

2.2.1 The causes of inflation

Marketers need to appreciate the causes of inflation in order for them to be able to conduct an assessment of the likely future path of general prices. The sources of inflationary pressure may originate from the supply as well as from the demand side of an economy. Three scenarios may occur:

- Demand-pull inflation. Demand exceeds ability to supply, prices rise and costs of production also rise as factors of production, such as wage costs, also inflate.

- Monetarist inflation. Attempts to manage inflation through management of the monetary supply by central banks.

- Cost-push inflation. Price rises are driven by increases in costs of inputs eg rises in the price of fuel and raw materials.

When inflation becomes rapid and uncertain it creates net costs for business and society.

- This poses difficult marketing mix problems for the marketer, especially those serving segments most seriously affected.

- In the extreme, **hyperinflation**, defined as price rises in excess of 50% per month, causes all confidence to be lost in paper money and barter re-emerges.

2.3 Balance of payments

> ▶ **Key term**
>
> **Balance of payments:**
>
> Balance of Payment (BOP) compares the value difference between imports and exports for a country. A negative BOP means that there is more money flowing out of the country than coming in. A positive BOP means that there is more coming in than flowing out.

The balance of payments is the systematic annual record of all exchange transactions between the residents of one country and the rest of the world. Exchange transactions include:

- A **visible** balance of trade
  - This is made up of foods/fuels/materials/semi-manufactured/finished products.

- An **invisible** balance of trade
  - This is made up of financial/travel/other services, government transfers, net earnings.

The balance of payments is not a desirable objective in itself, but rather, as a deficit worsens, it will become a tightening constraint on the government's ability to achieve other macroeconomic objectives.

2.4 The uses of national accounting data

In the United Kingdom the ONS collects and publishes economic performance data in the Blue Book. It includes estimates of GDP based on an analysis of estimates of income, expenditure and production.

This information provides the basis for forecasts and analyses of the current state of the economy. Care is required when assessing the potential of overseas markets using national income data as different countries have different values, tastes, needs and proportions spent on specific purposes.

2.4.1 The true value of data

- GDP data is normally expressed in nominal or current prices terms.

- Even if the calculations were entirely accurate, problems could still remain with regard to statistical information and the interpretation.

- GDP is no longer the undisputed measure of economic progress.

If GDP is going up by 3% and the size of the population remains the same it stands that individuals will be 3% better off. Even by adjusting to current price values, this measure does not successfully evaluate a society's sense of wellbeing.

2.4.2 Sources of information

The key source of economic data in the UK is the Office of National Statistics; their website has over 5,000 pages/articles/documents about the economy. Key data includes:

- Public sector finance
- Taxation and revenues
- Balance of payments
- GDP from income, expenditure and outputs
- Price indices and inflation
- Personal wealth and pensions
- Data analysed for regions and for sectors

All nations will have an equivalent data gathering and publishing organisation. In addition to this there are global and regional organisations with data covering international trade. Some of these are detailed in the further reading section of this chapter and the key sources are:

- World Bank
- World Trade Organisation
- Eurostat
- International Monetary Fund

Commercial sources include *The Financial Times* and *The Economist* as well as equivalent financial press from across the world.

3 The business cycle

▶ **Key terms**

Business cycle

'Also known as the economic cycle. The period of time during which an economy moves from a state of expansion to a state of contraction, before expanding again. A cycle can last anywhere between two and 50 years depending on which economic theory one adheres to. In practice, a cycle should contain a phase of expansion or recovery (to a peak) and a phase of slowdown or recession (to a trough). If the rates of growth and contraction are very strong, an economy could be 'booming' for a while at its peak, while the trough could see a phase of depression or stagnation. A trend governed by a business or economic cycle is termed cyclical.' (Financial Times Lexicon, 2012)

Recession

Despite tough economic conditions over a period of recent years the definition of **recession** tells us that the UK was not in recession during 2010 and 2011. Recession is defined as two consecutive quarters of a fall in GDP. This was last experienced by the UK in 2008/9. Through recent years there has been considerable reference to the credit crisis as if it were the same as recession. The credit crisis undoubtedly contributed to the recession but the term refers to the drying up of international and interbank lending.

The business cycle refers to the periodic fluctuation in economic activity that occurs in industrialised economies. Economies are rarely stable and tend to oscillate between periods of high activity, growth in employment and booming confidence, and periods of falling output, rising unemployment and general despondency.

Countries with low export and import ratios tend to have more stable economies. They are however not completely protected from adverse economic factors.

The business cycle represents the **average** of a multitude of individual industry cycles. Any one business may therefore be in advance of or lag behind the main cycle. Consequently, the marketer of a company must locate their own relative position since the published data always refers to the average. The duration of the cycle is also a variable. Up to 1945, it averaged 8–9 years in open economies while a less-consistent pattern has prevailed since.

The downturn can be a steep curve as was witnessed by many global economies in 2008. The challenge for economists is to use the business cycle not just to record past economic activity but to forecast future economic performance.

Figure 7.3   The stages of the business cycle

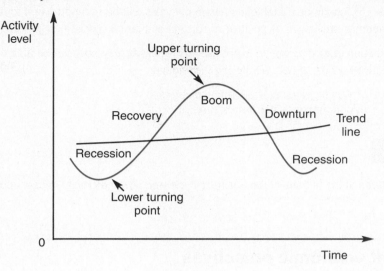

3.1 Recession

- Recession is defined as at least two successive quarters of **falling** GDP.
- Continued and deep recession becomes a depression.
- This is a difficult time for marketers.
- Consumption spending falls, competitive forces intensify.
- Profitability falls during any recession.
- Business confidence is usually low and any investment is reduced.
- The severity and duration of the phases vary from cycle to cycle.
- The marketer must anticipate fluctuating economic conditions.
- Recovery starts from lower turning point

  - Investment picks up.
  - Jobs are created and employment rises.
  - Consumer spending rises and business confidence begins to grow.
  - Prices are stable or rising slowly and profits also being to rise.
  - Income, output and expenditure rise at an increasing rate.
  - New investment planned as confidence recovers.
  - Inflation remains low as increased utilisation of capacity occurs.

3.2 Boom

- Starts from upper turning point.
- Consumer spending rises fast.
- Momentum through multiplier-accelerator.
- Outputs rise and firms may face capacity and resource problems.
- Increasing demand stimulates price rises (inflation).
- Interest rates rise sharply.
- Productivity is the only source of higher output.
- Business profits are high.
- Imports are sucked in.

3.3 Downturn

- Confidence and spending fall.
- Precautionary savings rise.
- Investment becomes unprofitable.
- Business failures rise and cutbacks multiply.

The upper and lower turning points are the key moments to identify as they signal a significant 'sea change' in economic conditions. Marketers aware of cycles will be more prepared to deal with the changes. Cycles can sometimes be viewed as positive opportunities that can assist new product launches and market penetration.

Prediction of turning points is not easy. Businesses may however be able to judge developments more effectively by using two monitoring techniques.

- Following leading economic indicators
- Monitoring industry trends surveys

ACTIVITY 7.2

Identify the key features of the phases of the business cycle and how they might impact upon marketers.

4 Government economic objectives

Wide fluctuations in levels of economic activity may be damaging to the overall economic wellbeing of society. The uncertainty and speculation which accompanies the cycle may be inequitable in their impact on different sections of the population, while the bottom of the cycle may bring high unemployment.

Sustainable economic growth and development is a fundamental objective because a growing economy allows a government to achieve many goals.

- Through economic growth and development, resources can be acquired.

- Growth does not always mean rising consumption.

- Poorer countries are more concerned with economic development involving a transformation of economy from one based on primary production to one based on manufacturing, services and information technology. This usually requires external funds to finance the dramatic improvements required in both the skill base and basic infrastructure.

However, governments tend to also have three other significant objectives:

- To maintain higher levels of employment or real jobs
- To control inflation
- To achieve a favourable balance of payments averaged over a period

Subsidiary goals might include:

- To keep the aggregate tax burden below 40% of GDP
- To achieve a balanced regional development
- To achieve sustainable resource conservation and respond to environmental concerns. For example, target to reduce carbon emissions by 60% by 2050.

The Chartered
Institute of Marketing

Greece

Technological advances and the culture of sharing information means it is no great surprise to find a website entitled 'Greek Crisis' a 'blog dedicated to the understanding of the current Greek (but also European) economic, political and institutional crisis' (Greek Crisis, 2012). Created by academics at the University of Athens the site describes Greece's debt as a percentage of GDP (165%), the size of its un-taxed 'shadow economy' (24% of GDP) and the percentage of the workforce employed in the public sector (9.4%). In February 2012 the Greek government approved a package of austerity measures in the face of significant social unrest.

Unemployment is often referred to as a social and economic drawback which can and does impact negatively on businesses. The seeming inability of many governments to achieve permanently lower unemployment and their acceptance of a certain unemployment rate as being unavoidable can be a reflection of a number of factors. These include:

- A rapid rate of technological change and the adoption of new and digital technologies to automate production methods, rationalise distribution channels and automate sales and customer service processes

- Customer orientation, changing tastes, intense competition and shortening life cycles cause rapid structural change that some find difficult to adjust to

- Inflow onto the job market exceeding outflow as married women's and foreign workers' participation rises

- Acceptance of a natural unemployment rate that is consistent with low and stable inflation

- A more turbulent environment, which makes business focus on job flexibility rather than job security

ACTIVITY 7.3

Assess the positive and negative economic impacts of a multinational company transferring its operations to a lower-wage economy (ie Indonesia, Bangladesh, China).

4.1 Economic indicators

- Governments use a wide range of economic indicators to decide on policy changes.

- Governments also use a range of methods to monitor their effectiveness.

  - Stock markets react quite strongly when publication of such figures diverges from expectations.
  - These indices are equally important for businesses in determining future marketing plans.

Key economic indicators to monitor include the following:

- Activity, growth and unemployment rates
- Inflation and interest rates
- Trade figures and exchange rates

5 The impact of international trade

The majority of countries are open systems and must deal with the realities of the international environment. Some economies, such United States of America, are so large that the domestic economy is the dominant

influence. Most are like the United Kingdom and are export-orientated and thus always susceptible to outside shocks.

Several factors encourage many countries in their eagerness to expand their international exposure. These factors include the following:

- World trade brings diversity of choice.

- National differences in culture, human skills, resource availability, ingenuity and technology lead to product, cost and price differences.

- A global market rewards specialisation and allows the exploitation of comparative advantage.

- International trade curbs monopoly power, increases competition, lowers prices.

- World markets offer scope for economies of scale and can significantly reduce costs.

- Access to world markets spreads risks and can counterbalance domestic activity.

- Trade or distribution networks encourage as well as enable the rapid diffusion of new ideas and inventions.

- Trade equals contact, mutual interest, cultural understanding, interdependence, co-operation.

- Liberalisation of planned economies allows integration into the world trading system.

- Growth in world trade has been continuous and offers expanding opportunities.

- Trade liberalisation agreements encouraged emerging economies to open their markets.

- The World Trade Organization (WTO), established in 1995, has a mandate to enforce world trade laws.

- Development of the internet, travel and trade links are producing a global culture. Consumers now think nothing of directly importing goods from international companies. The complex financial nature of asset-backed securities that brought about the 2008 credit crisis were managed and sold across international borders with the help of advanced technologies.

5.1 Globalisation

Globalisation is a process by which the world economy is becoming a unified interdependent system based on internationalisation of companies and the progressive lowering of trade barriers. It involves multinational businesses adopting worldwide strategies that apply the same or similar marketing mixes in all markets. A global marketing perspective implies a centrally co-ordinated plan directed towards a worldwide audience rather than the usual decentralised focus on local or regional markets.

The following are the advantages of globalisation:

- Enhanced scope for specialisation

- Enhanced scope for the standardisation of production and distribution

- Cost-effective research and development, product design and promotion

- Attractions of universal image advertising combined with the scope to adapt to suit local conditions

- Shorter new product planning cycle via learning/comparison from global experience

- Faster reaction to general customer preferences

- Superior marketing potential

- Transport cost savings

- Improved supply chain efficiency and leverage

- Direct investment gives tariff-free access to trade blocs if local content requirements are met

- Direct access increases local market knowledge and customer confidence

- Rivals derive competitive advantage out of their network of global activities

- Greater political stability: web of multinational subsidiaries and 'common' commercial interests

- Pressure on governments to conform to stable economic management as a condition for continued direct investment and a favourable reaction from global financial markets

The following are the disadvantages of globalisation:

- Cultural sensitivities force changes to global products

- Divergence in language

- Stage of economic development requires differentiation

- Concern over the American/Western cultural domination undermining national identity

- Risk of strategic dependence on multinationals whose strategy is globally not nationally driven

- Powerful companies can play one country off against another to secure incentive packages.

- Multinationals may use leverage to obtain favourable treatment and avoid profits tax via transfer pricing.

- Political tensions between the developed and developing countries

- The gap between the world's richest and poorest has doubled since 1960 suggesting an unfair trading and financial system.

- Subsidiaries may be closed for political reasons

Whilst organisations spread their activities across the world and consumers become familiar with global brands, success is sometimes dependent on careful adaptation to local tastes and cultures.

Significance of globalisation for marketers:

- The marketer must monitor a worldwide marketplace and the global environment.

- The threat of competition in domestic markets is significantly increased.

- Interdependence creates the potential for rapid communication of shocks through the system.

- Slower growth may produce protectionist responses since governments are concerned with national competitive advantage and face pressure from affected interest groups.

- Households do not want identical telephones or saloon cars.

- Manufacturers can gain competitive advantage and economies of scale by producing one main brand for an international market rather than many brands in low volumes for a purely domestic one.

- Gains from trade in this case do not necessarily derive from relative cost differences but rather from brand diversity and effective marketing.

- Entry into foreign markets requires a serious commitment. It is a strategic decision since a subsequent withdrawal due to lack of preparation would be expensive in terms of cost, brand image and credibility.

THE REAL WORLD

Jaguar Landrover (JLR) is a company with strong brands and a considerable British heritage but it is now owned by India-based multinational Tata. As global market conditions change, its success now depends on markets across the globe. Sales in China have now overtaken sales in the UK and JLR is considering establishing production in that country. This is a measure of globalisation but also a measure of the demand for premium products in China as their economy grows. This global approach has saved a company which, during the recession, turned to the government for assistance; it reported growth in sales of 21.9% during 2011 (Telegraph, 2012).

5.2 International trade agreements

Nations and businesses are increasingly vulnerable to global political and economic influences. The international environment presents the marketer not only with considerable opportunities but also with greater

challenges than the domestic market. Market decisions will be influenced by the existence and complexities of trade agreements which can be restrictive or can represent opportunities. The following are some of the popular trade blocs and organisations within the international environment:

- World Trade Organisation – formed in 1995 and replacing the General Agreement on Tarriffs and Trade (GATT). WTO has 153 nation signatories as at 2011 and together they represent 95% of world trade. It is a forum that aims to negotiate free trade by reducing restrictions and establishing fair trading rules. Signatories are not signed up to absolute free trade, however, their membership indicates an ethos in favour of free trade and against restrictive practices.

- EU – the European Union is a political and economic community of member states located primarily in Europe.

- AFTA – the ASEAN Free Trade Area is a trade bloc agreement by the Association of Southeast Asian Nations supporting local manufacturing in all ASEAN countries.

- SAARC – the South Asian Association for Regional Cooperation is an economic and political organisation of eight countries in Southern Asia. In terms of population, its sphere of influence is the largest of any regional organisation).

- NAFTA – the North American Free Trade Agreement (Spanish: Tratado de Libre Comercio de América del Norte (TLCAN)) (French: Accord de libre-échange nord-américain (ALENA)) is the trade bloc in North America created by the North American Free Trade Agreement (NAFTA) and its two supplements, the North American Agreement on Environmental Cooperation (NAAEC) and The North American Agreement on Labor Cooperation (NAALC), whose members are Canada, Mexico, and the United States.

- The Southern African Development Community (SADC) is one of several political and economic bodies representing the interests of economic development across regions within the African continent.

Figure 7.4 International influences on the organisation's domestic conditions

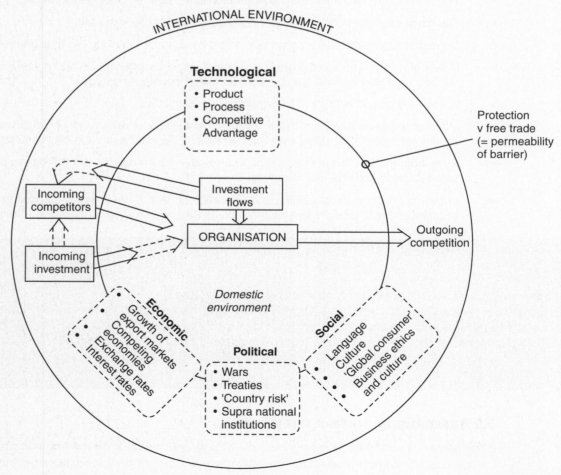

The Chartered Institute of Marketing

Match the terms with their correct definitions:

1   Tariff

2   Quota

3   Embargo

4   Non-tariff barriers

5   Terms of trade

6   Customs duty

(a)   Taxes on imported goods aimed at reducing their competitiveness with domestic equivalents

(b)   Various standards and regulations to which imports must conform

(c)   Tax imposed on imports in order to raise revenue

(d)   The index of average export prices compared to average import prices

(e)   A quantitative limit on the volume of imports per time period

(f)   Export prohibition on a particular good to certain countries, usually for political reasons

5.3 Frictions in the international environment

The powerful forces encouraging ever-greater participation in the emergent global marketplace can create conflict in international trade. These can appear arbitrary to the marketer but can be extremely damaging.

China and the United States, the two most powerful economies in the world, conduct significant levels of trade but frictions exist.

Economic analyst Wang Jisi, suggests in the New York Times (2012) that China considers the United States to be a declining power, fighting to retain its economic position. He speculates that China will be the winner in the long term, becoming the world's most powerful country.

6 Implications of economic factors for marketers

Marketers should recognise these criteria:

- Short-term and speculative capital movements can occur on a massive scale in the global economy.
- The exchange rate is an important 'price' but takes time to work through.
- The strength of reaction to a falling exchange rate may be uncertain.
- Unplanned exchange rate movements create risk.
- Currency appreciation is a serious threat to foreign sales (and domestic markets), as many international marketers have found to their cost.
    - Many governments prefer to aim for exchange rate stability given the uncertainties and costs associated with exchange rate fluctuations. This may cause it to manage its exchange rate or shadow the value of a critical currency such as the Euro or the Dollar.
    - A lasting policy response to correct the problem may be painful because only two policy options exist:
        - Expenditure reduction
        - Expenditure switching

- A deflationary scenario encourages protectionist instincts and threatens global prosperity.

- A tension exists between free trade advantages to the world as a whole and self-interest. One country can always gain from controls if all others continue to trade freely.

- Fear of international retaliation is often the main force against protectionism.

- Protection of infant industries is frequently used as a defence in developing nations.

- International marketers still face tariffs and quotas protecting domestic interests.

- Non-tariff barriers involve environmental, quality, health or safety standards and so may require expensive product modification.

- The marketer may also find a far from level playing field as domestic producers receive preferential assistance, for example, tax breaks, supports and patriotic attitudes.

- Many charities promote the cause of 'fair trade' for poor producers by encouraging consumers to pay a premium price for products that guarantee a fair price for producers and sustainable support for producer communities.

In brief:

- No marketer can remain insulated from this dynamic global economic system.

- The global economic system represents a major arena for profitable opportunity but equally a significant source of potential volatility and threat.

- Either way, the international environment cannot be ignored but must be closely monitored and carefully assessed.

- International institutions collect a wealth of information on the evolving state of the world economy and its constituent blocs, providing a database for marketing research on both trade potential and competitive risk.

CHAPTER ROUNDUP

In this important chapter, we have done the following:

- Analysed key aspects of the macroeconomic and international environment
- Investigated the circular flow to understand changes in income, output and expenditure
- Focused on the need for marketers to appreciate the meaning of economic indicators
- Obtained a grasp of future economic conditions will provide an important edge over rivals
- Assessed each of the main macroeconomic objectives
- Examined concepts such as the multiplier and the accelerator
- Looked at the meaning and measurement of GDP
- Identified the phases of the business cycle and how it might be managed to advantage
- Focused on the key indicators for marketers to monitor
- Outlined the impact of the main policy weapons on business and the marketer
- Examined the benefits and implications of expanding world trade
- Considered frictions in the international trade process
- Explained the importance of the economic environment for the marketer

FURTHER READING

Johnson, G. *et al. Exploring corporate strategy: text and cases.* 9th edition. Harlow, Pearson Education Ltd, Chapter 3.

Kotler, P. and Keller, K.L. (2011) *Marketing management.* 14th edition. London, Pearson Education, Chapter 3.

Palmer, A. and Hartley, B. (2012) *The business environment.* 12th edition. Maidenhead, McGraw-Hill, Chapters 13 and 14.

Palmer, A. *et al.* (2007) *Managing marketing.* Oxford, Butterworth Heinemann, Chapter 4.

Worthington, I. and Britton, C. (2009) *The business environment.* 6th Edition. Harlow, Pearson, Chapter 4 and 14.

Zimbalist, A. (2010) Is it worth it? http://www.imf.org/external/pubs/ft/fandd/2010/03/pdf/zimbalist.pdf [Accessed on 27 February 2012] Analysis of the impact of Olympic events.

Websites:

http://www.statistics.gov.uk

http://www.bis.gov.uk – Department for Business Innovation and Skills

http://www.ft.com

http://www.economist.com

http://www.worldbank.org

http://www.imf.org – International Monetary Fund

http://epp.eurostat.ec.europa.eu

http://www.wto.org/index.htm

http://www.oecd.org

http://www.adb.org for the Asian Development Bank

REFERENCES

Financial Times Lexicon (2012) http://lexicon.ft.com/Term?term=business-cycle [Accessed on 29 February 2012].

Greek Crisis (2012) http://www.GreekCrisis.net [Accessed 23 May 2012].

International Monetary Fund (2011) World Economic Outlook. http://www.imf.org/external/pubs/ft/weo/2011/update/02/pdf/0611.pdf [Accessed on 23 May 2012].

New York Times (2012) Chinese insider offers rare glimpse of US-Chinese frictions. http://www.nytimes.com/2012/04/03/world/asia/chinese-insider-offers-rare-glimpse-of-us-china-frictions.html [Accessed on 25 May 2012].

Riddick, G. (2012) Predictions for 2012: economic impact of Olympics and diamond jubilee. The Telegraph, http://www.telegraph.co.uk/finance/london-olympics-business/8969091/Predictions-for-2012-economic-impact-of-Olympics-and-Diamond-Jubilee.html [Accessed on 28 February 2012].

Telegraph (2012) *JLR profits make a bigger splash*. 15 February, Business p.3.

The Chartered Institute of Marketing (2012) Keep calm and carry on marketing. http://www.cim.co.uk/resources/emergingthemes/recession.aspx [Accessed on 29 February 2012].

VisitBritain (2012) Tourism 2012 Games. http://www.tourism2012games.org/tourism-opportunity.aspx [Accessed on 29 February 2012].

QUICK QUIZ

1   What are the four phases of the business cycle?

2   What is the main measure of economic activity within an economy? Is it sufficient as a single measure?

3   What are the acronyms BOP, WTO and CPI?

4   'Expenditure, output and income will all have the same value; firms pay households for factors of production and households pay firms for goods.' What is the concept being described?

5   What is the multiplier effect?

6   What are current GDP growth rates?

7   What is the technical definition of recession?

The Chartered Institute of Marketing

Activity 7.1

Multiplier effect examples:

- Investment in university-led research that can generate a hub of excellence
- The government investment in London 2012 as a catalyst for inner city regeneration and inbound tourism
- Controversial decisions surrounding the expansion of Heathrow or alternatives

Activity 7.2

Downturn

- Control stock in line with order slowdown
- The psychology is still one of growth and budgets must be managed carefully.
- This is the right time to conduct a Pareto analysis to weed out weak products and channel outlets.
- Recruitment should be halted and no further long-term commitments taken on.

Recession

- Be aware of brighter times ahead so retain skilled core and upgrade.
- Innovate through the marketing mix to provide value and retain customers.

Recovery

- Talk is still of recession but the rate of change in orders is upward.
- Start building stock and encourage distributors to do likewise.
- Start hiring and prepare new products for launch.

Boom

- Aim for sustainable growth and build market share
- Evaluate product portfolio to meet customer requirements

Activity 7.3

Themes included in your answer would ideally revolve around positive impacts such as profit contribution, retention of skilled research, development and management jobs and improving competitiveness. Negative impacts could include unemployment levels and taxation income lost.

Activity 7.4

1	a
2	e
3	f
4	b
5	d
6	c

1   Boom, downturn, recession and recovery.

2   GDP. GDP is a simple measure of growth – inflationary influences or population statistics are not taken into account and it takes no account of social measures that can influence perceptions of wellbeing.

3   Balance of payments, World Trade Organisation and Consumer Prices Index.

4   Circular flow of income.

5   An initial increase in expenditure will have a snowball effect, leading to further expenditures within an economy.

6   Clearly this will change with time. Across Europe in 2012 rates ranged from flat to modest rates of 2–4% per annum. In emerging economies higher growth rates in excess of 6% are the norm.

7   Two consecutive quarters of falling GDP.

CHAPTER 8

The political and legislative environment

Introduction

This chapter considers a political environment that embraces government, institutions, agencies and laws. These elements may influence and constrain both organisations and individuals in society. They also define freedom in terms of what can, and cannot, legally be done by companies today. Marketers are mainly influenced by the political dimension in general terms and by the legislative environment in detail. The objectives of law and regulation, an outline of the legal system, the costs and benefits of compliance as well as the impacts involved will all be discussed. Although marketers cannot control these, an appreciation is essential. Laws clearly differ around the world, an indeed within the UK, however, for marketers, there are some strongly consistent principles. In this chapter we will explore the UK's complex legislative framework and how it impacts upon organisations and their key stakeholders.

Topic list

3.5	Explain the political and legislative environments and, in general terms, their influence on and implications for marketing:
	■ Political activities resulting in legislative changes
	■ Green legislation
	■ Customer protection legislation
	■ Employment legislation, etc

1 The political environment

▶ **Key term**

Free trade promotes competition, but many pro-business governments do not wish to see their businesses affected. Some EU governments have, in the past, been hostile to Japanese investment in the UK. However, the single European market is designed to promote competition through free trade.

The political environment includes institutions, agencies, laws and pressure groups. Pressure groups have been previously explored in Chapter 2. These are now discussed in relation to lobbyists and the media. These elements may influence and constrain both organisations and individuals in society. They define freedom in terms of what can and cannot legally be done.

Marketers are mainly influenced by the political dimension in general terms and by the legislative environment in detail. Although marketers cannot control these, they must appreciate them.

■ The role and significance of government in a market economy is considerable.

■ The government is able to influence overall economic activity levels.

■ It enacts legal and regulatory frameworks that limit business freedom and enshrine business and customer rights.

   – Legislation and decisions of public authorities influence businesses.

   – Most aspects of marketing activity are covered by some form of legal control.

■ Businesses must monitor political activities carefully in order to:

   – Alert management to impending legislation

   – Mobilise efforts to represent stakeholder interests to the legislators

   – Develop awareness of intentions/decisions affecting business

   – Identify likely changes arising out of electoral shifts

   – Assess political manifesto implications/philosophy of ministers

Figure 8.1   Government policy influences

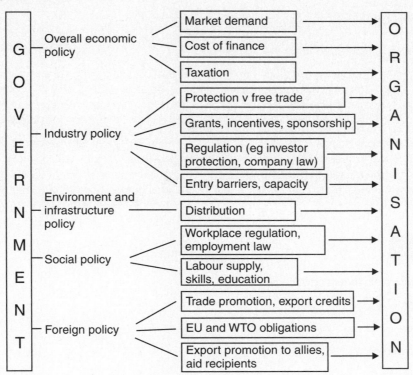

The government also controls the macroeconomic framework. Business has a collective interest in the relative burden of taxes and rates, and in trends in the size and composition of government spending on goods and services.

2 The political framework

- Political systems are located along a spectrum ranging from totalitarianism to popular democracy.

- Political power is the ability to bring about change through influencing the behaviour of others.

- Political stability is important, not least to investors who wish to minimise their risks. For example, multinationals are reluctant to invest in any economy experiencing political or labour unrest.

The inputs into the political system originate in wider society and arise out of changing attitudes, values, perceptions and demands. These are diverse and can be conflicting.

The main concern of businesses is for stability in political decision-making, a dependable planning horizon and a positive climate in which they can operate. Thus, the political environment is of vital importance to effective marketing.

China and Africa – a maturing political relationship

While Western governments are preoccupied with the Middle East, China is purposefully extending its influence across the African continent. Its investment is already significant and because of its endless drive for raw materials to sustain its own economic boom, its state-run enterprises are prepared to outbid most Western companies and come with no strings attached. Africa's trade with China has risen fourfold in the last decade and is now in excess of $100 billion.

The relationship is still evolving and competition for these raw materials is intensifying with Brazil and India the countries that are seeking to build links and increase trade. And in the west, politicians are anxious that China is acting as the modern day colonial exploiter. FT.com (2010) reported worries that 'Beijing's engagement is undermining western proselytising about democracy and letting corrupt and murderous leaders off the hook, just as governance was beginning to improve.'

ACTIVITY 8.1

Match the terms with their correct definitions:

1 Privatisation

2 Deregulation

3 Enterprise culture

4 Party manifesto

5 First-past-the-post.

(a) The candidate with the most votes cast is the election winner, irrespective of the distribution of votes to other contenders

(b) Removal of rules and requirements restricting competition

(c) A programme of intended policies, if successfully elected

(d) A climate that encourages self-reliance, entrepreneurship, individual wealth creation

(e) Transfer of 50% or more of the voting shares to private hands

ACTIVITY 8.2

Coalition – friend or foe

Conservative David Cameron was elected Prime Minister of the United Kingdom in 2010 with Liberal Democrat Nick Clegg as his deputy; Britain's first coalition government since 1945. Review the pledges and key policies of the coalition as they relate to the business environment. Apply a similar analysis to your own political environment if you are not based in the United Kingdom.

An interesting website for the marketer is http://www.number10.gov.uk as it gives an insight into political leadership and how the political parties in the UK seek to distinguish themselves.

2.1 The electoral cycle

Elections create political instability as they tend to 'influence' business cycles. Therefore marketers should be able to gauge the pertinence, feasibility and sustainability of the ideals and objectives advertised and promoted by the various parties in general as well as the government in power.

The Chartered
Institute of Marketing

The UK's coalition has attempted to quell some of this instability by introducing the Fixed-term Parliaments Bill which was finally passed in 2011, introducing a fixed term of five years and removing the Prime Minister's power to call an election at any time.

2.2 Central and local government

Parliament is the supreme legislative authority in the United Kingdom. Private members of the Parliament can propose bills, but the vast majority of the bills that become law are government sponsored or supported by the government; whatever the actual make-up and workings of the legislature. The political persuasion of the government in power can therefore significantly shape the principles and therefore the laws that will follow. The marketer should appreciate the origins of new laws as well as appreciate how businesses might influence their form and content.

Reflecting on the definition of marketing, one can consider that political parties themselves are aiming to satisfy customer (voter) requirements. The motive may not be profit but it will be sustainability of the government and a healthy and wealthy nation.

2.2.1 Local government

Local authorities are important stakeholders as they undertake urban planning and redevelopment, decide planning applications, maintain local roads and infrastructure and provide a variety of regulations that impact on local business.

- Marketers may interact with local or city authorities whose political representatives are often protective of their independence.

- The appropriate decision-making authority has, therefore, to be identified and lobbied.

- It is an aspect of the environment, therefore, where businesses should build positive and mutually beneficial relationships.

Pressure groups, already discussed in the micro environmental context in Chapter 2, represent a channel through which individuals and groups can make their views known to governments between elections.

- They are much more important than political parties in terms of membership and represent numerous, overlapping and competing influences within society.

- Pressure groups' effectiveness requires **commitment**, **cohesion**, **organisation**, **resources** and **strategic positioning**.

- Effective pressure group activity stimulates the development of counter-pressure.

2.2.2 Government through devolved powers

Unelected government agencies and other quasi-government bodies can help raise productivity and accountability. Some examples of UK non-departmental public bodies (NDPBs) or quangos that were retained following the government's 'bonfire of the quangos' are:

- Advisory Conciliation and Arbitration Service
- Higher Education Funding Council for England
- Low Pay Commission
- UK Trade International
- BBC
- Big Lottery Fund
- VisitEngland and VisitBritain
- Natural England

These bodies are not law makers but they may provide support, management and guidance functions and can influence future policy-making.

Investigate the services that UK Trade and Investment (UKTI) provide to businesses seeking to build exports. (See http://www.ukti.gov.uk).

---

3 Supranational bodies

3.1 The European Union (EU)

The European Union is now the most integrated and economically powerful bloc of countries in the world, representing a market with a total population of over 500 million. Membership of the SEM (the Single European Market), the European Monetary System and the Euro creates economic and legal obligations that imply a progressive loss of national sovereignty. The institutions relevant to the exercise of this transferred legislative authority include:

- The European Parliament
    - This is an elected body of Members of the European Parliament (MEPs).
    - It has gradually grown its power to veto budgets and support or reject proposals.

- The Council of the EU (Council of Ministers)
    - This is where the real decision-making power lies. It is composed of representative ministers, according to the issue under discussion.
    - Much of the voting is on a qualified majority basis. This implies that marketers and lobbyists wishing to influence outcomes must broaden their lobbying base and/or co-operate with other sympathetic groups.

- European Commission
    - This is the executive body of the EU (equivalent to UK's 'Whitehall').
    - It drafts regulations and directives to promote the objectives of the union. The outcome has been a large number of measures and directives to facilitate the evolution of an integrated market.
    - Compliance costs have arisen for business in the process, but so too have the opportunities for greater trade.

- The Court of Justice of the EU
    - It deals with any actions a business may wish to bring against EU institutions.
    - It also provides a means of individual redress where member states are not fully complying with their legal obligations.

Other EU bodies include the European Central Bank, the European Social and Economic Committee and the European Investment Bank.

3.2 Other regions

Other supranational bodies exist around the globe with varying degrees of input to legislative integration. They include:

- The Union of South American Nations
- Cooperation Council for the Arab States of the Gulf
- Association of Southeast Asian Nations
- Southern African Development Community

Political and legal business risk

Across the world the political and legal systems can represent opportunities and threats for businesses and indeed for the lives of people doing global business. The Foreign and Commonwealth Office offers advice on travel to other countries that is relevant for business and leisure travellers. Working in conjunction with the FCO, UK Trade and Investment offers authoritative advice on key issues related to the political stability and business security environments. For example current UKTI advice on the much troubled Zimbabwe (2012) is as follows 'Zimbabwe's next elections are due by 2013 but could be called sooner due to the current political impasse. They will likely bring a period of increased instability. In the meantime the government has been unable to make significant progress on political reform... Political tensions remain high with ZANU-PF employing state media to deliver sustained anti-western rhetoric.'

Corruption and bribery remain an illegal thorn in the side of fair business dealings. Global civil rights organisation, Transparency International, produces a corruption perception index which ranks countries/territories on how corrupt their public sector is perceived to be. In December 2011 the top three for low perceived levels of corruption were New Zealand, Denmark and Sweden. UK was joint 16th and the bottom three were Afghanistan/Myanmar (joint), North Korea and Somalia.

4 Lobbyists and the media

Lobbying may be defined as influencing members of a relevant legislature and solicitors of votes. Professional lobbyists can be of value to a business in the following ways:

Table 8.1   The role of professional lobbyists

Monitoring	An early warning service on forthcoming legislation
Interpreting	The implications of proposed legislation
Identifying	Political figures with a special interest in your issue
Informing	Political decision-makers about (your) industry developments
Preparing	Background briefs and cases for busy legislators
Co-ordinating	Constituency protest letters to political representatives
Advising	The business on strategy and tactics to adopt

- The mass media including press, radio and television can influence perceptions and opinions.
- They can influence decision-makers and their policies through their campaigns.

▶ **Exam tip**

Marks are awarded in the exam for format and presentation in Part B of the paper – long answer tasks. You can achieve these by giving part B a report style introduction, structuring tasks clearly, and using bullet points, tables and diagrams where appropriate. Consider how this book is laid out and how much harder it would be to read if it were solid blocks of text. Presenting information clearly and concisely is a valuable business skill and it will help you to gain more marks in your exam.

- Public Relations (PR) is an important aspect of marketing management.
  - Mutually beneficial relationships with the media must be created and maintained.
  - It is a two-way relationship based on principles similar to those between a minister and a pressure group.
  - PR aims to influence the media agenda and the tenor of debates.

5 The legal framework

Marketers should continuously reassess the political landscape to be prepared for shifts and impacts. The framework of law is the product of both legal and political influences and judgments adapt the law to reflect current attitudes and values within society. Entry into economic unions makes member countries subject to regulations and legal provisions (ie EU).

Authorities are normally responsible for the following roles:

- Rule making and their interpretation (eg regulations)
- Standards setting (eg emissions, food and hygiene)
- Inspections (ie usually unannounced spot checks due to complaints)
- Enforcement (ie various sanctions from fines to closure).

5.1 Role and objectives of legislation

Legislation involves a delicate process of balancing the diverse, and often conflicting, interests of the various stakeholders involved. Processes include:

- Counterbalancing the economic power of business
- Settling of disputes between stakeholders
- Governing what business can and cannot do

Media activities and community pressure groups such as the consumer's associations have made buyers more aware of their rights.

Figure 8.2 illustrates how not all the different types of pressure on businesses to deliver adequate products and services, come from the law alone.

Figure 8.2   Regulatory pressures on business in a broader view

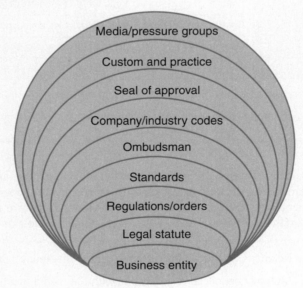

The Chartered
Institute of Marketing

Applying business law

Match the terms with their correct definitions:

1   *Caveat emptor* and *caveat vendictor*
2   Standards institute
3   Code of practice
4   Legislation
5   Directive
6   Ombudsman
7   Seal of approval
(a)   Let the buyer beware (no legal obligation to notify defects) and let the seller beware
(b)   The process of making laws
(c)   Voluntary guidelines to encourage desirable modes of behaviour
(d)   European legislation laying down result that member states must achieve.
(e)   An official appointed to investigate individual complaints of maladministration
(f)   Law laid down by government legislation
(g)   A mark, given by an expert, to confirm or guarantee a product.

The broad areas of laws affecting businesses are:

- Laws of employment
- Laws relating to competition (as described in Chapter 3)
- Protection of intellectual property rights
- Legislation controlling production processes

The government has the primary responsibility for the establishment, updating and operation of the legal framework. The resulting laws provide a means by which it can constrain business activities by defining the powers and responsibilities of owners and management.

Digital broadband technology and e-commerce raises the question of compliance with different national regulations with regard to advertising and promotion. One example of this is the complex international legal web of copyright regulations that the music, game and film industries are battling to navigate to tackle illegal copying and downloading.

5.2 Impacts and influences of legislation and regulation on business

Some of the drawbacks of legislation and regulation include the following:

- The extra costs incurred for training staff to conform to standards.
- Costs involved in recording, reporting and taking action where deviations arise.
- Conforming to legal requirements adds to costs and reduces foreign competitiveness.
- Conforming to safety standards delays introduction and returns.
- Complicated regulatory procedures may be an entry barrier to small companies.
- Environmental laws and regulations vary widely across the global economy.

  - It is difficult for multinationals to develop standard environmental policies.
  - The need to tailor to local regulations creates scope for double standards.

- Small companies are harder hit by regulations.
- Tariffs and quotas can help facilitate competition.

- All marketing activities are subject to a wide range of laws and regulations.
    - These may originate from or even overlap at supranational, national, state, regional or local levels.
    - They are often in a state of flux and can change unexpectedly due to public pressure or a change in government thinking.
- Marketers must keep up with all important changes.
- Legislation can clearly be double-edged: it can enhance or hinder competition.

6 The impact of legislation on the marketing environment

- Legislation can positively impact the marketing environment.
- Impacts of regulation are difficult to measure and more likely to be understated.
- Businesses may tend to be more inclined to measure the costs of compliance.
- The internet is a critical area for future legislation or industry self-regulation. Despite tremendous potential as a global marketing channel, there is ongoing concern about rising fraud, spam and privacy invasion.

> ▶ **Exam tip**
>
> **Improving your performance**
>
> When you receive your case study, think about the impact of laws on the case organisation. Familiarise yourself with these and include them in your PESTEL analysis.

ACTIVITY 8.5

Can you think of specific areas of concern for your organisation with regard to the internet?

Evaluate how legislation could help address these concerns.

The relevant legislation that impacts on the businesses in general and marketers in particular is clearly illustrated in Figure 8.3

Figure 8.3   The impact of legislation on business

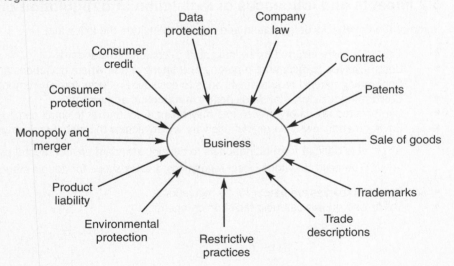

The Chartered
Institute of Marketing

Management needs to formulate a coherent policy in respect of legal matters:

- Establish policy guidelines and processes to ensure that at least minimum standards are attained so that liability is avoided.

- Set a policy regarding whether to take legal action against others and, if so, in what circumstances (eg when competitors infringe patents, bad debts).

- Seek the adequate external support (eg Department for Business Innovation and Skills).

Further considerations include:

- The expensive nature of legal actions

- The effect of actions on the company image

- Longer-term interest in ongoing business relationships

- Regulatory agencies may be content with assurances over future standards.

- Voluntary codes may be preferred to regulation and legal processes.

- Employment tribunals, which are quasi-judicial bodies, are used for cases of unfair dismissal, discrimination and related matters.

- Smaller companies are often exempted from certain legislation because of the high costs of compliance (ie employee protection).

6.1 Legislation and advertising

In the United Kingdom, the Advertising Standards Authority was set up by the industry to counter the need for legislation by ensuring that all who commission, prepare and publish advertisements comply with the required codes. It adjudicates complaints from the public and other interested parties. Other bodies, like the Broadcasting Standards Council, govern specific media like TV. The Independent Television Commission, however, licences commercial services, whether terrestrial, cable or satellite, and regulates advertising and other standards through its code of practice. Ofcom is the regulator that covers broadcasting, telecommunications and the internet. One notable regulation it has introduced is the banning of junk food advertising when younger viewers predominate.

THE REAL WORLD

Legal protection for the Olympic brand

The London Olympic Games and Paralympic Games Act 2006 was passed in order to enable the London Organising Committee of the Olympic Games (LOCOG) to prevent the undermining of rights granted to official broadcasters, sponsors, suppliers and licensees associated with the games. Its detailed elements prohibited unauthorised advertising, street trading and ticket sales. In addition to the above legislation, LOCOG brought together a complex web of protection for the games including:

- Trademarks including the London 2012 and Team GB logos

- Design rights eg for the mascots and medals

- Copyrighting of graphics, artwork, video and photographic elements of the games

- Compliance with advertising standards and rules for all partners including compliance with the Olympic Symbol etc. (Protection) Act 1995, amended in 2006

The laws protecting London 2012 were probably the most restrictive ever. Restrictions stipulated that use of two of the listed words associated with the games could constitute an infringement and these words included London, 2012, summer and games. The use of the Olympic rings, the combined colours of the rings, the Olympic-style torch/flame and images of the venues were also restricted.

Through these laws LOCOG hoped to avoid the repetition of cases from the past when advertisers such as Nike and American Express have used ambush marketing to gain exposure at Olympic Games without the high cost of sponsorship. Dutch brewer

Bavaria famously used ambush marketing at the 2010 Football World Cup by sending 36 young women wearing orange mini-dresses to a Netherlands match. The brand Budweiser had paid handsomely for the privilege of exclusive representation at the tournament and so the tightly clad ladies were ejected from the stadium, but only after pictures of their 'ambush' had been beamed to millions around the world.

(LOCOG, 2010)

6.2 Fair trading and the Consumer

> ▶ **Key term**
>
> **Compensation culture:** as a society, the UK is becoming more inclined to sue for compensation, enticed by sometimes significant financial reward. No-win-no-fee lawyers encourage claims and attention has recently fallen on the car insurance industry which has difficulty defending claims for whiplash, the cost of which has driven car insurance skywards.

6.2.1 Contract law

Contract law is the legality that regulates exchanges between buyers and sellers and it constitutes one of the most important areas of law for business. The three essential elements of a contract are offer, acceptance and an intention to enter into legal relations.

ACTIVITY 8.6

Make time to study the 'terms and conditions' attached to products or services supplied by your company. Compare these to the elements outlined above. Alternatively, study those you have to agree to when making a major purchase (eg an 18-month contract for a special mobile telephone rate).

> ▶ **Exam tip**
>
> If you are a non-UK candidate you have the option of relating your answers to the United Kingdom or your own country's legislation. If you decide to select your own country, you must familiarise yourself with the equivalent legislation. You should strive to achieve at least the same level of exploration as encompassed within this Study Text.

6.2.2 Protecting the consumer

This area of the law has grown incrementally in recent decades.

A permanent Office of Fair Trading (OFT) provides a pool of expertise and experience in consumer affairs. As a statutory body, it deals with suspected abuses and prosecutes offenders.

Local authorities are responsible for most of the day-to-day enforcement of consumer protection legislation. Key areas in which consumers have legal protection include:

- Consumer credit and the advertising of consumer credit
- Misleading advertising
- Selling online or distance selling
- Sale of Goods Act – stipulating that goods must be fit for purpose

The Chartered Institute of Marketing

In February 2012 Lloyds Bank announced a fall in profits as a consequence of having to pay £3 billion in compensation for mis-sold payment protection insurance (PPI). This was the expensive conclusion to a failed legal battle in which the courts decided that the banks had been guilty of wholesale mis-selling of PPI products to people who didn't need them or could never benefit from them.

6.2.3 Assurances offered to consumers by suppliers

- Acts govern how goods can be stored, described and sold.

- Voluntary industry codes have evolved as a means of more flexible regulation and are clearly a way forward for businesses:

    - They may provide a marketing edge to participating companies where the customer looks for a mark of service or quality assurance.

    - Many industries have such self-regulated codes including internet service providers, school caterers and visitor attractions.

    - The Office of Fair Trading now runs a scheme that gives official approval to voluntary codes of practice which meet a core set of criteria.

6.3 Data protection

New technologies have shaped fears with regard to:

- Access to information by unauthorised parties

- The likelihood that an individual could be harmed by the existence of data which is inaccurate, misleading or sensitive (eg medical details)

- The possibility that personal information could be used for purposes other than those for which it was requested and disclosed

The Data Protection Act 1998 addresses these concerns, protecting individuals with the following principles:

- Information must be obtained fairly and lawfully and held for specified and lawful purposes.
- Information must be accurate and, where necessary, kept up to date.
- It shall not be retained longer than is necessary for its purpose.
- Individuals have a right to information about their records.
- Information must be kept securely.

6.4 Employment law

Marketers as employers, and when fulfilling advertising for recruitment, need to be aware of employment law. This includes:

- Employees' right to a contract as described in the Employment Rights Act 1996

- Health and Safety legislation protecting the lives of employees

- Minimum wage legislation

- The EU's Working Time Directive under which workers cannot be forced to work more than 48 hours a week

- Equalities legislation preventing discrimination on the grounds of race, age, gender, disability, sexual orientation etc

6.5 Green legislation

Environmental issues have become more important over the last 10–20 years, with the emergence of the green movement and green economics. We look at wider environmental issues in Chapter 5, but it is clear that environmental legislation and regulations are growing. International pressure and pressure from the green-influenced vote has led to mainstream political parties taking these issues into their programmes. Most western countries now have laws to cover land-use planning, smoke emissions, water pollution and the protection of wildlife and habitats. Some examples are:

- The Energy Act 2011 which provides a legal framework for a range of energy efficiency measures
- The Climate Change Act of 2008 introducing legally binding targets for greenhouse gas emissions
- Waste Regulations 2011 – controlling disposal of hazardous waste
- WEEE – governing the disposal of electrical equipment

The Waste Regulations 2011 mean a significant change of approach for businesses. The new regulations stem from the EU Waste Framework Directive which provides the overarching framework for legislation across Europe governing the collection, transport, recovery and disposal of waste. The UK Environment Agency (2012) explains how this will affect businesses by placing emphasis on a hierarchy of priorities as follows:

- Preventing creation of waste eg through reduced packaging
- Preparing for re-use such as materials that can be recycled or re-used
- Recycling – optimising waste or by-products that are recycled
- Other recovery eg recovering heat from production processes
- Disposal

A final world on the legal environment is its tenuous links with the requirement for, and benefits of, corporate social responsibility. In 2012 large multinationals have been attacked by protest groups for their complex schemes to avoid tax. Tax avoidance (unlike tax evasion) is perfectly legal but businesses are beginning to find to their cost that stakeholders will quickly lose respect for organisations that fail to follow the spirit of the law as well as the letter of the law.

7 The international political and legislative environment

The complexities of legislation and politics from around the globe are beyond the scope of this Study Text, however, when investigating market threats and opportunities marketers will need to evaluate the legal environment in existing and potential markets.

This element of the macro environment is ever changing with trade advice and restrictions being added or lifted with regularity. Factors will include:

- Government attitudes to inward investment
- Levels of political stability
- Hard trade barriers such as tariffs or softer cultural barriers in the form of negative attitudes
- Border restrictions
- Corruption and bribery
- Censorship

UK Trade and Investment offers advice to UK companies wishing to export to other countries. They have a presence in many key markets including the USA, Argentina, Jordan, Hong Kong, India, Russia, China and Australia. Other countries have similar organisations to promote exports.

The Chartered Institute of Marketing

CHAPTER ROUNDUP

In this chapter, we have dealt with important aspects of the closely linked political and legal environments for marketers. In brief, these are as follows:

- The political process is complex but pressure groups and some processes are available to help business lobbies.

- The political environment is a source of uncertainty.

- The authority of supranational bodies, like the European Union, must now be accounted for and monitored.

- The media plays an important part in setting the political agenda.

- The influence of lobbyists is less readily detected but of greater potential importance to business interests.

- The law represents an evolving framework to reflect societal concerns and enable commercial activities to take place in a fair but effective manner.

- There can be an underlying tension between the needs of business to innovate and deploy resources efficiently over time, and the health, safety and equitable treatment of various stakeholders.

- Quasi-legal means of regulation, such as codes of practice, serve an important function.

- There are many considerations to weigh up before an organisation initiates legal proceedings.

- Failing to comply with at least the minimum legal requirements is bad business.

- Being forced to resort to law is potentially costly and time-consuming.

- Systems must be in place, plus staff suitably trained, to ensure compliance.

- Proposed legislation should be monitored and a proactive approach adopted.

- Employee legislation can reduce marketers' flexibility and freedom of action.

- Voluntary codes, if perceived as fair to stakeholders, can be cost-effective.

- Marketers can use superior legal standards as a source of potential competitive advantage.

- Compliance with exacting consumer legislation may put foreign competitors at a disadvantage and help create an image of 'best practice'.

FURTHER READING

Palmer, A. and Hartley, B. (2012) *The business environment*. 12th edition. Maidenhead, McGraw-Hill, Chapters 2 and 6.

Worthington, I. and Britton, C. (2009) *The business environment*. 6th edition. Harlow, Pearson, Chapters 3 and 7.

Websites:

http://www.direct.gov.uk is a gateway to a diversity of government information

http://www.ft.com

http://www.economist.com

http://www.thetimes.co.uk

http://europa.eu/index_en.htm for information on the European Union

http://www.labour.org.uk/home

http://www.conservatives.com

http://www.parliament.uk – latest news from the house of commons and house of lords

http://www.number10.gov.uk – the official site for the British Prime Minister

http://online.businesslink.gov.uk – includes advice for business on the legal environment

http://www.ukti.gov.uk – advice on political and economic conditions in international markets

http://www.fco.gov.uk – advice on safety and conditions in overseas countries

http://www.sadc.int – Southern African Development Community

REFERENCES

Environment Agency (2012) Waste (England and Wales) Regulations 2011. http://www.environment-agency.gov.uk/business/topics/waste/128153.aspx [Accessed on 23 May 2012]

LOCOG (2010) Brand protection. http://www.london2012.com/documents/brand-guidelines/statutory-marketing-rights.pdf [Accessed on 2 March 2012]

Transparency International (2011) Corruption perceptions index 2011. Available at: http://cpi.transparency.org/cpi2011/results/ [Accessed on 2 March 2012]

UKTI (2012) Overseas business risk – Zimbabwe. http://www.ukti.gov.uk/export/countries/africa/southernafrica/zimbabwe/overseasbusinessrisk.html [Accessed on 2 March 2012]

Wallis, W. and Burgis, T. (2010) Continent drives a harder bargain. FT.com, http://www.ft.com/cms/s/0/85632536-74ed-11df-aed7-00144feabdc0,dwp_uuid=e11d5c1a-74ee-11df-aed7-00144feabdc0.html#axzz1nsGwo02u. [Accessed on 2 March 2012]

QUICK QUIZ

1   Describe the principle of free trade.

2   How does government social policy impact upon an organisation?

3   What is the term that the UK government uses to describe quangos?

4   Name three of the bodies operating at European supranational level.

5   Name the main legislation aimed at protecting consumer data and privacy.

6   Name four areas of legislation/regulation of the relationship between employees and employers.

The Chartered Institute of Marketing

Activity 8.1

1 e
2 b
3 d
4 c
5 a

Activity 8.2

The coalition government has place significant emphasis on supporting SMEs, innovation and training and the removal of bureaucratic barriers to growth. Some examples are: support and investment in the tourism, energy, aerospace, media and fashion industries. At the same time it has abolished the Regional Development Agencies who once led sector and geographical initiatives to support growth. Students should always be listening to the organisations around them and hearing views on governments – are they helping or hindering business growth?

Activity 8.3

UKTI employs international trade advisers and has representation at offices in 96 markets across the globe. Services include information, advice, trade fairs, access to buyers, events, seminars and information on latest business opportunities.

Activity 8.4

1 a
2 d
3 c
4 b
5 f
6 e
7 g

Activity 8.5

The internet has opened up many new communications channels for organisations, making the issues of compliance more complex for the marketer. Legislation covering areas such as trade description, distance selling, copyright, data protection and (for the public sector) freedom of information all have implications for information and/or transactions online. Employment law also comes into play when considering staff access to and use of online resources or social media.

Activity 8.6

Terms and conditions do vary enormously depending on the nature of the product or service and the size of the contract. One might see clauses describing cancellation terms, product returns, payment, confidentiality, use of sub-contractors and force-majeure (unforeseen events beyond the control of a contracting party).

1   Freedom for businesses to trade across national borders without financial penalty or prohibitive legislative restrictions.

2   Workplace regulation, employment law, labour supply, skills and education.

3   Non-departmental public bodies.

4   The Court of Justice of the EU, European Commission, the Council of the EU (Council of Ministers), and the European Parliament are the main bodies.

5   Data Protection Act

6   The EU's Working Time Directive, minimum wage legislation, Health and Safety and Employment Rights Act. The long list of European bodies and their roles and responsibilities can be found at the EU website detailed in Further Reading below.

CHAPTER 9

The technical/information environments

Introduction

We live in a technological society whose effects impact on all aspects of our life. Our working environment is particularly subject to such influences. Many major transformations have occurred in recent years in the majority of industries and occupations. So too have our means of transport, how we shop, the ways we spend our leisure time, how we learn, the houses we live in and the way our health is monitored. Only our sleeping habits seem relatively unaffected, although new drugs, insulation, bed designs and environment control are affecting the lives of many in this respect too. Internet-based UK retail sales are rising yearly. Consumption of media such as TV, the internet, and mobile phones is also increasing. In this chapter we explore the need for marketers to understand the role of technology and the changes taking place and to be sensitive to new developments, recognising the importance of monitoring and forecasting technical change.

Topic list

Technology ① 1

Technological change ② 2

The technological diffusion process ③ 3

Convergence of technologies ④ 4

Technology and the workplace ⑤ 5

Marketing: using Information and Communication Technologies (ICT) and the internet ⑥ 6

Future applications of technology ⑦ 7

3.8	Explain the evolution of the technical and information environments and consider its actual and potential impacts on organisations, employment, marketing and communications:
	■ The technical diffusion process
	■ Technology and the workforce
	■ Technology and the impact of social change
	■ The convergence of technology ie, telecommunications linked with media communications
	■ Digital superhighways
	■ Credit transfer
	■ The internet and other technology based communication tools

1 Technology

Developments in technology are happening at an ever increasing pace. The rapid appearance of new products such as high definition television, and the obsolescence of their predecessors, highlight the fast rate of change that markets can exhibit. No organisation will be unaffected by the technological environment so marketers must strive to understand the changes taking place and be sensitive to new developments.

■ Skills must be acquired and continuously updated. Individual and organisational survival may depend on this.

■ Much of marketing is underpinned by technology. Consider the influence of technology on the marketing mix:

– Innovative product development is fed by innovation.

– New technology can be part of the product itself eg streamed films and mobile applications.

– Promotion increasingly relies on communication technology.

– Technology can provide the platform for complex pricing structures such as for rail travel.

– Technology can result in efficiencies and reduced costs and prices.

– Distribution and logistics are dependent on efficiencies driver by technology.

– Market research pivots on information systems used to more easily gather and analyse data.

– Management of data is supporting more efficient and effective processes in dealing with customers.

■ The successful development of new technology comprises seven distinct stages:

– **Knowledge** of the current state of technology is the foundation upon which research takes place.

– **Research and invention** is the generation of new ideas, or improvement of existing ones.

– **Development** is their useful application to specific products or processes.

– **Innovation** relates to the commercial exploitation of a development or new idea.

– **Diffusion** refers to the rate of its adoption through the potential target population concerned.

– **Refinement** exploits the full potential of the technology. It often forms the basis of product differentiation in the growth and early maturity stages of the life cycle.

■ Re-investing profit back into the maintenance of technological or design leadership can ensure companies' long-term profits and competitive edge.

■   Characteristics of technology

    – Technology affects most of the marketing environment.
    – Significant dependencies include the internet and mobile phones.
    – Marketers should consider threats at distinct levels.

ACTIVITY 9.1

(a)   Give six examples of industries with big cost-saving innovations over the last five years. Can you think of any industry that had no significant cost-saving innovations?

(b)   What products and services that are taken for granted today did not exist 30 years ago? Think in terms of organisation.

THE REAL WORLD

The Human Genome Project

A collaboration of scientists from the United Kingdom, China, France, Germany, Japan and the United States enabled the understanding of the precise genetic code that makes us human. This is arguably one of the greatest scientific breakthroughs in human history. It heralds the era of biomedicine that corporate biotech giants can exploit. Genomics may indeed open up enormous commercial opportunities for biotechnology companies.

Potential advantages of this project include the following:

■   More rapid development of treatments for cancer, birth defects and common ailments. (This includes development of Delta 32, the so-called 'survival gene', which is one of ten mutant genes carried by those who are resistant to AIDS.)

■   Life expectancy could be doubled by curing those previously incurable with personalised body repair kits.

■   Despite private sector involvement, this may be freely available to everyone.

■   Genetically based antidotes to Spanish flu-like viruses are now being developed.

■   Healthcare with gene therapy could revolutionise medicine.

■   Cancer could be viewed as a chronic but manageable illness within 20 years.

Potential drawbacks of this project include the following:

■   The temptation to engineer human beings (ie designer babies)
■   Possible invasion of privacy (discrimination against genetically disadvantaged)
■   Insurance/loan restrictions on individuals known to be susceptible to disease
■   Companies may demand genetic tests before recruiting new employees
■   Lack of ethical guidelines (eg human cloning from harvested embryo stem cells)
■   No guarantee that genetic testing will be affordable by the poor (healthcare gap)
■   Excessive control over life-saving diagnosis/treatment by firms patenting genes
■   Development of 'white plague' diseases genetically engineered to kill specific biological groups

This focus on the human genome reminds us that technological change has a wide interpretation and the scope of impact on our societies and our economies is substantial. If we focus purely on the use of information technology we may miss significant advances on knowledge, ways of working and the collaborative efforts that see our society advance.

2 Technological change

There are a number of factors that have assisted in the increasing pace of technological advances towards the information society that we see today, including:

- The convergence of technology – eg telecommunications linked with media communications. The Apple iPhone is a prime example of this, and now includes, for example, video calling, high definition video recorder, maps, GPS, internet browser, ebook reader, music player as well as standard calling function.

- In 2011 it was estimated by the International Telecommunications Union that subscriptions to mobiles across the world were 87 per 100 people. In the developed world this can be a penetration of as much as 130% (more than one phone per person) but in the developing world mobile telecoms services are the main driver for ICT growth. For example in Africa mobile technology penetration is much higher than that of PCs so broadband connectivity is being led by mobile broadband. Other statistics published by ITU (2011) are:

  - One third of the world's population online
  - Almost 6 billion mobile-cellular subscriptions
  - Almost 1.2 million mobile broadband accounts

- Digital superhighways are unifying information, communication and multimedia – close to two thirds of people in the developed world have access to the internet. Access is increasingly seen as a 'right' much like infrastructure such as sewage and roads.

- Electronic funds transfer – rather than cash based transactions are fast becoming the norm.

The technological environment is not just about computers and information technology; it is much wider than that. From innovations such as 3M's Post-it® note, to the Dyson vacuum cleaner and the current trend for high-definition flat screen TVs, we can see that technology has an impact right across society, into the workplace and into our homes. However the importance of information technology and the internet should not be underestimated.

2.1 The social impacts of technological change

The impact of recent technological change has potentially important social consequences:

- Increase in homeworking and remote working supported by mobile technology and a growing ability to work in virtual teams.

- Skills in the interpretation of data and the management of information processes are becoming more valued than manual or physical skills.

- Technology helps to increase productivity and more people are required to work in the service roles that support and fulfill production with an emphasis on customer service.

- More information is available more readily than ever before. This has many effects, from greater consumer awareness and increased competition (through readily available price comparison) to the homogenisation of global cultures.

> ▶ **Key term**
>
> **Information society**: industrialisation led to an acceleration of technological development that was not seen previously. As developed nations now become **'information societies'**, the pace of technological development is increasing.

Jobs of the future:

Today's educators stress that they don't really know what jobs their charges will be working in. Some existing jobs will go and some new careers might appear:

New jobs that might be considered jobs of the future (some are already here):

- Home companion-caretaker – enabling people to carry on living at home
- Online education broker – tailoring bespoke education packages for clients
- Traceability manager – sustainable global supply chains
- Hydrogen fuel station manager – onsite production and sales

Jobs that might disappear:

- Hospital consultant – technical tasks could be performed by robots (but the patient care of nurses will always be required)

- Shop assistant – as purchases move online

- Construction trades – computers will model and manufacture components for assembly onsite

- Soldiers – robotic technology performing frontline roles, protecting lives

- Life, death and taxes go on… so there will still be roles for writers, entertainers, lawyers, politicians undertakers and tax collectors

(The Guardian, 2010)

2.2 The role of business

Most technological change is incremental and progressive in nature, but breakthroughs can and do bring sudden and dramatic change. Organisations must monitor their technological environment. The drive to seek innovation depends on a number of factors:

- Stage of the product or technology life cycle
- Size of the firm
- Nature of competition in the market
- The pace of change in consumer tastes

Global competition is one of the imperatives forcing technological innovation.

The rate at which technology and competitive strategy dominance occur within different industries depends on two factors:

- The stage of evolution of that industry
- The type of technological and competitive forces within that industry

3 The technological diffusion process

Innovation in the market place can take many forms, from radically new products incorporating new technology to changes in packaging. The rate at which firms adopt innovations is the rate of diffusion and involves cost and risk as well as the prospect of return.

Figure 9.1   The technological diffusion process

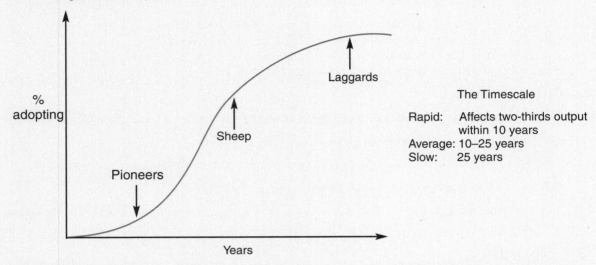

- **Pioneers**: Also referred to innovators or early adopters, these people are eager to try new ideas and are often perceived to be risk takers. They are likely to have greater exposure to mass media than later adopters and are certainly more willing to change.

- **Sheep**: This is a more conservative segment who will tend to purchase after some thought and may need some persuading.

- **Laggards**: This is a small group of traditionalists who are unwilling to change. They may be forced to changes only when their previous choice is obsolete and no longer available.

Think of this model and these descriptions in terms of digital radio or smart phones. Where are we now on the diffusion process?

Factors that determine whether the rate is rapid or slow include:

- Profitability – the extent to which the change will improve profits

- Deterrence – what happens if the organisation does not adopt technology?

- Scale of investment and access to capital

- Market structure – oligopolies will tend to have the resources to adopt technologies quickly and globally.

- Characteristics of the new product or process

- Potential range of applications and business benefits

- Environmental acceptability

- Change agents. There is often resistance to change in organisations, both from management and the workforce and from customers. Champions for new technology, or change agents, can lead decision-makers or drive initiatives to support diffusion.

 The Chartered Institute of Marketing

The internet is attractive as a channel of commerce due to a variety of reasons:

- Low entry cost
- Rapid return on investment
- Flexibility of investment
- Connectivity and ultra-rapid communication
- Alignment to growing information needs
- Wide scope for reaching potential targets

ACTIVITY 9.2

Dependence on technology

Suppose that an unusual electrical storm unaccountably disrupted the workings of all microprocessors that have ever been produced.

What do you think would be the immediate effects on the following?

- A motorist
- A household
- A marketing department

4 Convergence of technologies

> **Key term**
>
> **Cloud computing**: the advent of cloud computing has been part of this convergence as data can be held in a 'cloud' so programmes, data and messages sit not on a user's PC but in a cloud; or more accurately in distant mega servers that are accessed by all cloud users. The ability to share and work on data with other users and to access files and programmes from any device opens up new opportunities and ways of working.

As communications technologies have developed, facilities and capabilities have converged. Examples of convergence in the home are:

- Watching TV online
- Using TV to purchase online
- Making telephone and video calls online using eg Skype
- Mobile banking
- Using game consoles to access the internet and buy online

These trends are particularly relevant for marketers who need to understand how their customers are communicating and transacting with them. The convergence of media has changed the face of advertising from the world of mass media to a complex web of channels, devices and interest-led opportunities.

THE REAL WORLD

Technology and innovation businesses will keep a particularly sharp eye on technological advancements as these can pose new threats or open up new opportunities in the market. Vetronic Services is a small UK-based business designing and manufacturing hi-tech equipment for use in veterinary practice.

Business owner Keith Simpson describes the company's approach to technological change: 'Technology is moving forward at a frightening pace and to maintain a hold in the market-place we need to embrace these emerging technologies and incorporate them in our products. This means either integrating them into our existing products or designing them into new products. We have identified wireless and remote access technologies as the improvements likely to have the greatest impact on how our products are used and perceived. To this end we have been designing in wireless functionality to all of our monitoring products since 2008 and producing software allowing world-wide remote access to any data arising form these monitors. Technological advances are usually commercially driven and perhaps never more so than the lightning development of movement technologies.

The most striking example of this is the technology now being used in hand-held console games such as Wii. For us, movement detection means a very different thing from game designers; it means indication and in some cases, quantitative assessment of life. We are now designing equipment to utilise this technology in our patient monitoring products.'

This unique combination of professional skills, covering both veterinary science and technology, is the cornerstone of Vetronic's success.

5 Technology and the workplace

5.1 Employment patterns

Technological development affect employment patterns over the whole economy, as new industries and activities develop:

- Skills: effective production control in a computerised environment depends on the ability of the workforce to interpret and manipulate abstract data and to do this they need an overall theoretical knowledge of the system. A critical, questioning attitude towards data presented on the screen is needed.

- Decision-making: dealing with problems thrown up by systems requires an ability to discuss, co-operate and reach decisions.

- Empowerment: user friendly ICT (Information and Communication Technologies) and the automation of routine tasks means that employees can gain more control over their work.

- Cost cutting and adding value

At a practical and tactical level, advances in technology offer business the following:

- Improved production and cost control systems and computerised production and project planning

- Point of sale technologies that transact payments electronically but also record data and link with Customer Relationship Management systems

- Management information and performance measurement systems

THE REAL WORLD

The end of corporate conferencing?

The conference industry is worth more than £10 billion to the UK as businesses gather together to meet and discuss ideas, share best practice and follow industry news – activities that can all happen online. There may be fewer live conferences as a consequence but the industry is working to ensure that face-to-face conferencing remains but technology is used to add value. Key Note (2011) surveyed the industry to gather views on the likelihood changes resulting from new technologies.

More than 50% of respondents agreed that the following technologies might be commonplace.

- Live video streaming to remote participants
- A social network before, during and after the event
- All presentations, video etc downloaded to mobiles
- Event running in parallel in virtual meeting sites

5.2 Business processes

5.2.1 Production management

Production management information systems provide information to help with the planning and control of production. One application which is frequently used is production planning, involving the provision of a production plan to meet the requirements of customers and stockists as efficiently as possible. Stock control systems or modules range from simple batch processing systems that update a stock file from daily movement records, to online (real-time) systems providing instant, up-to-date information on stock availability and reducing working capital tied up in stocks.

5.2.2 Point of sale devices

Even the smallest business is now likely to utilise Electronic Point of Sale (EPOS) and Electronic Funds Transfer at the Point of Sale (EFTPOS) devices using bar coding to trigger cash registers and terminals connected to a main computer or a web-based transaction system. These can of course produce detailed transaction information in an instant. Contactless payment systems are also increasingly available eg Visa's payWave.

5.2.3 Communications

Email communications, computer-integrated telephone systems, mobile messaging and social networks are all changing the ways in which organisations communicate internally as well as with customers and other stakeholders.

---

6 Marketing: using Information and Communication Technologies (ICT) and the internet

The internet represents several opportunities:

- An international source of information
- A communication tool
- A channel for marketing activities
- A channel for e-commerce
- A major engine of potential future job growth
- An escape into virtual reality (eg secondlife.com)

6.1 Technological forecasting

> ▶ **Key term**
>
> **Marketing mix**: the 7Ps of Product, Price, Place, Promotion, People, Process and Physical evidence. These represent the mix of tactics employed by marketers. Although not a core part of the syllabus for this unit the mix is relevant and may appear in questions as a framework for evaluating the impact on marketing of significant changes in the marketing environment.

A technological forecast should be the foundation block of long-term plans, based on effective collusion between the technologist, designer and marketer. This is necessary to achieve the essential balance between creating and satisfying the needs of the customer.

Alternative or substitute product or process technology is more difficult to forecast than core technology, and requires a more qualitative analysis. Steve Jobs famously described the development of the iPad as being the result of imagination and creativity rather than robust research; Apple developers needed to think beyond what customers were asking for and take a view on future ways of living.

- The progress of technology can be assessed in three distinct ways as follows:

    - Evolution of the current technology

    - Morphological. The exploration of technological opportunities by systematically defining the basic features of current technology, identifying the known alternatives and looking for feasible alternatives.

    - Scenarios. These provide views of the future and insight into developments.

- Organisations must have frequent and systematic processes in place to evaluate technological factors.

> ▶ **Exam tip**
>
> Make short notes on other technological developments in each element of the marketing mix:
>
> - Product (ie design cycles)
> - Place (online and mobile channels)
> - Promotion (interactive TV, computer-designed samples, social networking – conversations with customers, QR codes)
> - Price (bar code scanning, electronic pricing)

ACTIVITY 9.3

To the general public, these were all in the future, five years ago – where are they now?

- A chequeless society
- Commercial space travel
- Drive-by-wire electronic systems for congestion-free 'intelligent' motorways
- Speech-responsive computers
- Windscreen maps in cars
- Digital signatures for transactions

6.2 Information Technology and marketing applications

Advances in technology have made the marketer's job easier: access to a greater depth of data for market analysis; direct access to consumers through a wide range of digital media and new online channels of distribution. It has, however, also made the marketers job much harder: customers expect an individualised customer experience; promotional messages are surrounded by the 'noise' of the thousands of messages that consumers are estimated to encounter on a daily basis; and fashions and trends switch quickly making today's winners tomorrow's losers, and vice versa.

Table 9.1   Information technology in the context of the marketing mix

Mix element	Impact of technology
Product	Enabling detailed research processes and analysis
	Branding appropriate to digital channels
	Computer aided design of products
	Digital products such as software, music, games, film and e-books
	Mass customisation eg build your own specification of computer online with Dell
Price	Supporting complex pricing structures and frequent (and automated) market-led price changes

Mix element	Impact of technology
Place	Sales no longer restricted to physical premises
	Online sales channels including web sites and digital distribution partners
	Significance of mobile m-commerce
	Efficient ordering processes through extranets
Promotion	Managing the range of communication channels and tactics: multiple digital broadcast options, web sites and micro sites, social media, mobile, apps and viral campaigns
	Campaigns and communications personalised to the customer
People	Distance learning for staff
	Digital internal marketing
	Management of the non-human customer service experience
	Customers providing information and support to other customers
Process	Expectations of 24 hour service
	Outsourcing eg call centres
	Electronic payment methods
	Customer relationship management systems
Physical evidence	Greater need for trust where physical encounters are limited

THE REAL WORLD

'The internet has revolutionised the way in which consumers make their travel decisions. Web-based marketing campaigns have become an increasingly important means of promoting destinations and tourism services. Social networking websites provide forums for tourists to discuss the places they have visited. More and more people are booking online.'

(European Travel Commission, 2012)

Travel is one of the top sectors for online sales and this has resulted in many significant changes for the industry:

- The number of high street travel agents has fallen dramatically and the mix that they use has had to evolve to provide added value for customers and competitive pricing against online channels.

- The industry itself has gone through significant vertical and horizontal integration in the drive for competitiveness and in the UK market is led by two major groups; Tui Travel and Thomas Cook. These companies have had to rethink their product offering as customers are tending to 'build' their own holidays, negating the need for the services of tour operators.

- Thomas Cook, the world's oldest travel firm, reported a £91 million loss in the first quarter of 2011/12 blaming very tough trading conditions.

- Customers are now less likely to buy a package holiday and more likely to directly purchase flights and accommodation. Online retailers and providers facilitate 'dynamic packaging', where the customer's independently selected elements are rolled into a single purchase.

- Accommodation providers and airlines, once dependent on the big tour operators, can now benefit from direct sales online – saving commissions.

- Even small guest houses can sell on the world stage using simple E-commerce booking and payment systems.

7 Future applications of technology

7.1 From information to commerce

Increasingly, websites have shifted from merely providing information to enabling interactivity and two-way communication as well as sale of products and services. Further opportunities may include:

- More effective and flexible collaboration with business partners
- Competitive advantage for the whole supply chain
- Capture and analyse information to help improve sales
- Small firms can secure deeper discounts from pooled purchasing
- Operational efficiencies reduce transaction costs
- Improved feedback makes suppliers more responsive to customers' needs
- Crowdsourcing – using customers' input to drive change
- The potentially global network of suppliers widens choice and reduces cost
- Smaller suppliers can be integrated into supply chains at minimal cost
- Balance of power shifts to buyers due to price transparency

THE REAL WORLD

My Starbucks idea

Starbucks has over 16,000 outlets around the world and can be seen as a corporate giant but it is eager to engage customers and local stakeholders in the future of the company. Technology has enabled Starbucks to take customer engagement to the next level. Mystarbucksidea.force.com is a website dedicated to encouraging customers to shape the future for their stores. At the time of writing they have received 28,256 ideas for new or evolved products, 12,555 ideas on the atmosphere in stores and location of stores and 8,000 ideas on involvement in social responsibility programmes. This conversation with customers has already resulted in, for example, the rollout of apps across Europe, taste testing events and the return of some previously dropped blends. It also has over 28 million 'fans' on Facebook.

ACTIVITY 9.4

Identify four product areas where you think restructuring due to the rise of internet sales has been the greatest so far. Identify four product/service areas where you think the impact of the internet sales has been the least. Explain your reasoning.

The Chartered Institute of Marketing

7.2 Mobile marketing

Mobile marketing includes all activities which are conducted to communicate with customers through the use of mobile devices. Activities could include:

- Promoting products or services
- Providing information or offers
- Permission based SMS or MMS (multimedia messages)
- E-commerce or M-commerce as it is generally described
- Mobile Geographical Information Systems (GIS)
- Quick Response (QR) codes for smart phones
- Mobile banking

Factors which enhance its attraction for marketers include the following:

- The mobile phone is a very personal device.

- One mobile for one user

- The mobile accompanies the user

- Faster dissemination of information

- The recipient can respond straightaway

- Wider reach than email

- Production costs to marketers are negligible.

- Opt-in mechanisms may reduce irritation and intrusion.

- Excellent for reaching young adults but older customers are also catching up.

- Internet advertising can be viewed by internet connection on mobile device

- Time-based information and location-based information as well as real MMS are increasingly becoming more widely available and popular

- Precise targeting can be facilitated.

- Five to ten times more click-through rates compared to internet advertising messages.

- As mobile phones primarily favour a two-way communication, companies should incorporate two-way aspect in any of their M-campaigns.

- There is significant growth in m-commerce, mobiles being used for transactions.

- The technology enables the seamless customer journey from initial interest and contact right through to after sales.

- The whole process is tailored to the individual: their interests, their favourites and their preferred way to pay.

The task of marketers becomes one of encouraging and enabling; making it easy for customers to access the information and services that are relevant to them as individuals.

7.3 Social media

The phenomenal rise of social media presents new opportunities and threats to marketers. Across the world millions of users are registering to be part of social media services including Facebook, LinkedIn, YouTube, Pinterest, Google and Twitter. Although their use can be seen as 'social' and therefore restricted to lifestyle consumer products, they are also used to great effect by B2B marketers. Benefits to marketers are:

- Facebook polls
- Video chat as a customer service tool

- Engaging with business news and events

- Video demonstrations and client testimonials

- Responding to customers through social media (but should this be at the expense of speed of response to customer service enquiries through traditional channels?)

- Building networks for customer generated content

Together, social media channels need to be seen as the route to e-commerce, driving customer content and to some extent replacing other promotional routes such as search engine optimisation and pay-per-click campaigns.

7.4 Digital (broadband) and internet television

Digital or interactive television encompasses a range of properties:

- Viewers can interact with programmes and use interactive services.

- This technology is interactive. Therefore it enables the following:
  - Email
  - Home shopping

- It also allows significantly more programmes and on-screen peripheral information to be broadcast.

- It also offers much more flexibility.

- This arguably leads to more audience fragmentation.

- It can also lead to the enhanced ability to target audience segments with adverts and direct response promotions.

- The ability to filter out adverts may lead to more programme sponsorship.

- This medium offers new possibilities for marketers.

- Tailored interactive advertising content such as the following can be used:
  - Programmercials (programme sponsorship)
  - Messages on the electronic programme guide
  - Bannering during programmes
  - Product placement
  - The technical properties of this medium can help marketers to build relationships with viewers.

- Increasingly all of these services are accessed through internet TV, sometimes on mobile devices.

7.5 Automated customer handling

- Automated customer handling is increasingly being used within businesses.

- Some fundamental criteria are associated with this:
  - The technology offers several advantages to customers and companies.

  - FAQs enables basic information to be communicated thus savings afforded for both parties.

  - Touch-tone phones and automated exchanges direct customer contacts through a series of prompts (and classical music) eventually leading to the right person in the right department or a precise automated message.

The Chartered Institute of Marketing

- Additional factors for consideration:

    - Care must be taken to minimise or avoid alienation arising from the lack of human interface and other potential frustrations.

    - This could negatively impact customer relationship management.

    - It remains to be seen whether development of videophone technology, with pleasing digitalised 'human' images, will resolve problems.

7.6 Other means of technological advancements

- Teleworking, telecommuting or the electronic cottage involves working from home or the car using telecommunications and computing equipment.

- Teleconferencing/electronic meetings are increasingly becoming part of business practices.

- Virtual companies usually have few or no assets but they provide services through the use of third-party contractors. They are expected to become increasingly successful in the future.

- Cloud computing – access to digital resources through web-based tools rather than through in-house servers.

7.7 CIM – a digital community

The Chartered Institute of Marketing was first founded as the Sales Managers' Association in 1911. Like virtually all organisations, it is moving forward and making use of digital technology to improve its services for members and for the profession. An electronic library enables members to search online for both digital and paper-based resources. Agenda 'papers' are published and disseminated online. Members are part of national interest group networks and regional networks, sharing ideas and building knowledge and connections. Continuing professional development events, real and virtual, are hosted around the world. You can follow CIM on Twitter @CIMinfo. Online webinars are held for studying members and LinkedIn forums are used and monitored to aid learning. Many more technological advances will no doubt follow.

7.8 Resistance to change

- Technology has been the major engine in the development of mass affluence.

- Employees, consumers, distributors and managers may resist change for various reasons.

- Change may also be resisted by external forces such as pressure groups, concerned with the impact on the environment.

- Concerns about security and the fear of 'Big Brother' watching your every move

    - Laws and regulations also constrain what is possible.

    - The Data Protection Act required that mailing list organisations register and abide with its provisions, so scope for direct marketing is limited.

▶ **Exam tip**

Technology is an all-pervasive aspect of a business environment that knows no boundaries. Companies of every nationality will be seeking to exploit its potential for competitive advantage. It is therefore likely to be a popular aspect of the macro environment for examination questions, given its general applicability to all CIM students. Look at past papers and think carefully about question wording. You may be asked to identify technological implications, in which case a list with limited detail should suffice, but you may be asked to analyse or evaluate impacts in which case a more detailed answer is required and you will need to reflect more deeply on the true impact on organisation, good and bad.

CHAPTER ROUNDUP

In this chapter concerning the technological environment:

- Some of the main characteristics of technology and its main phases were identified, culminating in the information or communications era, which developed economies are currently entering.

- The critical role of business was examined and the factors encouraging innovation.

- Technical imperatives driving the pace and diversity of technological change were identified and explained.

- The diffusion process was explained and the need for technological forecasting emphasised. Sources of information by which a business can keep track of potential developments were outlined.

- Various applications to sales and marketing were discussed with reference to the supply chain. Some future applications were assessed including telecommuting and marketing databases.

- An exploration of M-technology and digital communication was also offered.

- Technological change is very much a double-edged phenomenon.

    - Its accelerating pace has accommodated rising populations but produced future shock challenges among many seeking to cope with the myriad changes involved.

    - It has provided convenience through increasingly intelligent products and services but also unforeseen consequences as the effects have rippled through society.

FURTHER READING

Egan, J. (2008) *Relationship marketing: exploring relational strategies in marketing*. 3rd edition. Harlow, Pearson, Chapter 11.

Gummesson, E. (2008) *Total relationship marketing*. 3rd edition. Oxford, Butterworth Heinemann, Chapter 3.

Palmer, A. (2009) *Introduction to marketing: theory and practice* 2nd edition. Oxford, Oxford University Press.

Palmer, A. and Hartley, B. (2012) *The business environment*. 12th edition. Maidenhead, McGraw-Hill, Chapter 4.

Palmer, A. et al (2007) *Managing marketing*. Oxford, Butterworth Heinemann, Chapter 10.

Worthington, I. and Britton, C. (2009) *The business environment*. 6th edition. Harlow, Pearson, Chapter 16.

Websites:

http://www.amazon.co.uk as an example of how internet technology may be harnessed to the provision of innovative customer service

http://www.what is.com is a directory of internet terminology.

http://www.clickz.com for a business perspective on internet developments.

http://viewswire.eiu.com – the Economist Intelligence Unit's forum for news, issues and analysis on technology.

http://www1.oecd.org – statistics and news on global technology developments for the Organisation for Economic Co-operation and Development.

The Chartered Institute of Marketing

REFERENCES

European Travel Commission (2012) New Media Trendwatch. http://www.newmediatrendwatch.com/ [Accessed on 3 March 2012].

International Telecommunications Union (2011) The world in 2011 – ICT facts and figures. http://www.itu.int/ITU-D/ict/facts/2011/material/ICTFactsFigures2011.pdf [Accessed on 3 March 2012].

Key Note (2011) *Exhibitions and conferences*. 12th edition. Richmond Upon Thames, Key Note.

Simpson, K. [email] sent 6 March 2012, 08:09 and information adapted from website: Vetronic (2012) About us. http://www.vetronic/aboutus/php [Accessed on 16 February 2012].

Starbucks (2012) My Starbucks Idea. http://mystarbucksidea.force.com [Accessed on 18 June 2012].

Wylie, I. (2010) Jobs of the future. The Guardian, http://www.guardian.co.uk/money/2010/jan/09/jobs-of-the-future [Accessed on 2 March 2012].

QUICK QUIZ

1   Give three effects of technology on the workforce.

2   Fill in the blank. _____ systems hold customer data and can be used to align products and services to better meet customer needs.

3   List some promotional uses of the internet.

4   Explain the difference between E-commerce and M-commerce.

5   Identify four of the top social media sites/services.

6   Define technological convergence.

7   Describe the stages of the technological diffusion process.

ACTIVITY DEBRIEFS

Activity 9.1

(a)   Examples are numerous, for example IT, pharmaceuticals, chemicals, car design, and financial services. Most industries have been affected by IT systems. Craft goods and personal services may have been among those least affected.

(b)   Many of the information technology-based consumer products and services were not available, eg PCs, laptops, mobile phones, airbags, chip and pin cards, microwaves, camcorders and sophisticated computer games.

Activity 9.2

The motorist would be stranded since microprocessors control ignition, steering, braking and inboard control systems on modern cars. Traffic lights would cease to function, as would petrol pumps. Households would grind to a halt as controls for heating, telecommunications and electronic equipment fail. The marketing department relies on 'information systems' defined as the products, services, methods and people used to

collect, store, process, transmit and display information. It also relies on the telephone, now controlled through digital exchanges, not to mention televisions that receive advertisements. Product information derived from bar code scanners would be lost and banking and credit systems would fail.

Activity 9.3

The degree of diffusion varies but only intelligent motorways appear to be further into the future. According to General Motors, within 50 years, six biofeed sensors in dashboards will detect incipient slumber and vibrate to wake the driver. The motorist could steer into a 'nap lane', set a course using the car's satellite-guided navigation system, engage the autopilot and go to sleep. Computer chips embedded in the tarmac will 'read' the road. Hydrogen-powered fuel cells will replace petrol engines and a joystick will control all movements including braking and accelerating.

Activity 9.4

Product areas most significantly affected by the rise of internet sales could include books (digital and print), music, film, travel, electronic goods and consumer durables. These products are particularly suited to online purchase as they are relatively standardised and delivery can be fulfilled online or through efficient distribution channels. Organisational structures have evolved to meet the needs of these markets and channels.

The internet has had a lesser impact on services such as trades (plumbers, tree surgeons etc.) and professions (lawyers, dentists etc). However, any successful business will recognise the role of digital communications in building relationships with customers before, during and after a sale.

QUICK QUIZ ANSWERS

1. Requires new skill, some jobs become redundant, productivity increases, new service and knowledge roles appear.

2. Customer Relationship Management

3. There are lots of ideas within this chapter including, email and text campaigns, websites and social media.

4. E-commerce (electronic) is the term used to describe online transactions; probably using PCs. M-commerce is where transactions are conducted using mobile technology. M-commerce (mobile) is effectively an element of E-commerce.

5. YouTube, Facebook, LinkedIn and Twitter. Others include Pinterest, Google+ and Foursquare. The popularity and effectiveness of these channels is evolving and should be monitored. This list may look outdated in a matter of months.

6. The ability to use a range of devices for a range of different purposed eg video streaming on mobiles, buying online through your TV.

7. The figure in this text uses the terms pioneers, sheep and laggards. Similar models may use the terms early adopters, early majority, late majority and laggards.

CHAPTER 10

Corporate social responsibility

Introduction

In this chapter we develop our discussion of the organisation's relationship with its external environment further by looking in detail at corporate social responsibility (CSR), sustainability and ethics. We examine the concepts and the impacts that they may have on what the organisation tries to achieve. This builds on the discussion of CSR as a competitive strategy in Chapter 4. The aspects of social responsibility an organisation chooses to focus on will depend on its core activities. It's also worth remembering that in some areas, for example human rights, avoiding negative publicity and damage to reputation can be as important as demonstrating credentials as good corporate citizens. Organisations, through their values and their actions have the power to promote changes in social values in society at large.

Topic list

Corporate social responsibility ①

Corporate citizenship ②

Human rights ③

Sustainable development ④

Shareholder and consumer activism ⑤

Programmes and initiatives ⑥

CSR and marketing ⑦

3.9	Evaluate the impact of economic and environmental sustainability on an organisation's CSR agenda including the impact is has on the organisation, its vision, mission and objectives: ■ Environmental information systems ■ Impact analysis ■ Codes of conduct ■ Social/conscience marketing/human rights ■ Ethics ■ Environmental sustainability ■ Shareholder activism (green shareholders)
3.11	Review the emergence of social marketing as an increasing trend in establishing social values associated with CSR: ■ Growth of social and cause related marketing ■ Traceability/Transparency ■ Fair trade/Local product policy ■ Government initiatives eg, packaging, labelling, recycling, etc

1 Corporate social responsibility

We introduced the concept of CSR in Chapter 4 in the context of competitive positioning but the drivers for increased responsibility come from within the macro environment. Think back to the horrific wake up call of the 1984 Bhopal disaster in India in which a leak from an American-owned chemical factory resulted in the deaths of over 2,000 people. That tragedy arguably marked a turning point in relentless global expansion of multinationals, beyond which wider societal issues could be at the top of the agenda – over profit. Through recent decades human rights and environmental issues have also been a key focus.

- CSR can, in practice, be used to refer only to social impacts but more commonly it is analysed in terms of the triple bottom line framework of sustainability mentioned in Chapter 4, measuring:

  - **Social** progress that recognises the needs of everyone
  - Effective protection of the **environment** and prudent use of natural resources
  - Maintenance of high and stable levels of **economic** growth or employment

- Consider that there are a range of perspectives on this:

  - Sustainability for whom? There is often a conflict between social and environmental sustainability.

  - Sustainable where? Should the developing world be encouraged to reach and sustain the same level of economic development as western economies?

  - Does sustainability equal preservation? Does social sustainability means preserving the existing institutions and customary behaviours of society?

  - For how long? For this generation, the next generation, the next millennium?

  - At what cost? Should ecosystems be protected at the costs of jobs and present-day wellbeing?

  - Sustainable by whom? Meaningful global international agreements are limited at present so the focus is on nations, individuals and businesses.

- An alternative framework for analysing CSR is put forward by Caroll & Buchholtz (2000, cited in Jobber, 2010) who maintain that there are four main layers of CSR:

  - **Economic responsibilities**: Companies have an economic responsibility to shareholders demanding a good return, to employees wanting fair employment terms and customers seeking

good-quality products at a fair price. Businesses are generally driven by financial performance and so economic responsibilities form the basis of all others.

- **Legal responsibilities**: Since laws codify society's moral views, obeying these laws must be the foundation of compliance with social responsibilities. Although in all societies corporations will have some legal responsibilities, there is perhaps more emphasis on them in continental Europe than in the Anglo-American economies. In Anglo-American economies the focus of discussion has often been whether many legal responsibilities are unnecessary burdens on business.

- **Ethical responsibilities**: These are responsibilities that require corporations to act in a fair and just way even if the law does not compel them to do so.

- **Philanthropic responsibilities**: According to Carroll & Buchholtz (2000) these are desired rather than being required of businesses. They might include charitable donations, contributions to local communities and providing employees with the chances to improve their own lives.

ACTIVITY 10.1

Why do marketers have a key role to play in the process of promoting corporate social responsibility?

2 Corporate citizenship

The concept of corporate citizenship provides a different perspective on organisations and society. It seeks to determine how much and in what ways organisations engage with society. Again there are different views of how far it should extend.

- **Limited view**: This is based on voluntary philanthropy undertaken in the organisation's interests. The main stakeholder groups that the corporate citizen engages with are local communities and employees. Citizenship in action takes the form of limited focus projects.

- **Equivalent view**: This is based on a wider definition of citizenship that is partly voluntary and partly imposed. The organisation focuses on a broad range of stakeholders and responds to the demands of society. Self-interest is not the primary motivation; instead the organisation is focused on legal requirements and ethical fulfilment.

- **Extended view**: This view is based on a partly voluntary, partly imposed view of active social and political citizenship. Corporations must respect citizen's rights, particularly as governments have failed to provide some of the safeguards necessary for their citizens. Corporations can make a big impact since they are amongst the most powerful institutions in society.

THE REAL WORLD

Northern Rock featured in the December 2011/March 2012 case study and reference was made to the setting up of the Northern Rock Foundation, 'an independent charity that aimed to tackle disadvantage (be it age, infirmity or poverty) and improve the quality of life for people in the North East of England and Cumbria' (CIM, 2011). An exam task asked students to consider the benefits to Northern Rock. Northern Rock was seen as supporting social causes as a means of creating goodwill, awareness or loyalty. A further controversial issue raised by the case was the payment of large performance bonuses to senior staff after the crisis and as a nationalised organisation; a sore point with UK taxpayers who have had to bear the brunt of the government's bailout of the struggling bank.

3 Human rights

Publicity on human rights can often have a negative impact on a business's reputation. Equally, organisations can achieve positive benefits from a good human rights record.

Multi-nationals, with turnover higher than many individual countries, wield great power and influence over standards but the same issues exist for smaller businesses and can include:

- Environmental health eg pollutants affecting health directly, or indirectly through food production
- Child labour in agriculture and in manufacturing
- Workplace safety
- Freedom of expression

The FTSE 4 Good Indices and Dow Jones Sustainability Index both measure the performance of companies against globally recognised corporate responsibility standards including human rights. The Dow Jones Sustainability Index assesses and organisation's human rights records through the following criteria:

- Public policy statement including a clear declaration of support for the Universal Declaration of Human Rights

- Clear board responsibility

- Commitment to internationally recognised labour standards

- Commitment to respect indigenous people's rights

- Employee human rights training

- Stakeholder consultation

- A human rights impact assessment

- Production of a human rights report

Dow Jones's 2011 review lists organisations that are best in sector including BMW, PepsiCo, Xstrata and Air France-KLM.

4 Sustainable development

The most often quoted definition of sustainable development comes from the Brundtland Commission 1987 (cited IISD, 2012).

> 'Sustainable development is development that meets the needs of the present without compromising the ability of future generations to meet their own needs...'

At a local and national level, planning authorities will assess the suitability of proposed developments in terms of the impact on the local environment, the economic contribution the development will make in terms of taxation income and jobs and the contribution to the social or cultural wellbeing of an area.

At a global level, the International Finance Corporation (part of the World Bank Group) offers a framework for institutions reviewing the sustainability of investments, which indicates that projects should be appraised on:

- Assessment and management of social and environmental risks and impacts
- Labour and working conditions
- Resource efficiency and pollution prevention
- Community health, safety and security
- Land acquisition and involuntary resettlement
- Biodiversity conservation and sustainable natural resource management
- Indigenous peoples
- Cultural heritage

The Chartered
Institute of Marketing

In 2011 the UK government produced a draft National Planning Policy Framework which aimed to replace over 1,000 pages of planning guidance to just 12 pages with an emphasis on sustainability. While protecting local heritage and natural sites the framework aims to:

- Facilitate further expansion of renewable energy regeneration
- Encourage support for green transport
- Tackle light pollution

The Department for Communities and Local Government (2011) described the how the framework could be used in conjunction with local economic development planning.

'The draft Framework also underlines the need for councils to work closely with communities and businesses and actively seek opportunities for sustainable growth to rebuild the economy; helping to deliver the homes, jobs, and infrastructure needed for a growing population whilst protecting the environment. A presumption in favour of sustainable development means that proposals should be approved promptly unless they would compromise the key sustainable development principles...'

5 Shareholder and consumer activism

5.1 Shareholder activism

Sustainability and environmental performance is of increasing importance to many shareholders. Groups of shareholders and networks, such as the Ethical Shareholders Group, exist to promote the concerns of 'green' shareholders and to ensure that relevant issues make their way onto companies' agendas. Shareholders can influence in the following ways:

- Voting in favour of ethical and environmental resolutions
- Suggesting improved practices
- Letter writing campaigns to directors, senior management and politicians

Some shareholders will invest in a company's shares in order to have a voice. Others may be selecting shares on the basis of ethical and sustainable management. There has been significant growth in 'ethical' investment funds aimed at this latter group.

5.2 Consumer activism

Consumer associations and campaigning organisations exist to support the rights of consumers. New media has enabled the consumer movement to spread messages and encourage consumers to act:

- Protesting against issues that matter to them such has human rights or environmental protection – such protests can gain significant publicity and prove embarrassing for targeted companies.

- Boycotting products and services – this has the potential to cause real harm to corporate performance.

Ethical Consumer is one organisation encouraging consumers to vote with their feet and in 2012 their active boycotts included:

- Tesco for selling live turtles in their stores in China

- Nestle – the longest running boycott which started in 1977 – for sales of baby milk products in developing countries

- The charity British Heart Foundation for use of animals in medical research

- Royal Bank of Scotland for its involvement in the Canadian oil sands

Ethics on the high street

In 2011 UK high street chain, Topman, part of the Arcadia Group, was criticised through social media websites for a T-shirt design that was perceived to be glamorising domestic violence. *Marketing* magazine (2011) was amongst the media reporting the story and the store's apology. The T-shirts were swiftly removed from sale. Pressure groups may act as the catalyst but it is the significant power of consumers, aided by social media communications, that can result in very quick actions from businesses keen to maintain a positive image. The same group (Arcadia) hit the headlines just a year earlier over its tax avoidance strategies (see Chapter 2).

During the 1990s, the rights of workers, many of them women and children, were highlighted and the awareness of these issues resulted in the growth of campaigning organisation. Ethical Consumer (2012) produces detailed ethics reports on various sectors including banking, food and transport. Their research on the high street reveals the ethical good guys and bad guys, covering issues such as:

- The promotion of positive body images for women (as it impacts on female health eg anorexia)
- Worker's rights along the supply chain
- Production waste and water usage

The resulting index places brands such as Bonmarche, New Look and Gap at the ethical end and supermarket brands from Sainsbury's, Tesco and Asda at the bottom of the ethical scale.

6 Programmes and initiatives

The principles and practices of corporate social responsibility are extremely wide ranging and businesses, in establishing a position that reflects their values, may consider a range of programmes, initiatives or principles such as:

- Fair trade
- Traceability
- Local purchasing

6.1 Fair Trade

> **Key term**
>
> **Fair trade marketing** 'is the development, promotion and selling of fair trade brands and the positioning of organisations on the basis of a fair trade ethos.' (Jobber, 2010 p196) Customers are prepared to pay a price premium for the peace of mind that producers (in developing countries) are being paid a fair wage for their produce. Coffee, bananas and cocoa are just some of the products that have captured a significant share of the wider market.

The term fair trade is most commonly used in connection with the relations between producers based in the developing world and retailers based in advanced economies.

- Producers, traditionally the weaker partner in this relationship, are guaranteed a fair price.

- Long term supply relationships are set up enabling communities to invest.

- Agreements often mean financial support for wider community facilities and initiatives.

- The ethos is supported by consumers in the form of higher prices.

A number of certification bodies exist to reassure customers that the appropriate standards and terms for producers are being met. Fair Trade International is a global network of 25 fair trade organisations setting and controlling standards.

The Chartered
Institute of Marketing

In 2009, Britain's top chocolate brand, Cadbury, began a move towards fair trade with the UK's Fair Trade Foundation. Both Cadbury's and the Fair Trade Foundation have featured as case studies for Assessing the Marketing Environment.

> ▶ **Exam tip**
>
> Consider how different elements of the syllabus for this unit may be linked. For example CSR as an increasingly significant macro environmental factor will have an impact on how an organisation meets the needs of its stakeholders. Practise this approach by investigating the benefits of fair trade for a range of stakeholders.

6.2 Traceability

Organisations are increasingly expected to be able to trace the flow of all raw materials and ingredients from producers through to manufacture:

- Traceability of food so that consumers can be assured of production standards.
    - Consider the recent arguments about the difference between 'outdoor-reared' and 'outdoor-bred' pork.
    - Food safety can be enhanced as the source of any contamination can be easily traced.
- Traceability of wood products so that customers are aware of the sustainability.
    - Forest Stewardship Council (FSC) is one recognised badge.

6.3 Local products and services

Promotion of local products can also link with societal marketing and sustainability.

- It can be a means of sustaining local industries such as agriculture or fishing.
- Wealth is retained and circulates within the local economy.
- Carbon footprints can be reduced as movement of goods is reduced.

The food and drink industry has been a key campaigner for 'buy-local' but it can also impact upon wider procurement policies in large organisations aiming to demonstrate commitment to a community.

7 CSR and marketing

> ▶ **Key term**
>
> **Marketing ethics**: Jobber (2010) describes **marketing ethics** as 'the moral principles and value that guide behaviour within the field of marketing, and cover issues such as product safety, truthfulness in marketing communications, honesty in relationships with customers and distributors, pricing issues and the impact of marketing decisions on the environment and society'.

The ideas and practices of corporate social responsibility are underpinned by the concept of ethics.

The ethical perspective of marketing in relation to the marketing mix is as follows.

- Product eg food safety, issues around alcohol and tobacco, production and manufacturing processes and the impact that this can have on stakeholders and the environment.

- Price eg the price and availability of medicines to the developing world.

- Place eg access to services such as libraries or GPs and the equality of access where some services are available only online.

- Promotion eg tasteful, reflecting appropriate diversity and not misleading. Considering the use of non-renewable materials. Choice of media consistent with ethical brand values.

A corporate ethics code typically contains a series of statements setting out the organisation's values and explaining how it sees its responsibilities towards stakeholders. Such codes might cover:

- Regulating employee behaviour and relationships with suppliers and subcontractors
- Specific areas such as gifts, and anticompetitive behaviour
- They tend to be formal documents and employees may be asked to sign that they will comply
- They can be used to shift responsibility from senior managers to operational staff

7.1 Chartered Marketer's Code

> ▶ **Key terms**
>
> **Societal marketing**
>
> Aims to promote the consumer's long term interests rather than gratifying their immediate needs. This means not just avoiding marketing activities that may not be in people's best interests, but actively promoting sustainable, ethical issues.
>
> **Cause related marketing**
>
> This refers to marketing activities in which a business forms a partnership or association with a charity or cause in order to promote a product, brand or issues, for mutual benefits.
>
> - The term is sometimes used more broadly for any type of marketing on behalf of social and other charitable causes
> - Cause marketing differs from corporate philanthropy as philanthropy generally involves a donation, whereas cause-related marketing is a relationship not generally based on donations.
>
> Examples of cause related marketing include:
> - Sponsoring community or arts events
> - Raising funds on behalf of charities
> - Providing resources or seconding staff to assist in initiatives tackling social or environmental problems
>
> Benefits:
> - Cause related marketing can create mutual gains and positive synergy when the business and charity have similar target audiences and similar messages
> - Businesses can achieve better public relations and gain marketing opportunities
> - Enhanced morale amongst staff
> - Charities may gain more than money eg reaching new supporters through an organisation's customer base

CIM's Chartered Marketer status is framed in a Code of Professional Standards for members. The clauses within the code stipulates that a Chartered Marketer should:

- At all times conduct himself with integrity in such a way as to bring credit to the profession of marketing and CIM.

- Not by unfair or unprofessional practice injure the business, reputation or interest of any other member of CIM.

- At all times, act honestly in professional dealings with customers and clients (actual and potential), employers and employees.

- Not knowingly or recklessly disseminate any false or misleading information, either on his own behalf or on behalf of anyone else.

- Keep abreast of current marketing practice and act competently and diligently and be encouraged to register for CIM's scheme of Continuing Professional Development.

- At all times seek to avoid conflict of interest and make prior voluntary and full disclosure to all parties concerned of all matters that may arise during any such conflict.

- Keep business information confidential except from those persons entitled to receive it, where it breaches this code and where it is illegal to do so.

- Promote and seek business in a professional and ethical manner.

- Observe the requirements of all other codes of practice which may from time to time have any relevance to the practice of marketing insofar as such requirements do not conflict with any provisions of this code, or CIM's Royal Charter and Bye-laws.

- Not hold themselves out as having CIM's endorsement in connection with an activity unless CIM's prior written approval has been obtained first.

- Not use any funds derived from CIM for any purpose which does not fall within the powers and obligations contained in the Constitution and Member Group Guide, and which does not fully comply with this code.

- Have due regards for, and comply with, all the relevant laws of the country in which they are operating.

Consider this in relation to CIM's definition of marketing:

The Chartered Institute of Marketing

The management process responsible for identifying, anticipating and satisfying customer requirements profitably.

Jobber (2010, p186) introduces two societal concerns for marketers:

- **Materialism**: marketing promotes materialism which may not be in the best interests of a society. Consumers crave brands, not because it will give them a better life but because organisations spend millions persuading them to buy.

- **Short-termism**: products are developed to satisfy current preferences at the expense of longer term wellbeing.

ACTIVITY 10.2

Identify societal marketing approaches that may be in conflict with the more immediate customer wants and needs.

THE REAL WORLD

Zero air miles

Devon-based Riverford Organic Vegetables is a network of farms that produce, source and sell organic produce, delivering to over 40,000 customers a week around England. While supermarkets will sell for example green beans flown in from Kenya, Riverford have a firm 'we never airfreight' policy which means that their customers are encouraged to build menus around produce with a lower carbon footprint. Air freight (particularly short haul) has the highest carbon footprint of any freight transport method.

ACTIVITY 10.3

What steps do businesses need to take to develop brands that are successful **and** sustainable?

- Corporate social responsibility is an overarching theme across the macro environment.

- The triple bottom line represents one framework for analysis of impacts.

- CSR can comprise economic, legal ethical and philanthropic responsibilities.

- An extended view of corporate citizenship suggests that business can have a responsibility beyond that of governments.

- Human rights represent a significant area of challenge for global corporations and is one measure that is increasingly being used to appraise investments.

- Sustainable development principles are driving investment, planning and development decisions at local, national and global levels.

- Shareholder and consumer activism has the power to contribute positively or negatively to corporate performance and direction.

- CSR principles shape the marketer's role and are embedded in the Chartered Marketer's Code.

- Marketers hold a critical role as they influence two-way communications and the tactics in the marketing mix.

- Cause related marketing is a specific area of activity that marketers can use.

FURTHER READING

CIM (2007) Marketing and the Triple Bottom Line. http://www.cim.co.uk/resources/ethics/tbl.aspx [Accessed on 9 March 2012]

Jobber, D. (2010) *Principles and practice of marketing*. 6th edition. Maidenhead, McGraw-Hill, Chapter 6.

Palmer, A. and Hartley, B. (2012) *The business environment*. 12th edition. Maidenhead, McGraw-Hill, Chapter 5.

Worthington, I. and Britton, C. (2009) *The business environment*. 6th edition. Harlow, Pearson, Chapter 17.

Websites:

http://www.sustainability.com – a sustainability consultancy

http://www.forumforthefuture.org – a not-for-profit sustainability organisation

http://www.ethicalconsumer.org – alternative consumer organisation

http://www.corporatewatch.org – a research organisation supporting anti-corporate campaigns

http://www.fairtrade.net – international network of fair trade organisations

http://www.wrap.org.uk – Waste and Resources Action Programme

REFERENCES

Chapman, M. (2011) Topman removes T-shirt glamourising domestic violence. Marketing Magazine, http://www.marketingmagazine.co.uk/news/1092116/Topman-removes-shirts-glamourising-domestic-violence/ [Accessed on 8 March 2012].

The Chartered Institute of Marketing (2011) *Assessing the Marketing Environment*. December 2011 Case study.

The Chartered Institute of Marketing (2010) Professional Marketing Standards. http://cim.co.uk/filestore/about/codeofprofessionalstandards10.pdf [Accessed on 8 March 2012].

Communities and Local Government (2011) Dramatic simplification of planning guidance to encourage sustainable growth. http://www.communities.gov.uk/news/corporate/1951729 [Accessed on 9 March 2012].

Dow Jones (2011) Dow Jones sustainability indexes. http://www.sustainability-index.com/djsi_pdf/news/PressReleases/SAM_Presentation_110908_Review11_final.pdf [Accessed on 9 March 2012].

Ethical Consumer (2012) Active boycott list. http://www.ethicalconsumer.org/boycotts/currentboycottslist.aspx [Accessed on 9 March 2012].

Ethical Consumer (2012) Shopping guide to high street clothes shops. http://www.ethicalconsumer.org/buyersguides/clothing/clothesshops.aspx [Accessed on 8 March 2012].

FTSE (2012) FTSE4Good index series. http://www.ftse.com/Indices/FTSE4Good_Index_Series/index.jsp [Accessed on 8 March 2012].

International Finance Corporation (2012) IFC's sustainability framework. http://www1.ifc.org/wps/wcm/connect/topics_ext_content/ifc_external_corporate_site/ifc+sustainability+framework/2012+edition/2012-edition#SustainabilityPolicy [Accessed on 8 March 2012].

International Institute for Sustainable Development (2012) What is sustainable development? http://www.iisd.org/sd/ [Accessed on 9 March 2012].

QUICK QUIZ

1   What are Carroll & Buchholtz's four levels of corporate social responsibility?

2   Complete this definition: The Brundtland report defines sustainability as 'meeting the needs of the present without _____'

3   What is meant by societal marketing?

4   How do retailers support producers under fair trade?

5   Give three examples of cause related marketing.

Activity 10.1

The CIM paper on the triple bottom line emphasises the marketer's role as a two-way link between customers and businesses. Marketers can feedback customers' increasing concerns about sustainability, fair trade, local sourcing and human rights and communicate to customers what the business is doing to address these issues. Because of their good communications skills, marketers are good candidates to champion CSR.

Activity 10.2

Societal marketing conflicts could include: retailers reducing use of packaging in a way that fails to meet the needs of consumers; energy providers installing smart metres that could encourage lower usage; retailers changing policies on selling provocative clothes in young teenage sizes.

Activity 10.3

Steps could include:

- Thorough brand evaluation including values
- Detailed understanding of customers' needs, wants and aspirations
- A CSR policy that is embedded throughout all marketing areas (not just promotion)
- Incentivising performance on measures related to CSR and long-term impacts
- Communicating CSR messages effectively and consistently

QUICK QUIZ ANSWERS

1   Economic, legal, ethical and philanthropic

2   'Meeting the needs of the present without compromising the ability of future generations to meet their own needs.'

3   Meeting the needs and wants of its target markets but doing so in a way that preserves or enhances the consumers' and society's wellbeing.

4   Primarily by guaranteeing fair prices and long-term trading relationships

5   Examples could include partnering with relevant charities, engaging customers in charitable activities, pay-back schemes that return profits to communities or other beneficiaries and encouraging and enabling staff to volunteer.

CHAPTER 11

Coping with the challenges of the environment

Introduction

This concluding chapter focuses on the effective management of the future marketing environment as covered in the fourth and final section of the syllabus. First we consider the importance of information and the need for organisations to develop an effective marketing information system. This is concerned with the collection, presentation and effective interpretation of important marketing information, and with the creative manipulation of that information into a form that is useful for the strategy and planning processes of the organisation. We discuss the key problems in dealing with the dynamism and uncertainty of future change and the role of forecasting and the tools and techniques available to the marketer to assist in predict future market conditions. Multi-faceted and in most cases interactive, change in one part of the marketing environment causes reactions elsewhere. Marketers must understand the complex relationships and processes at work and, if possible, be part of the change itself rather than merely responding belatedly to its effects. This chapter draws together the strands of the whole marketing environment syllabus.

Topic list

Monitoring the marketing environment	1
The importance of information	2
The Marketing Information System (MkIS)	3
The importance of marketing research	4
Coping with the environmental challenge	5
Forecasting	6
Marketing audit toolbox	7

3.10	Evaluate different methods for undertaking analysis of environmental trends:
	■ Environmental audits ■ Quantitative and qualitative forecasting techniques ■ Trend impact analysis ■ Scenario building ■ Delphi method
4.1	Explain the process of undertaking the internal and external market environment audit:
	■ Environmental scanning ■ Collecting internal and external marketing information ■ PESTEL analysis ■ A competitor comparison of key competitors ■ Assessing opportunities and threats ■ Reviewing environmental and resource constraints
4.2	Describe the meaning and role of various analytical tools in the marketing auditing process:
	■ PESTEL ■ Five Ms ■ Ansoff's Growth Strategy Matrix ■ SWOT

1 Monitoring the marketing environment

Organisations compete and collaborate with a variety of primary stakeholders and interact as interrelated parts of the wider marketing environment. The environment is subject to continuous change, which organisations must monitor and adapt to. To be effective the business organisation must possess the following subsystems:

■ A sensing system to access information and appraise developments using secondary sources or market research to acquire market understanding.

■ An information classification system to convert data into useful information.

■ An information processing system to give information meaning.

■ An information database and retrieval system to collate, store and mine data.

■ A control system to establish any deviations from established objectives.

■ A planning and policy-making system so decisions can be based on choices identified and evaluated by the marketing information system.

■ A communication system to receive and distribute information internally and externally.

1.1 Undertaking a marketing audit

> ▶ **Key term**
>
> **Marketing audit**
>
> 'A marketing audit is a comprehensive, systematic, independent and periodic examination of a company's – or business unit's – marketing environment, objectives, strategies and activities with a view to determining problem areas and opportunities and recommending a plan of action to improve the company's marketing performance.' (Kotler, 1994)

In the context of this unit the focus of the audit is on the internal and external marketing environment. A marketing audit does not exist in the compulsory formal sense that an external financial audit does. For proper strategic control, however, a marketing audit should be:

■ **Regular:** for example, completed once a year

■ **Comprehensive:** reviewing all internal, micro and macro elements

■ **Systematic:** it should be carried out according to a set of predetermined, specified procedures and methods.

The Chartered
Institute of Marketing

- **Independent:** A consultant can be used or a member of staff with an unbiased overview (significant internal weaknesses may be identified and this could be contentious).

A structured approach to auditing the marketing environment should reduce the need for crisis management and identify information needs but its key role is in forcing decision-makers to analyse and evaluate the current situation and, moving forward, develop appropriate marketing strategies.

A checklist of questions to answer when undertaking an audit of the internal and external environment might be:

Internal environment:

(a)   Is the current legal status appropriate for the organisation's current and future position?

(b)   Are internal resources adequate and efficiently used?

(c)   Do leaders and staff have the required competencies to meet future challenges?

(d)   Are internal strengths and weaknesses identified and evaluated?

(e)   Are the organisation's mission and vision, strategies and objectives clear, appropriate and do they reflect the values of the organisation?

Micro environment:

(f)   Are stakeholders identified and evaluated in terms of their power and influence?

(g)   Are stakeholder relationships monitored and evaluated?

(h)   How well is the organisation performing in achieving customer satisfaction through the product portfolio?

(i)   How is the marketing mix used to competitively deliver value to customers?

(j)   Is the organisation's competitive position assessed and are strengths, weaknesses and key success factors of competitors monitored and evaluated?

(k)   What are the impacts of competition regulation on the organisation in any of its markets?

Macro environment:

(l)   What significant legislation affects the organisation and how might political influences impact regulation or market conditions in the future?

(m)   How are the economies of the organisation's markets performing and what are the potential impacts?

(n)   How are demographic or cultural factors changing and what are the likely impacts?

(o)   How do technological changes impact upon the production of, or the demand for, the organisation's products and services?

(p)   What are the significant pressures on the natural environment and what actions can the organisation take to mitigate negative impacts?

(q)   How are changes in any of the above areas monitored and future scenarios forecast?

2 The importance of information

Information and information management is vital to enable the organisation to respond to the above checklist of questions.

Organisations need to ensure that the information and knowledge engendered is utilised effectively to achieve competitive advantage.

Information is of limited value unless it meets the following criteria:

- Data must be collected from the right sources.
- Data must be accurate enough to form the basis of effective decision-making.
- Data should be collected at a time relevant to decisions to be taken.
- Data should be processed into market intelligence.
- Information should be made available to appropriate parties.
- Data should be collected, processed, stored and distributed in a timely and cost-effective manner in line with the three crucial stages of database management.
- The information should be presented concisely and in adequate depth.

Information needs to be collected, processed and communicated for four important marketing purposes:

- Planning
- Strategy formulation
- Decision-making
- Control

Information communication technologies help organisations in many ways. They:

- Improve dialogues and relationships with important stakeholders
- Improve the ability to learn from others, past trends and patterns
- Allow instantaneous customer-focused response to complaints
- Increase speed and cost-effectiveness of research
- Communicate with customers

> **▶ Exam tip**
>
> Have you visited the CIM website and consulted past papers? Have you reviewed the Senior Examiner's comments on these and been attempting sample questions under examination conditions? Have you also consulted the specimen paper? At this stage, it is all about preparing SWOT and PESTEL analyses and revising theory with relevance to specific cases. This is also part of what you are expected to do with the case study given before the exam.

2.1 Marketing skills: information at your fingertips

- Sophisticated databases and data mining procedures enable better-quality information to support decisions.
- Information analysis can also help companies take advantage of opportunities enabled by tastes becoming less standardised and predictable.
- The business press knows what is going on in the marketing environment.
- Marketers need a network of business contacts.
- Social media offers many new routes to information gathering.

The Chartered Institute of Marketing

3 The Marketing Information System (MkIS)

The role and purpose of the MkIS was outlined in Chapter 4, in the context of analysing the micro environment. In bringing together all of the elements of the marketing environment, the MkIS serves as a tool to manage all data from all areas of the marketing environment. As Kotler and Keller (2011) have defined it, a Marketing Information System consists of people, equipment and procedures needed to gather, sort, analyse, evaluate and distribute needed, timely and accurate information for decision-making. How is the information gathered and stored? What is the likely scope for its range and depth? How is the resulting information likely to be used?

Information for a Marketing Information System (MkIS) comes from three main sources:

- Internal data
- Marketing intelligence
- Marketing research

A marketing information system can be used by organisations for a variety of reasons:

- To generate new knowledge or access it from external sources
- To represent knowledge in documents, databases, software, promotions and so on
- To embed knowledge in new processes, products and services
- To diffuse existing marketing information throughout an organisation
- To apply accessible knowledge to effective marketing decision-making
- To facilitate more knowledge through market research and competitor intelligence
- To measure the value of marketing knowledge assets and their impact
- To identify opportunities and/or create value

Market research can provide some important specific feedback, but a marketing intelligence gathering system is the main means of identifying emerging trends. A balance has to be struck between the benefits of additional information and the costs of collection and of inaccuracy arising from insufficient data.

ACTIVITY 11.1

List types of information on the macro environment and the micro environment.

THE REAL WORLD

Lego

Perhaps perceived as a traditional and even old-fashioned organisation, Lego has in fact thrived in the battle against hi-tech toys and digital gaming cultures. Indeed, although the company's basic product remains the Lego brick, its full product portfolio includes licensed products related to blockbuster films and of course its own range of online games. The Danish company featured as the case study for the Assessing the Marketing Environment exam in September 2009 and the case described the Company's use of 'listening posts' in key markets around the world to gather critical information on macro and micro market factors and trends.

Figure 11.1 shows that any business needs an integrated internal and external information system to provide the means for dovetailing organisational and marketing developments with environmental change.

Figure 11.1   An integrated internal and external information system

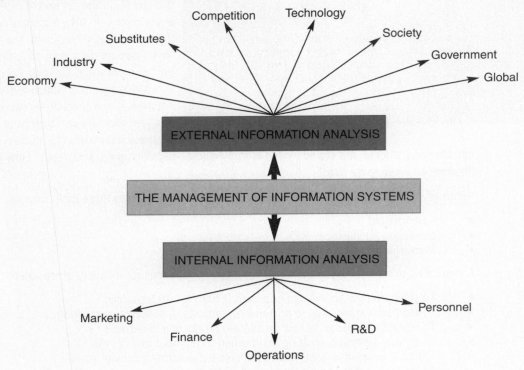

3.1 Online business information

- Databases are revolutionising management information systems.
- They are simply an electronic file of information.
- Data gathering can be cost-effectively automated.
- They provide ease, speed of access and can be analysed.

Figure 11.2 shows some of the main sources of information available and virtually all of this data is published online.

The Chartered
Institute of Marketing

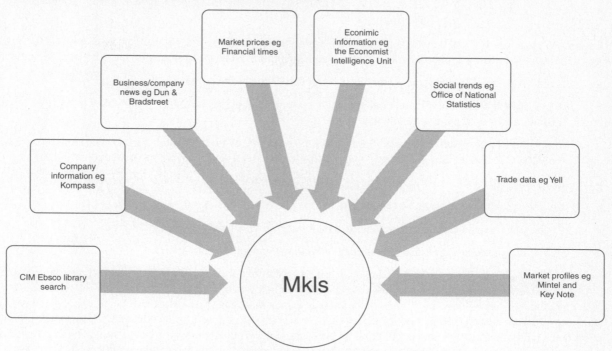

- Online searching offers additional benefits compared to traditional methods.

- Business database applications should ideally include:

  - Market research and marketing plans
  - Marketing presentations and customer relations/communications
  - Market/sales analysis and sales force co-ordination

- Limitations of Information and Communication Technologies (ICT):

  - Balance is needed between the need for information and the cost
  - Danger of information overload
  - Reliance on experience and intuition rather than cross-referencing
  - Dependence on human interpretation/judgement of the information
  - Physical and psychological communication barriers and resistance

Personal privacy is a hot topic and fear of loss of personal data is rising. In fact, technological advances have enabled people and businesses to know a great deal more about us as consumers. How are businesses gathering and using data about you?

- Over 4 million CCTV cameras – more than the rest of Europe combined.

- A £12 billion investment in a national computer system linking GPs, hospitals and medical records although the scale of this unmanageable project was axed in 2011.

- The world's largest DNA database (3.6 million profiles or 6% of the population) with 40,000 added monthly as a result of the 2003 Criminal Justice Act extending coverage to anyone arrested even if not subsequently charged.

- Spy in the sky satellites/GPS/road pricing technology to track and store vehicle movements and monitor how we drive

- Recording of phone messages, emails and mobile phone conversations

- Online purchases, till scanners, loyalty card histories and credit card transaction records

- Online usage recording details of searches, interests, connections and spend

Both Facebook and Google have in the past fallen foul of customers and lost goodwill by introducing changes to privacy policies that ultimately give these companies greater commercial scope for using information about you. For example, information you provide to Google can be used by them to commercially exploit market opportunities through Google search and YouTube. Businesses will be paying Google to put their message in front of you – their perfect customer! This depth of data is arguably great news for marketers, who can reach the right audience, and to consumers, who get to see relevant advertising. However, the privacy concerns remain high and are raising questions of social responsibility and human rights.

▶ **Exam tip**

One of the most common causes of poor examination performance is the failure to address the question. To prevent this:

- Practise on as many questions as possible

- Conform to the format and context requirement

- Underline the instructions for example explain/compare/give implications/illustrate/discuss

- Define key words that represent the central issue of the question eg stakeholders/macro/micro/internal

- Once you have understood the question, make a list or a mind map of your main points and check these when you write your answer

- If asked for an evaluation of **two** factors, don't waste valuable time covering more

- While you are writing your answer, if more points come up, add these to your list and then go back to where you were with your answer.

- Once you have completed your answer, go back to your main points and verify if you have addressed all of them.

Leave a bit of space at the end of each task – you have time to revisit it and add more detail.

4 The importance of marketing research

- The quality of marketing decisions is directly related to the quality of information that underpins them.

- Fundamental characteristics of marketing research:

    - It is an important marketing tool which generates information.

    - It systematically collects, researches and analyses information about specific marketing problems or potential marketing opportunities.

    - It is a continuous process in an environment of change.

    - It feeds into the Marketing Information System (MkIS) through environmental scanning of the PESTEL factors.

    - It helps monitor change in the behaviour of customers and competitors.

    - It improves the ability of the marketer to make timely decisions.

4.1 The information benefits of marketing research

Information features in all of the key stages of the marketing research process:

- Defining the research problem
- Setting specific research objectives
- Designing a research plan
- Determining information needs
- Defining secondary sources and gathering information
- Planning quantitative and qualitative data collection
- Selecting research techniques and implementing research plan
- Data analysing, interpretation and reporting of findings

The information benefits that flow from the market research process includes:

- Focus on the organisation-specific information requirements
- Assistance in defining the nature of your marketing problems
- Detail that is unavailable from mere scanning of secondary sources
- Information tailored to current and future needs of the organisation
- Information unavailable to competitors; thus potential competitive advantage
- In-depth survey of secondary sources and identification of primary data needs
- Appropriate and cost-effective research approaches to gather primary data
- Objective interpretation of timely information can form basis for action

Can you match up the definitions to the marketing research terms?

1   Exploratory research
2   Observational research
3   Causal research
4   Descriptive research
5   Qualitative research
6   Quantitative research
(a)   Test hypotheses regarding cause-effect relationships
(b)   Gather primary data by people, behaviour and situations
(c)   Gather preliminary data to help define problems or suggest relationships
(d)   Collect interview data in sufficient volume to allow statistical analysis
(e)   Help describe markets and marketing problems, for example market potential
(f)   Uncover customer motivations, attitudes or buying behaviour using personal or small group techniques

5 Coping with the environmental challenge

- Many businesses have a planning horizon of five to ten years, long-term strategies.

- As turbulence undermines predictability, such approaches can be questionable.

- Potential consequences of bad forecasts are so significant that organisations need to consistently consider a few factors such as the following:

  - Which are the right forecasts?
  - How significant are the different trends?
  - Where are the turning points?
  - Which are the discontinuities?
  - What is the pace of change?

- Possible business responses to forecasting problems could include:

  - Abandonment of all forecasting pretensions
  - Concentration on short-term adaptive planning
  - Improvement of the quality of conventional forecasts

- The problem with forecasting is not a lack of the necessary statistical techniques but rather the quality and availability of the necessary data.

- Organisations should evaluate from where they are collecting their data, what and how they are inputting and review their primary information.

The Chartered
Institute of Marketing

6 Forecasting

Forecasting market potential and expected sales can be regarded as both an art and a science. Forecasting techniques that rely on historic information of projecting current trends into the future can be misleading as future determinants of the market for a particular product can be significantly different to those existing in the past or in the present. However, businesses do need to make long-term strategic plans which means they need to have a reasonable degree of certainty over significant environmental trends and developments.

Some forecasting methods are:

- Statistical techniques

  - Moving averages – removing fluctuations by averaging results of a fixed number of periods to eliminate seasonal variations

  - Time series analysis – used to identify seasonal and other cyclical fluctuations and the long-term underlying trends

  - Econometrics – the study of economic variables and their inter-relationships using computer models

- Delphi method – in this method a number of experts are asked to independently and anonymously give their opinions and insights on a particular trend and how it may develop. These initial results are summarised and the summary is returned to the experts who are then asked to respond again. The process is repeated until a consensus is achieved.

- Scenario building – a scenario is a detailed and consistent view of the ways in which the business environment of an organisation might develop in the future. Scenarios inevitably deal with conditions of high uncertainty so they are essentially qualitative in nature. They are a tool to help set the scene for decision-making, showing managers some of the key factors that need to be considered and the potential effect on the business. They therefore represent a tool for preparing for the future rather than definitive forecasts of what the future might hold.

7 Marketing audit toolbox

Marketers have a toolbox of models, techniques and frameworks to help them understand a turbulent environment including internal audits, external audits, the environmental set, impact analysis, PESTEL analysis/SWOT analysis, the product life cycle and forecasting methods.

7.1 5 Ms Model of organisational inputs

The 5 Ms model, as introduced in Chapter 1, refers to inputs that an organisation requires in order to function and add value. They are:

- Men
- Money
- Machines
- Materials
- Minutes

The competence and skill employed within the organisation should be used in a way to enable the transformation of these inputs into something valuable of importance to the customer. This forms a framework for analysis of the internal marketing environment.

7.2 Environmental audits

Environmental audits are the means of acquiring knowledge through the regular identification and collection of relevant information on the current situation.

Audits include:

■   The internal environment – competencies and resources

■   The micro environment – markets, connected stakeholders and competitors

■   External environments and key macroeconomic indicators.

Audits help organisations with a variety of functions, namely:

■   Systematic understanding of the environment

■   Provision of critical input into the strategic planning process

■   Indication of areas an organisation should be adapting

■   Underpinning projected diversification or extension to foreign markets

■   Complementing an internal or marketing audit to assess effectiveness in meeting marketing objectives

■   Determining how well marketing activities and actions matched opportunities and constraints of the environment

■   Providing necessary inputs to construct a marketing plan

7.3 The environmental set

Every organisation faces a set of environmental factors over which it may have some influence but seldom any direct control. All organisations operate in the context of a shifting set of what are in fact potential threats or opportunities.

■   The set that concerns any specific business will be individual to its own particular situation.

■   It will change over time as the elements in the set shift in relative importance and actual impact upon the business.

   –   The board of directors and marketers must monitor changes in their set.

   –   The set is the starting point for environmental assessment with SWOT analysis providing the basis for formulating a strategic response.

ACTIVITY 11.3

Produce a current environmental set for your own organisation. Rank the elements to identify and consider their probable significance in 12 months' time.

7.4 Impact analysis

This assesses the probable impact of environmental changes on an organisation or its competitors. It measures sensitivity of key parameters to changes in environmental variables. A number of tools may be used to provide a more informed view of the implications of environmental change.

The Chartered
Institute of Marketing

- **Competitor impact grid**: Competitors vary in their ability to withstand threats of exploit opportunities.

Figure 11.3 shows the effect of potential/probable environmental changes on direct competitors in multiple groceries.

Figure 11.3   Competitor impact grid

Environment future	Sainsbury's	Tesco	Asda	Lidl	Aldi
Edge-of-town planning restrictions tighten	– –	– –	– – –	–	– – –
New Food Agency regulations	–	–	–	–	0
Serious recession	–	–	0	+	++
Genetically modified foods backlash	– –	– –	++	0	0

The effect is rated on a scale from + + + to – – – with 0 representing a neutral impact

A positive score suggests improvement in profits and competitiveness.

This analysis encourages the marketer to assess the effect of environmental change in advance and respond accordingly

- **Environmental impact grid**: Environmental forces critically impacting on elements of the business are identified and awarded a weighted assessment. For example, how will changes to the transport network of a country impact on different rail travel customer groups?

- **Trend impact analysis**: A graph can be used to identify and extrapolate trends and this is used to highlight significant change in impact.

- **Influence diagrams**

  - These are flow charts designed to provide marketers with clear perception of the critical environmental influences on the business.

  - These can then be closely monitored in order to provide early warning of threats or opportunities.

  - A response to the contingency can be planned and executed.

THE REAL WORLD

Renewable energy

Against a backdrop of climate change, EU Directives have driven targets for reduced greenhouse gas emissions which have in turn helped to shape a fast changing marketing environment for the renewable energy industry. Government incentives and strong social support have for example led to significant demand for solar panels. Across the country households have fitted the gleaming panels onto their roof-tops, sales points have sprung up in supermarkets and malls, online campaigns and conversations abound. With additional wind and wave power generation, the consequence is an increase in renewable power generation as a percentage of total power generation from 4.3% in 2005 to 6.8% in 2010 (Department of Energy and Climate Change, 2011). Organisation constructing, fitting and selling panels have quickly responded to their marketing environment and up scaled to take full advantage. As the funding ceases they may scale down or they may be looking for the next construction/energy/sales opportunity.

7.5 The Ansoff matrix

Ansoff's product/market matrix is used for the analysis and determination of growth strategies. It can be borne in mind when conducting a marketing audit because it may help to frame the context of the information gathered. Four generic alternatives/business options are offered:

- Market penetration: existing market/existing product

- Product development: existing market/new product

- Market development: new market/existing product

- Entry into new market: new market/new product

The matrix can also be used to identify and compare levels of risk for differing growth strategies.

The rigid and rational approach can be limiting. Time is also not considered, for example diversification may be a preferred option but this may be long term and dependent on short-term growth in other segments of the matrix.

Figure 11.4   Ansoff product market growth matrix

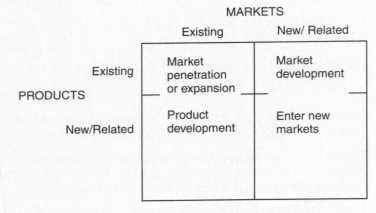

7.6 SWOT analysis

SWOT is a very commonly used tool used to summarise the current situation of organisation, teams or individuals as a step to building strategies for improvement and growth. It forms a key element of this unit as a tool for bringing together a summary of all of the significant issues in the internal and external environments and how they can impact upon future performance. This analysis can be the foundation for developing strategies to enable the organisation to tackle threats and take advantage of opportunities.

- Strengths and weaknesses are internal factors that represent where the organisation is now.

- Opportunities and threats take into account the external factor from both the competitive or micro environment and the macro environment.

- The organisation aims to build on strengths in order to take advantage of opportunities, while addressing significant weaknesses and responding appropriately to threats.

- The role of the analysis is to focus marketing thought on future plans to exploit the 'right' opportunities and/or defuse serious and imminent threats.

- The whole purpose of the technique is to encourage marketers to be outward-looking by appreciating relevant environmental developments and impact.

- Organisations must also consider:

    - The availability of resources
    - The feasibility of alternative courses of action to exploit them
    - Risk analysis/assessment

Build on strengths ⇒ take advantage of opps!

Addressing weaknesses/threats.

The Chartered
Institute of Marketing

7.7 PESTEL Analysis

Analysis of the macro environment summarises all of the factors that might impact upon the organisation but over which it has no control. Chapters 5 through to 11 have investigated these factors in some detail. The skill of the marketer is to ensure that relevant factors are regularly monitored and that robust data is being used to evaluate the threats and opportunities that these represent now and may represent in the future. The elements of PESTEL, which should be familiar to you by now, are summarised below.

Table 11.1   Elements of PESTEL

Factor	Examples
Political	Changes in government, stability/instability in domestic and overseas markets and foreign trade policies
Economic	Business cycles (boom, recession, recovery), interest rates, exchange rates, availability of finance, inflation, employment rates and energy costs
Socio-cultural	Population structures, socio-economic measures, lifestyle and fashion trends, consumption and media habits, business and social customs and consumer values and concerns
Technological	New products and processes, risk of obsolescence, virtual team-working and digital communications
Environmental/Ethical	Sustainability, energy use, recycling, packaging, pollution control, ethical trading and ethical investment
Legal	Laws regulating employment, manufacture (eg health and safety) trading and consumer rights

▶ **Exam tip**

As you prepare your PESTEL analysis you may find it helpful to identify all of the factors that may be relevant, explain why they are relevant and also evaluate their relative significance. This depth of detail will help you to respond to tasks in the exam. Please remember that although a number of models have been discussed in this chapter and throughout the text, it is only SWOT and PESTEL that can be in the prepared analysis that you can bring into the exam.

7.8 Conclusion

Through use of these various tools, skilled and knowledgeable marketers can bring together a detailed picture of the organisation and its place within the marketing environment. When auditing the marketing environment, marketers will rely on information from many sources and will require an analytical approach to evaluate that information. Use these tools to analyse the current situation but also to anticipate the changing factors that will impact upon the organisation in the future.

Throughout this text the many factors affecting the organisation have been discussed. Globalisation and technological advances have combined to create a market that is fast changing and sometimes unpredictable and no organisation is immune to these changes. The true skill of the marketer is to make justifiable decisions based on robust analysis of the marketing environment: from the day to day issues on the shop floor and the precarious position in the market place to the dramas of the global world of business.

CHAPTER ROUNDUP

In this chapter, we have seen that:

- It is crucially important for the marketer to monitor change in the marketing environment.

- Information is the critical resource and needs to be organised within the framework of an MkIS.

- There are problems in making accurate forecasts when the environment is turbulent and unpredictable, but scenarios can provide management with useful alternative views of the future.

- Frequent audits provide the necessary inputs for impact and SWOT analyse.

- The marketer must be future-orientated and be wary of the patterns of the past.

- Issues and environmental challenges should be scanned for continuously with a view to determining the ones that constitute potential threats or opportunities for the organisation.

- There is continuing potential of the internet and electronic databases in accessing information.

- A turbulent environment demands adaptability and flexible strategic planning.

FURTHER READING

Palmer, A. and Hartley, B. (2012) *The business environment*. 12th edition. Maidenhead, McGraw-Hill, Chapters 15 and 16.

Palmer, A. *et al* (2007) *Managing marketing*. Oxford, Butterworth Heinemann, Chapter 11.

Worthington, I. and Britton, C. (2009) *The business environment*. 6th edition. Harlow, Pearson, Chapter 18.

Websites:

Many of the websites listed in previous chapters will be of relevance here but in terms of the marketing audit students should be reflecting on cases and scenarios that show how organisations are analysing and responding to the evolving marketing environment.

National business news website for all quality press.

Global business consultancies:

http://www.pwc.com

http://www.mckinsey.com

Annual reports for plcs are generally published online and will indicate environmental factors and strategic responses.

REFERENCES

Department of Energy and Climate Change (2011) Energy trends.
http://www.decc.gov.uk/assets/decc/11/stats/publications/energy-trends/2076-trendsjun11.pdf [Accessed on 3 March 2012]

Kotler, P. (1994) *Marketing Management: analysis planning and control*. 8th Edition. New Jersey, Prentice Hall

Kotler, P. and Keller, K. L. (2011) *Marketing management*. 14th edition. London, Pearson Education.

The Chartered
Institute of Marketing

1   What is a marketing audit?

2   What is the business environment?

3   What is a scenario?

4   State five categories of internal inputs that describe the operation of the internal organisation.

5   Which two of the SWOT elements are shaped by the internal organisation?

6   What is a Marketing Information System?

7   What is the name of the technique where experts provide views on the future which are reviewed to reach a consensus?

8   What framework would you use to analyse the macro environment?

ACTIVITY DEBRIEFS

Activity 11.1

Micro – eg industry reports, trends and research, competitor information, markets and market segments data and supply and distribution chain trends.

Macro – eg government reports and statistics, global economic news, population trends, technological developments, and national and supranational legislation.

Activity 11.2

1   c
2   b
3   a
4   e
5   f
6   d

Activity 11.3

Defining an environmental set for your organisation (or the case organisation) can be done by considering all elements of the environment and classifying those that are of significant or insignificant importance. For example you may scale PESTEL factors in a range from +3 to –3 to note their potential positive or negative impact. If the significance is '0' then arguably this is not part of that organisation's environment set.

1   A detailed analysis of marketing capacity which enables plans to be made with the aim of improving company performance.

2   All factors that impact on the company's operations within the industry and within the wider marketplace.

3   A detailed and consistent view of how the business environment of an organisation might develop in the future.

4   Men, money, machine, materials and minutes.

5   Strengths and weaknesses.

6   The framework for day-to-day management and structuring of information gathered regularly from sources both inside and outside the organisation.

7   Delphi

8   PESTEL

Index

The Chartered
Institute of Marketing

The Chartered
Institute of Marketing

The Chartered
Institute of Marketing

The Chartered
Institute of Marketing

The Chartered
Institute of Marketing

The Chartered
Institute of Marketing

The Chartered
Institute of Marketing

Review form

Please help us to ensure that the CIM learning materials we produce remain as accurate and user-friendly as possible. We cannot promise to answer every submission we receive, but we do promise that it will be read and taken into account when we update this Study Text.

Name: _____   **Address:** _____

_____

_____

1. How have you used this Text?
(Tick one box only)

☐ Self study (book only)

☐ On a course: college_____

☐ Other _____

3. Why did you decide to purchase this Text?
(Tick one box only)

☐ Have used companion Assessment workbook

☐ Have used BPP Texts in the past

☐ Recommendation by friend/colleague

☐ Recommendation by a lecturer at college

☐ Saw advertising in journals

☐ Saw information on BPP website

☐ Other _____

2. During the past six months do you recall seeing/receiving any of the following?
(Tick as many boxes as are relevant)

☐ Our advertisement in *The Marketer*

☐ Our brochure with a letter through the post

☐ Our website www.bpp.com

4. Which (if any) aspects of our advertising do you find useful?
(Tick as many boxes as are relevant)

☐ Prices and publication dates of new editions

☐ Information on product content

☐ Facility to order books off-the-page

☐ None of the above

5. Have you used the companion Assessment Workbook?   Yes ☐   No ☐

6. Have you used the companion Passcards?   Yes ☐   No ☐

7. Your ratings, comments and suggestions would be appreciated on the following areas.

	Very useful	Useful	Not useful
Introductory section (How to use this text, study checklist, etc)	☐	☐	☐
Chapter introductions	☐	☐	☐
Syllabus learning outcomes	☐	☐	☐
Activities	☐	☐	☐
The Real World examples	☐	☐	☐
Quick quizzes	☐	☐	☐
Quality of explanations			
Index	☐	☐	☐
Structure and presentation	☐	☐	☐

	Excellent	Good	Adequate	Poor
Overall opinion of this Text	☐	☐	☐	☐

8. Do you intend to continue using BPP CIM products?   ☐ Yes   ☐ No

On the reverse of this page is space for you to write your comments about our Study Text. We welcome your feedback.

Please return to: CIM Publishing Manager, BPP Learning Media, FREEPOST, London, W12 8BR.

TELL US WHAT YOU THINK
Please note any further comments and suggestions/errors below. For example, was the text accurate, readable, concise, user-friendly and comprehensive?